MEDJUGORJE
The Message

Medjugorje – A Shining Inspiration
Other titles available from Paraclete Press

MEDJUGORJE
The Message

WAYNE WEIBLE

PARACLETE PRESS
Brewster, Massachusetts

33 32 31 30 29 28 27

Copyright © 1989 by Wayne Weible
Library of Congress #: 89-62243
All rights reserved.
Published by Paraclete Press
Brewster, Massachusetts

www.paraclete-press.com

ISBN #: 1-55725-009-X
Printed in the United States of America

To The Blessed Virgin Mary
Who always leads us to her Son;
And to my wife Terri,
Without whom this book would not be.

Contents

Foreword

When I was a small child I remember one day my brother ran out of the house filled with excitement. "There is a man in the house!" he said. "And he is not Catholic! He is a Protestant!"

I immediately thought this man must be different, and I ran into the house to see him. I wanted to see if he had a nose and a mouth and ears like ours. Never before had I seen or known anyone who was not a Catholic.

Much to my surprise, I found this man, this "Protestant," to be exactly like us in looks and mannerisms. Today, I know that this was a simple but very important early step in my conversion to the teachings of Jesus Christ. I realized through the simple observations of a child one of the most profound truths of God: He creates every human as an equal.

My friendship and association with Wayne Weible has led me to new and very special steps in my awareness of the universal brotherhood of every human being on earth. It has also led me to be more fully aware of the beauty of that reality. Hours of prayer, work, and conversation with Wayne in the setting of Medjugorje have led me to recognize that there is nothing God has put between us to separate us. It is as if I am hearing anew the words of Jesus spoken to His mother from the cross in a broader sense: "Woman, *these* are your sons."

This is the real experience of conversion at Medjugorje. When God leads His people, they convert and relate to one another with a deeper understanding. Everyone who listens with his heart to the Word of God comes to a full self-realization, a union with heaven and earth. It is then that the sense of fear and unrest begins to disappear.

This book is not an anticipation of any final judgment about the events in Medjugorje. It is a testimony to the faith and conversion experience of people who allow the Spirit present there to lead them.

Svetozar Kraljevic, O.F.M.

Prologue

The first words of this book were written at the foot of the cross on Mount Krizevac in the tiny village of Medjugorje, Yugoslavia. That is as it should be. It was there at that special place that the full meaning of the gift God gave us of His Son became for me a single-minded reality.

The cross is a universal symbol of Jesus Christ, a visible sign ever reminding us of His passionate death, given that we might have individual peace and life eternal. That, in substance, is the basic message coming from the reported apparitions of the Blessed Virgin Mary at Medjugorje; it is an invitation to receive them through reconciliation with Jesus. It begins with total conversion to His Way — the Way of the Cross.

Since June, 1981, the message of conversion and reconciliation with God has been uniquely reaffirmed by the Blessed Virgin Mary in the unlikely little village of Medjugorje. She has been appearing there daily to six young people who live in the valley that lies in the shadow of the cross on Krizevac. According to the youths chosen for this special mission of renewal, the mother of Jesus is bringing an urgent plea from her Son to all mankind to turn away from a world terminally ill with the disease of sin and reconcile with Him.

From this phenomenon has come a world-wide response. Millions of people have converted their lives to living in the ways of God; millions continue to visit the site. In the midst of a modern, high-tech lifestyle which has steadily led us away from the essence of God's grace, the symbol of the cross is being wonderfully renewed.

The cross on Krizevac is a 15-ton, 36-foot high concrete monolith which stands majestically on the highest summit of the hills and mountains surrounding the Medjugorje valley. It can be seen for miles, and it has become the landmark for this holy place. That, again, is as it should be.

In 1933, villagers struggled up the steep, rocky, thicket-covered mountainside, laden with heavy buckets of water and concrete. They were determined to build a monument to their faith to celebrate the 1,900th anniversary of the cross. The project became so meaningful for them, they changed the name of the mountain from Sipovac, to Krizevac, which means "Mountain of the Cross." Such a profound act of faith so many years ago highlights the area's special grace as the chosen site of the Virgin Mary's appearances today.

The cross on Krizevac is no thing of beauty. Years of harsh weather have aged, discolored and chipped away chunks of cement from its edges. But its beauty goes far beyond the exterior. Krizevac becomes the mental image implanted in the hearts of the millions who come to Medjugorje. It becomes a permanent reminder of an experience that gives a beauty within the soul that knows no earthly comparison.

Almost every pilgrim who comes to Medjugorje makes the difficult trek up the rocky pathway to the foot of the cross. Rugged and breath-taking, it is a climb of approximately a mile. Still, they come in droves; the young and the old, the healthy and the sick. People who normally have trouble with physical effort due to age or health somehow find the will and the strength to make it to the top.

All come looking for healing through fervent prayers, whether it be physical or spiritual — or both. There is a story told of a man with no legs who pulled himself to the top of the mountain, finishing exhausted and bloodied, but triumphant. Another is told of a man of slight build who comes to the mountain often and always carries his crippled wife on his back to the base of the cross. Hundreds of similar stories concerning this special cross exist. For those who come here from around the world, they serve as fuel for the fire of conversion and reconciliation that occurs from this supernatural phenomenon.

For those souls filled with such spiritual hunger, the cross on Krizevac is Calvary and Jesus at His darkest hour. Yet, it is also His triumph. It is the fulfillment of God's new covenant with mankind promising eternal life through His Son's sacrificial death.

Millions continue to come to the tiny village of Medjugorje to hear this covenant renewed by Mary's message from her Son. I was one of them. I wrote this book as the personal witness of one spiritually hungry soul who found peace and love in that message by way of the cross on Krizevac.

— Wayne Weible

*"Hatred creates division and does not see
anybody or anything. . . act with love
in the place where you live. . . ."*

1

The Messenger

It was a beautiful May afternoon, transforming the entire Irish countryside into a travel poster. We drove along with our windows down, enjoying the fresh air. The narrow road was flanked by stone fences guarding deep green fields. Every so often we would catch a glimpse of a thatched-roof stone cottage that might have been there for three centuries or more. There was a feeling that here in County Donegal, time was somehow suspended.

Cresting the next hill, we suddenly braked for a flock of sheep being herded along down the middle of the road by a young girl. I was glad I wasn't driving.

Our driver, Vera McFadden, was unfazed. She and her two women friends in the back had come over to Letterkenny in her tiny British motorcar to take me to their church in Derry, where I would be speaking that evening. I sat in the left-hand front seat, still unused to the lack of a steering-wheel on that side. Otherwise, I was thoroughly enjoying Ireland's northernmost county.

"I can't believe how green the grass is," I murmured.

"Ah, you would if you knew the rain we get!" Vera chuckled. " 'Tis a fine day indeed," she added in her thick Northern brogue, "but a rare one, what with the sun shining."

I smiled and nodded, even though it was difficult for me to understand her. It was my second speaking tour in Ireland in the past year, and I had experienced the cool, rainy weather that typifies the country.

We rounded the next corner, and suddenly all smiles vanished. Directly ahead of us was another obstruction blocking the road — a horizontal pole with red and white stripes that identified it as a British checkpoint at the Northern Ireland border. In front of it stood two soldiers in full battle dress, their rifles cradled at the ready. I was shocked, frightened and angry all at the same time. Beyond the pole a dozen troopers similarly clad were lounging on the grassy bank beside the road. They were chatting and smoking cigarettes — but their weapons were close at hand.

Vera stopped the car, and one of the soldiers came up to her. She passed him her identification papers which he inspected without a word. Then he nodded to the other soldier who raised the pole. No one had said anything, I realized, as we started up and drove through the checkpoint into Northern Ireland. The day seemed to lose its sparkle.

We had not gone half a mile when Vera suddenly swerved to the left, as a British armored personnel carrier overtook us and pulled in front. As it did, I noticed that its rear steel doors were slightly open, and through them a soldier was aiming his gun directly at us. I had the cold thought that this was the closest I had ever been to the business end of a gun. The vehicle then accelerated out of sight around the next bend.

I sat there burning with anger and disbelief. "What was that all about?"

Instead of answering, Vera swerved again, as a second armored vehicle roared past. Like the first, its rear doors were cracked open, and another soldier menaced us as before. Then it, too, was gone.

"What's going on?" I demanded, shaken by the sudden thought that things were not all that safe here.

"They always travel in pairs," Vera explained. "To avoid ambush."

"But we're civilians! We're supposed to be allies with them. I can't believe this!"

Vera shrugged. "We're also Catholics," she said, nodding at the rosary beads hanging from the rear-view mirror, "and you're with us so they assume that you're Catholic, too." She sighed. "I can't really blame them; their mates are being blown up by car bombs and shot at all the time."

All at once the full impact of the tragedy of Northern Ireland struck home — Catholic terrorists killing British occupying soldiers and innocent Protestants; Protestant terrorists killing innocent Catholics, with each atrocity heaping fresh wood on the fires of revenge. It had been going on for generations and there was no sign of change. There was only the ingrained tradition of hate, with children on both sides raised to hate as their parents did.

"How can you live this way?" I wondered aloud.

"Well, we do have to go on living now, don't we?" Vera replied with a faint smile. "Of course it's not all like that. I have neighbors who are Protestant, and we get along fine. And our prayer group is mixed. Really, it's the rads who cause all the trouble," she said, referring to the radicals on both sides. "You know, sometimes you just have to laugh at them. One time I was about to go into a bank, when a man with a black stocking over his head grabbed me and put a gun to my head. There was another lad with him also wearing a black stocking for a mask, and I gathered that they were about to rob the bank, using me as a hostage."

"Who were they?"

She shrugged again. "IRA? INLA? It doesn't much matter; the two are fighting each other all the time. Anyway, they were then joined by a third man, only the stocking over his head was *brown*, not black. All at once I began laughing, and I said to him, 'You're out of dress, lad! You're not in the proper uniform!' I don't know why I said it or why I began laughing, because I was terrified." She started to giggle in the telling of it, and there were more giggles coming from the back seat. They had obviously heard the story before.

"Well," she went on, "that so unnerved them that they turned and left, running as fast as they could. I thought the bank ought to give me a reward!"

The three of them were now convulsed in laughter. Amazed that they could find humor in such near-tragedy, I realized how important it was that they were still able to laugh.

After they had subsided, Vera said quietly, not taking her eyes from the road, "I know of no more tragic place on earth than these six counties that make up Northern Ireland. Maybe it's because I know some of the new widows and the grieving families and the kids who will grow up with no fathers." She shook her head. "With so many Christians on both sides, you'd think — but we pray and pray, and nothing seems to change. Sometimes I wonder if God hears us." She turned to me. "Maybe the message you bring tonight will make a difference, please God!"

We lapsed into silence. I gazed out at the countryside, its beauty belying the despair of its people. The "message" I would be bringing them came from the reported appearance of the Blessed Virgin Mary, mother of Jesus Christ, to a group of young Croatians in the mountain village of Medjugorje, Yugoslavia. Her central message of peace and love had steadily made its way around the world, bringing millions of people back to God. Tonight a Lutheran Protestant would be talking about a religious phenomenon considered to be predominantly Catholic, in a land ripped with strife between the two faiths.

Could the message of Medjugorje really make a difference in a conflict that was more than 800 years old? Was it possibly a tiny drop of the oil of peace on these terribly troubled waters? There was no doubt in my mind that the answer was yes! God *did* care and He *did* hear. Tonight I would share the evidence and the hope. . . .

All at once I was struck by the irony of that: not too long ago I was without any hope myself; now, I would be bearing an extraordinary message of hope to a land that had lost it. My mind went back over the incredible chain of events which had brought me here. It had begun on an October evening three years before as I sat in the den of our home in Myrtle Beach, South Carolina. The torn and bleeding heart of Northern Ireland could not have been further from my mind . . . .

"I have come to tell you that God exists,
and that He loves you. . . ."

2

Beginnings

I looked down at the videotape in my lap, impatiently waiting for Terri to finish putting our kids to bed so that we could watch it together. Having already read a book that had been given me along with the tape, I knew what it was essentially about: in a tiny village in the mountains of Yugoslavia, the Virgin Mary, mother of Jesus Christ, had reportedly been appearing to a group of local teenagers, beginning in June, 1981, and continuing every evening since.

Every evening. . . what if there was something to this? What if it wasn't a hoax or mass hallucination or the fantasy of a self-deluding, superstitious people? What if a religious phenomenon was actually taking place in this little town with the unpronounceable name? At the very least, it would make a good story for my weekly newspaper column. That was my main interest.

"Terri, you about ready?" I called down the hallway knowing full well that she wasn't. I could hear our five-year-old son Kennedy asking for a drink of water, a usual step in the nightly routine. His year-old sister Rebecca was already asleep.

"I've promised him a story," Terri answered. "I'll be there in a few minutes."

More like twenty minutes, I thought to myself, smiling. Terri was a loving, caring mother. I wondered if Kennedy knew how lucky he was. Of course, I was pretty lucky, too. She was the best thing that had ever happened to me. Having gone through a traumatic divorce after fourteen years of a marriage that had produced four children, I had given up hope of ever finding my way out of the emotional tunnel I was in — when she had come along.

Terri was interested in what was going on in this little mountain town also, but for different reasons. If there *was* something to this, and it involved changes in the world, then it could affect our children.

We had first learned of the reported phenomenon during a Sunday school class at our Lutheran church. As a teacher of one of the two adult classes, I occasionally picked an optional subject for class study. The regular Lutheran curriculum was often stiff and difficult to teach, and our class, mostly younger marrieds and singles, wanted more variety. For this particular class in late October, 1985, I had given them an unusual assignment: to bring in news stories or other material concerning modern-day miracles.

Enough of them did their homework so that we had an animated discussion. As we were winding things up, Becky Ginley, a friend of Terri's, piped up, "Here's a good one: have you all heard about what's happening in Yugoslavia? There's a little village there where the Virgin Mary is supposedly appearing to six kids, and they say it's been happening for more than four years."

The rest of the class stared at her. Becky beamed back, pleased at having been able to surprise us.

As far as I was concerned, 'surprised' was putting it mildly. As a newspaper columnist, it was difficult to come up with new and interesting topics each week. This one, I sensed, was hot. And with Christmas nearly upon us, the timing would be perfect. About the only time most people ever thought of the Virgin Mary was at Christmas, usually from setting up or seeing manger scenes where she would be positioned kneeling beside the baby Jesus. Personally, I had never given her more than two thoughts.

"Where did you hear about this?" I asked Becky.

"From a friend who's Catholic."

"What's Catholic got to do with it?"

"Well, you know, this sort of thing usually happens in the Catholic church."

"It does?"

She looked at me, her head tilted. "You never heard of Fatima, or Lourdes?"

"No, I —"

Just then the bell marking the end of class rang, and everyone headed for the door. "Hey, we'll talk more about this next week, okay?" I yelled as they were leaving. I quickly asked Terri to see if Becky had any more information on it. As she rushed to pick up her two children from the nursery, we hurried down the hall after her.

"Becky, wait a minute!" Terri called. "Where can we find out more?"

Becky looked at her watch and bit her lip. "You know Mary Jeffcoat?"

"Yes." Mary was a city councilwoman who had previously been public relations director of one of the local hospitals, and we knew her through our work at the newspaper.

"Well," said Becky, backing down the hall, "Mary's the one who told me about it; I think she's got more information."

"What has she got?"

"A videotape, I think — and maybe a couple of books. Look, I've got to go. Give me a call," she said, turning and dashing off to the nursery.

Terri and I discussed the reported apparitions on the

way home and on and off throughout the day. I knew it would make a really good story. In my mind I was already working out the tie-in. . . A modern-day miracle might be taking place in a Yugoslavian village at the same time we prepared to celebrate the miracle of Christmas. My only reservation was that such an odd religious topic might damage my journalistic credibility.

That evening, Terri called Mary Jeffcoat. "Well, she's going to drop the tape off here on her way home from work tomorrow. She also has a book on it that she'll lend us."

The following day, my journalistic curiosity was in overdrive. I wanted to read the book as soon as I could get my hands on it. So did Terri. Like a couple of kids with a new toy, we squabbled good-naturedly over who would read it first. When it was my turn, I devoured it in two hours. It was not that long — just 98 pages. Co-authored by a Catholic priest and a nun, Robert Faricy and Lucy Rooney, it told the story of the first days of the apparitions at Medjugorje.

In the mountainous Hercegovina region of central Yugoslavia, about an hour's drive from the Adriatic Sea, was a village so small that it did not appear on most maps. Those published after June 25, 1981, however, might well include the little farming community of some 400 Croatian families. On that day, shortly before sunset, a sequence of events began that was destined to change forever the history of the town and the surrounding countryside— and perhaps the world.

Ivanka Ivankovic, 15, and her friend, Mirjana Dragicevic, 16, having finished their field chores had gone for a walk on the dirt road that wound from their hamlet of Bijakovici, along the base of the hill known as Podbrdo. On their way home, Ivanka happened to glance up and was startled to see the shimmering figure of a woman up on the hill, bathed in a brilliant light. "Mirjana, look: it's *Gospa!*" (Our Lady) she exclaimed without really thinking about what she was saying.

"Come on," replied her friend with a wave of disgust, not even bothering to look, "Why would Gospa appear to *us?*" and she continued down the road towards home. But Ivanka in a high state of excitement pleaded with her to believe that she really had seen something. When they came near the home of Milka Pavlovic, 13, she was just coming out to bring in the family sheep. Ivanka begged the two of them to return with her to see if the figure was still there, and when they reached the place where Ivanka had seen her, now Mirjana and Milka also saw her.

They were soon joined by Vicka Ivankovic, 17, a close companion of the two who had gone looking for them. Seeing them waving excitedly to her from the road, she hurried to join them. When they told her they were seeing the Madonna, she was too scared to look and ran away, wondering how her friends could tease about something so sacred.

But driven by curiosity she returned a short while later with two boys who had been picking apples along the roadside, Ivan Dragicevic, 16, and Ivan Ivankovic, 20. (None of the youths involved were closely related; many of the villagers had the same last names.) The younger Ivan ran away, but the other stayed and also saw what he would later describe as "something completely white, turning."

Vicka, having clearly seen the apparition upon returning, was more explicit. She described the figure as wearing a silver-grey gown, having dark hair and a pale white complexion: she stated that the figure, who appeared to be holding a baby in her arms, beckoned for them to come up the hill, closer, but they were too frightened to move. (With the exception of Christmas, this would be the only time that the apparition would appear with her Son.)

Some of the youths began to cry; others prayed. They stayed until dusk and a light mist began to fall. Returning to their homes, they told their families what had happened — and were scolded and teased, the parents fearful that the neighbors would call them liars. Vicka's sister playfully teased her saying, "Maybe they saw a flying saucer!"

The next day, after completing their work in the fields, they felt an inner urge to return to the hillside, although not all of them were able to do so. Milka's mother, not really believing her daughter, had taken her to a distant field to work that day, and when she, too, felt the urge to return, it was too far. When the others stopped by Milka's house to get her, they were told by her older sister, Marija, 17, that she wasn't home. So they asked Marija to come with them. Jakov Colo, only 10 years of age and a cousin of Milka and Marija, was also at the house; at the urging of Marija, he decided to go with them.

Ivan Ivankovic who was several years older than the others decided that going to see "visions" was for children, and he declined to return. (A few days later he would become a staunch believer and regret not having returned; shortly thereafter, he would be arrested and jailed for two months for going up on the hill against a police order forbidding the young visionaries and their followers to do so.) The other Ivan did go, possibly embarrassed at having run away the day before. A number of villagers followed at a distance, curious to see if the "rumor" of the Madonna's appearance was true.

Shortly after 6:00 PM the figure appeared again, gesturing to them to come to her. This time they did. In fact, they ran up the hill at an astonishing rate of speed, and when they reached the figure they fell to their knees.

Some of the onlookers tried to follow but could not keep up. They reported that the six young people seemed to be looking up at something slightly above them and a few feet away. The youths began praying the Lord's Prayer, because, as Vicka would later explain, "We didn't know what else to do." This second-day visit lasted approximately fifteen minutes, during which the figure identified herself as "The Blessed Virgin Mary."

Again there was some teasing when they returned to their homes, but with the witness of other villagers, it was mild. They knew these children were not given to fanciful exaggeration or playing pranks, and, they definitely would not lie about something so sacred to them. If they said they'd seen something, then they had seen it — even if no one else could.

Word traveled fast among the five hamlets that made up the parish of Medjugorje — especially word of the most extraordinary occurrence in common memory. The following afternoon several thousand people gathered on the hill with the children. They seemed to have come from everywhere — some from as far away as the town of Ljubuski and even from the city of Mostar, more than a half-hour's drive away.

On this third day a glowing light appeared on the hillside, and it guided the six seers to the site of their next encounter with the *Gospa*. Others could see the light but could not see what was inside of it. Milka was also present, her mother realizing after Marija's experience the second day that her younger daughter had actually been telling the truth. She allowed Milka to go, at Marija's insistence that she, too, would see. But sadly, she did not see the Gospa — that day or since.

This time the six, having gained courage from the previous day's experience, asked the figure several questions: why had she come to their village? And why to them? And what did she want of the people?

"I have come here, because there are many devout believers here," was her response. "I have come to tell you that God exists, and He loves you. Let the others who do not see me, believe as you do."

Jakov reported it a little differently. According to him her reason for coming was that all might be at peace and be reconciled one to another. (I found it more credible that the six young visionaries did *not* repeat verbatim the same story; in fact, given the natural independence of young people that age, I would have found it suspicious if all their reports were word-for-word identical.)

By the fourth day, the government authorities at their regional headquarters in nearby Citluk had become alarmed; the situation was getting out of control. They summoned the six young people to the police station where they were intensively interrogated and examined by a doctor — who pronounced them perfectly normal, healthy teenagers. Frustrated, the authorities next sent for the Franciscan pastor of St. James Church in Medjugorje, Father Jozo Zovko, who had just returned from Zagreb where he had been leading a retreat. They informed him that the gatherings on the hillside were to stop, and they held him personally responsible. Yugoslavia, after all, was a Communist nation; officially, God did not exist. Nonetheless, theirs was an 'enlightened, progressive' Communism; religious assembly was tolerated, provided it took place in the churches, on appointed days, at appointed times. Those parameters most emphatically did not include spontaneous mass demonstrations on hillsides.

Father Jozo assured them that he was no less concerned than they about the sensational events which had occurred in his absence. He did not tell them that he had already met at length with the youths, not as an advocate but listening intently, trying to catch them in any slip which would give them away. Having heard that one of the group had brought drugs from a distant city (Mirjana lived in Sarajevo and spent only the summer months at Medjugorje), he feared that they had experienced a drug-induced hallucination — and had become trapped in it, with no alternative but to continue the charade.

His associate pastor, Father Zrinko Cuvalo, was considerably harsher with the children in the course of his own interrogation. Fearing the possibility that a grotesque hoax was being perpetrated, he pressed in; compared to the incalculable harm that could be done — to the village, to the faith, to the Church in Yugoslavia — the temporary emotional discomfort of six young people was of little consequence. He questioned them and re-questioned them, separately and together. He made no attempt to hide his skepticism and impatience, deliberately trying to provoke them into making contradictory statements.

A third Franciscan priest, newly arrived to the events at Medjugorje, had an even more radical solution: exorcise the lot of them. But at this proposal, the other two priests balked. That was a bit too harsh. Whatever else these young people might be guilty of, they were not demon-possessed, a judgment with which the newcomer agreed as soon as he had a chance to meet with the six himself. The three priests, well aware of the enormity of the responsibility that now rested on their shoulders, were proceeding with deliberate caution. Regardless of the eventual outcome, the world, the Government, and the Church were going to be holding them personally accountable.

Through it all, the six youngsters remained unshakeable in their testimony. In Citluk, as the time of the next afternoon apparition approached, the government officials dispatched another doctor, Darinka Glamuzina, to observe the events on the hillside. A self-proclaimed atheist who served with the ambulance corps, Dr. Glamuzina could be counted on to return with a report which would justify their shutting down the whole affair at once.

As sundown approached, practically the entire hillside was covered with people —thousands upon thousands of them. The visionaries got separated and lost sight of one another in the vast crowd. It was fast turning into a circus-like gathering. Marija was accompanied by Father Zrinko, who was in civilian clothing, not wanting to be recognized by the authorities (it was the first time that any of the local priests had come to the hillside), when she saw the special light and ran up the hill towards it. The other children must have seen it, too, for they soon joined her and began to pray.

According to observers a few feet from the six youths, all at once their praying stopped. They became enraptured with the sight of something that only they could see. Each seemed to be asking the apparition questions, sometimes one on top of another, yet each seemed to receive an individual answer which satisfied him or her. Among the questions they asked was: did she have anything she wanted them to tell the priests?

"Let them believe strongly and guard their faith," was the later-reported reply.

When the vision was over, onlookers recounted that Dr. Glamuzina descended the hill hastily, a look of shock on her face. She refused to file a report or have anything further to do with the apparitions. The reason given by one of the young seers was that Dr. Glamuzina had brazenly asked to "touch" this figure the young people claimed to see. One of them asked the apparition if the doctor could touch her. She replied, "Let her come forward; there will always be Judases who do not believe."

The fifth day was Sunday, and in his sermon Father Jozo, still skeptical, made no reference to the happenings on nearby Podbrdo Hill. Instead, he emphasized the importance of the *traditional* observances of faith. If he had intended to sound a cautionary note, it went unheeded; that evening, there were more people on the hill than ever. It seemed as if every man, woman and child within a 50-mile radius was there.

At approximately 6:40, the apparition appeared. (Though the site might change, the time would remain fairly consistent.) Interviewed later, the young visionaries reported that one of the questions they asked was: "Dear Lady, why don't you appear in the church so that everyone can see you?"

Her response, as later related by one of the visionaries, was the same as her Son's had once been: "Blessed are they who have not seen and believe. . . ."

Monday morning in Citluk, the authorities held an emergency meeting. There were now reports of miraculous healings: a paralyzed child was walking, a blind man's sight had been restored, numerous minor infirmities had been reportedly healed. The situation was becoming critical. If word of such phenomena were allowed to spread, they felt they could not control the crowds that would descend on the tiny village. Once again, they sent for the visionaries, and this time they took them to the neuro-psychiatric department of the hospital in Mostar. Surely there they would be diagnosed as hallucinatory or otherwise deranged. But again, they were found to be sound and healthy and sent back home.

That afternoon the narrow roads leading to Medjugorje were clogged for miles. Huge multitudes made their way to the hill. As the visionaries approached, the crowds began to press in on them, and in desperation the local villagers, urged by Marinko Ivankovic who lived across the road from Marija, joined hands and formed a circle around them to give them room to pray. As had become the custom in the past days, they began with the Lord's Prayer, and the Hail Mary. In the middle of one of the prayers, the apparition appeared. This time one of the questions they asked was: how long would she continue to appear to them?

The answer was startling: "As long as you wish."

The following morning two women from the village who were government social workers came by in their car and offered to take the children sightseeing. Knowing them well, the six readily accepted and spent a pleasant day. But as the time of the apparition drew near, they became anxious and wanted to return to the hillside. The social workers just smiled and continued as if they hadn't understood. Realizing what was happening, the young seers threatened to jump out if they did not stop the car immediately and let them out. Hastily they pulled over.

As they did, all of them including the social workers saw a ball of light coming towards them from the direction of the hill. The children knelt a short distance from the roadside, and in a few moments began to converse with the apparition. Thoroughly shaken by the light and the up-close witness of the apparition, the workers returned the seers to their homes. The next day they resigned their positions with the government and later moved entirely from the area.

Now the authorities were adamant: there would be no more hillside meetings with some supernatural person. If the seers wanted to go on making fools of themselves, they would have to do so in the church. But they were to remain out of sight, so as not to make fools of others. The situation had become intolerable; people were walking off their jobs to go to the hill. No one was interested in working anymore. The entire region was in a state of paralysis. The authorities made it abundantly clear that if the children did not comply, it would go very hard on their families. In a Communist country, where the Government controlled work permits and everything else, the young seers knew the threats were hardly empty.

But the next day, Wednesday, one week from the first apparition, the authorities abruptly changed their minds: the foolishness must be stopped entirely. They dispatched the police to Medjugorje to take the seers into custody.

It became a nightmare for the visionaries. People dutifully reported to the police that they had seen the children — in the fields, in the village, near the church — but wherever the police rushed, they seemed to just miss them. The six proved adept at this dangerous game of hide-and-seek. They always kept on the move, running down the vine rows, crouched over so as not to be seen, cutting through the woods, and even changing clothes to throw off their pursuers. It was a harrowing experience that eventually led them to the church.

Father Jozo was in St. James, kneeling quietly in the front of the church, praying fervently for direction. God had spoken clearly to Abraham and to Moses in times of great trial, and so, he begged, what was he to do?

In the stillness of the empty church he suddenly heard the words: *Go out now and protect the children.*

Stunned by the clearly audible message, he got up and ran to the back door of the church. As he opened the door, around the corner came the children on the dead run. "Help us, Father! Please, help us!" they cried as they gathered about him in tears.

Father Jozo hastily escorted them to the nearby rectory, expecting the police at any moment. Admonishing them to remain absolutely silent, he went back outside and waited. Sure enough, three policemen came running towards the rectory. "Quickly, have you seen those children?" they demanded breathlessly.

"Yes," replied the priest, preparing to defend them at

all costs. But instead of delaying long enough to ask him where, they took off in the direction of Bijakovici, the little hamlet where all of the children lived. Father Jozo waited until they were out of sight, then re-entered the rectory. After calming the frightened and exhausted seers, he gave them something to eat.

Later that afternoon the apparition took place in St. James Church, with the people of the village gathered there at the request of their pastor. If there was any doubt left in Father Jozo about the authenticity of the apparitions, it was instantly dispelled: dumbfounded, he was given to see the Virgin exactly as the children did. From then on, he was the leading defender of the apparitions, a stand that would soon cause him to be imprisoned for 18 months at hard labor for refusing to shut down the church to put a stop to the phenomenon.

Father Jozo had decided he would give the people the one thing that mattered above all else: he scheduled a Mass for 6:00 p.m. that evening, asking Father Zrinko to precede the Mass with the prayer of the Rosary. Later when he went to the church, it was literally packed, including the altar area. The pastor who had initially been so skeptical of the apparitions because no one was coming to the church or wanting to come to confession, now had difficulty in raising his arms to say, "The Lord be with you." The people were no longer passive spectators at a supernatural event; they had become active participants in a phenomenon that would touch the lives of millions the world over.

That service set the pattern for what would eventually become a daily routine. The apparitions occurred wherever the children might be, as a group or individually, and Father Jozo had them meet in a small sacristy just to the right of the altar in St. James Church. Now, the same villagers who had always worked late into the evening were filling the church at 5:00. All fifteen decades of the Rosary were prayed, and later a blessing and healing service were added. Including the Mass, many were finding themselves in the church for three hours each evening. The conversion of Medjugorje had begun.

Conversion to the ways of Jesus was the basic message given by the Madonna. She said the way to conversion was through prayer, fasting and penance. These would lead to conversion of the heart and individual peace. Truly, the people of Medjugorje were now trying to live that message.

The early bliss of holiness would not always remain for them, however; on August 18th, their pastor was arrested and charged with spreading sedition. (He had made some comments in a sermon which were construed to be anti-Government.) It was a desperate act on the part of the Government in the hope that it would bring an end to the apparitions, and the large gatherings they were attracting. Father Jozo had expected it; when they came to arrest him, he was ready. But neither he nor the parishioners expected what happened next. The church was ransacked. Religious articles were scattered and knocked over; the church was ordered closed.

As the bells tolled, however, the church filled, the people defiantly ignoring the order not to enter. A numb silence ensued, as they witnessed the devastation. Father Zrinko then stepped to the altar and informed the people of the arrest of Father Jozo, although by this time most of them knew it. In a voice filled with emotion he told them, "This is the most difficult day of my life." The church was filled with the sound of weeping.

The Mass began. But when the people started to sing the opening hymn, the words stuck in their throats. It was the same with the prayers; during the Our Father,

Father Zrinko had to ask several times for them to repeat the line, "as we forgive them."

After the Mass, the custom of saying the traditional seven Our Fathers, Hail Marys and the Glory Bes with the visionaries leading them, began. Suddenly, they stopped the prayers and hurried into the side room off the altar. The priest informed the parishioners, "Our Lady has called them aside." There followed a hush, with all eyes fixed on the door to the little room. Little Jacov then came out with the others, and going to the microphone he told the people: "Our Lady called us to that room where she was waiting for us. She told us to tell you not to be afraid, that she wants us to be happy and to show joy on our faces. She said she will protect Father Jozo."

After a moment of shock, there was a burst of applause, and then they began to sing — with great joy. The prayers were soon finished, but many stayed beyond them, not wanting to leave.

Medjugorje would continue to have its share of troubles. But as far as the villagers were concerned, it was evident that the Madonna was still in control. . . .

I looked up from the book in my lap and shook my head; it was all so strange! My newspaper training had taught me to be skeptical first and reserve judgment until I had the cold, hard facts. But this had been going on for more than four years — and it involved uneducated children. How could they be part of a hoax for such a long time? Still, my only aim was a story, so what did I care?

"Well, what are you waiting for? Put the tape in, and let's see this miracle of miracles!" Terri said with a teasing smile as she came into the room and took a seat.

I got up and put the tape in the machine. Now we would judge for ourselves whether the apparitions of Medjugorje were real or just another exaggerated children's story.

3

The Message

The video began with a long shot of the mountain behind St. James Church, which had a huge cement cross on its summit. Then, as the sound track carried singing from the Croatian Mass, the camera closed in on the church with its twin spires and the throngs of people in front of it. An American Catholic priest was interviewing people — from France, Italy, Germany, everywhere. There were couples, families, and many teenagers, and he was asking them why they had come and what they had found. This went on for approximately fifteen minutes. The focus then shifted to the six youngsters who had involuntarily become "visionaries" and conduits of the apparition's message.

As the Faricy book had reported, they looked like normal, healthy teenagers. Instinctively I began making notes: each had a strong, well-developed personality and seemed happy and at ease. They were nice-looking kids but entirely average. The video had been made earlier that year, four years after the events described in the book, and things had settled down considerably. The evening apparition had become routine now, and Government authorities were less hostile, a change of attitude caused primarily by the unexpected influx of tourist currency.

As the camera observed the seers up close just before the start of the apparition, all my journalistic objectivity drained away. I found myself shaking my head and murmuring, over and over, "This is unbelievable!" But I sensed immediately in my heart that it was real. But — how could it have been happening for such a long time, and no one in this country seemed to know about it?

The seers began to pray. Suddenly they stopped in mid-sentence and fell to their knees. Vicka was smiling and apparently conversing, but there was no sound coming from her moving lips. Ivan was also holding a silent conversation, but his lips were not in synchronization with Vicka's. Marija was just gazing upward, smiling in veneration. They all were staring at the same spot, oblivious to the crowd pressing around them or the flash bulbs going off in their faces.

As I watched in fascination, I suddenly felt a strange sensation: someone — was speaking to me! It was not an audible voice but one that seemed to be within me. Incredibly, I somehow knew that it was the Virgin Mary.

I felt a numbing sensation throughout my being. Everything in the room seemed to fade away, until there was just me and what was happening on the television screen. And the voice within, with its message: *You are my son, and I am asking you to do my Son's will. . . .*

Unable to breathe, I managed to glance at Terri: had she heard it, too? She was watching the screen, interested but relaxed. I realized it was happening only to me. My heart was pounding; I thought I was going to pass out. The message continued: *Write about the events of Medjugorje; this will become your life's mission if you choose to accept it. You will no longer be in your present work.*

The remainder of the video was a fog. When it was over, we just sat and stared at each other. Should I tell

Terri what had happened? Would she believe me? "Well, that was certainly interesting — better than the book," she said at length. "Funny thing is, I don't have any difficulty believing it."

All I could do was dumbly nod. She looked at me, waiting for a reaction. Then, noticing the strange look on my face, she asked, "What's the matter with you?"

"Terri, I know this sounds crazy, but — she just spoke to me. . . "

"Who?"

"The Virgin Mary; she just spoke to me. She's asking me to spread this message —" I ran out of words.

She stared at me quizzically for a moment. "Don't you think you might be overreacting to this just a little?"

"Terri, I'm telling you, it *happened!*" I couldn't blame her for doubting, but I was still disappointed that she didn't believe me. "I don't know how or why but I'm telling you: it really did happen!"

She smiled and tried to put it in a light vein. "Well, why don't you take a couple of aspirin and come to bed; you'll be okay in the morning."

"You go ahead," I said, shaking my head. "I couldn't sleep anyway."

She got up, came over and gave me a little hug. By now she realized that whether it had happened or not, I had been deeply affected by the tape. "Don't worry about it. If it's real, you'll soon know it. I'm going to bed; just come whenever you feel like it."

For a long time I just sat and stared at the blank television screen, going over and over in my mind what had happened. Then, taking a deep breath, I determined to get a handle on the whole thing. Nothing in all my experience had prepared me for this. There were only two possibilities: either I had gone crazy, or I had just received a message from God through the Virgin Mary.

Had something tilted me over the edge? There was a lot of pressure in my life, but there had always been pressure. For nine years we had owned and operated four weekly newspapers and a printing company. Pressure was a daily companion with deadlines, competition, employee problems, and so on. In all probability, I had never been more sane than I was right now.

Yet the alternative was even more difficult to contemplate. . . . Jesus Christ had suddenly become real — a real, flesh-and-blood Jesus. *Alive,* then and now. And His mother who was appearing to these young people in Yugoslavia. . . had just spoken to me.

As the reality of that suddenly hit me, I fell to my knees and began to pray, as I'd never in my life prayed.

*"I invite all of you to start living in
God's love. . . I want to lead all
of you to perfect holiness. . . ."*

4

You Are My Son. . . .

I don't know how long I knelt there, saying over and
over "My God, my God, why me?" I wasn't qualified for
this; I knew nothing about apparitions or the Catholic
Church. And the only thing I knew about the Virgin Mary
was that she had been chosen to give birth to Jesus Christ.
Why would she ask *me* to spread this message she had
brought to the little village of Medjugorje?

I felt completely unworthy to be involved in anything
so — holy. That feeling of unworthiness was not from
humility; it was a painful realization of the many wrong
things I had done in my life. All of the guilt that I had
ever felt over my divorce now welled up in me, like salt
in fresh wounds.

Yet as wretched as these thoughts were, a sense of the
presence of God's love never left me. It was as though
another message inside of me was assuring me that
however unacceptable I might be in my own eyes, I was
not unacceptable to Him.

I remembered then what I had so often heard in church
and had even taught in Sunday School classes: Jesus died
on the Cross so that our sins — all of them — could
be forgiven. All we had to do was ask, with a sincere,
contrite heart. But teaching it or hearing it was one thing;

actually experiencing it was another. I felt like a little child, bathed in love and acceptance after being severely disciplined.

For a long time I just knelt there, too drained to do anything. Then I got up, started the tape again, and collapsed on the couch.

This time as I watched, I was inundated by a flood of insight which went straight to my heart, bypassing my intellect. I didn't have to understand how or why this was happening to me; I just knew that it was — and that was all that was necessary.

When the tape came to the part just before the apparition, the message I had received was renewed. I knew that I was to do more than just write about Medjugorje. More than just live its message of love and individual peace. From that moment on, Medjugorje was going to be my life.

Exhausted but too keyed up to sleep, I sat on the couch reliving the milestones in my life. Certainly the divorce was one of the most traumatic. How could I have been so foolish to marry so young, and then to allow a family with four beautiful kids to disintegrate into a tragedy of hate and alienation. I thought it could never happen to me. . . .

Bored with high school, I had dropped out after the tenth grade and joined the Navy. After being discharged I went to Columbia, South Carolina, to visit my sister and her new husband. It was to be a quick visit, for I was on my way to Tempe, Arizona, to attend Arizona State University with a service buddy who lived there.

I never got to Arizona. I met a young, Southern Baptist girl, and we began dating. It was my first serious relationship, and I was certain that if I didn't marry her, I'd never get another chance. She was shy, from a small mill town, and she went to church regularly. I began to attend with her, though my family background was Lutheran. Actually I didn't care where I went — or even if I went. In less than a year we were married.

One Sunday shortly after the wedding, I felt an urge to attempt to give my life to God. I didn't know why I wanted to do it; maybe it was the altar call for conversion that was a regular part of the Baptist service, or perhaps it was the sermon on that particular morning. All I knew was that I needed to change my way of living. I got serious about church after that, attending every Sunday morning and Wednesday evening.

But even with the commitment to church, our marriage was troubled; there were simply too many differences between us. It seemed to cool almost from the first weeks, but I was not about to lose the little security and love it offered. We would simply have to make it work.

A few months later, on returning from one of our frequent visits to my wife's parents, I found acceptance papers to the University of South Carolina in the mailbox. I was shocked. I had earned the GI Bill during my four years in the Navy and had applied mainly because my brother-in-law who was attending pharmacy school there had talked me into it. I did it simply to get him off my back, never dreaming that I would actually be accepted.

Now that it was fact, I couldn't wait to get started. I made plans to major in journalism, having always wanted to be a writer. At first it was exciting — with no thought of how hard the next four years would be.

No sooner had I started, though, than I learned we were about to become parents. Suddenly I was a full-time student who also had to work a full-time job. Four years and three children later, I received my coveted degree, but the strain had taken a terrible toll on our marriage.

I went to work for the local newspaper company — not as a reporter but as an advertising salesman in the classified department. It was a big letdown, but selling classified ads paid far better, and with three children and another on the way, I had no choice. My position turned out to be providential; I made rapid progress, soon rising to management level. I still wanted to write, but at least I was a "success."

In 1971, I got my big break. The company had purchased three small weekly newspapers in and around the coastal resort city of Myrtle Beach. I was offered the assignment of building the circulation of the largest and transforming it into a daily. If I could do it, I would be its publisher. I jumped at the opportunity.

My wife, however, did not share my enthusiasm. Her family was then only a little more than an hour's drive away, and the thought of losing them and all of our friends to move down to Myrtle Beach 150 miles away was more than she could bear. So, I commuted. Our relationship continued to deteriorate. Each Sunday evening I left to the wails and tears of my children. And at work I was soon putting in 15 to 17 hours a day. When I arrived home Friday night, I was totally wiped out.

Everyone but me saw the divorce coming. As unhappy as the marriage was, I wanted it to work, if only for the sake of the children. But it was not to be. When the end came, it tore me apart and left me bitter at a lot of people, especially church-going hypocrites. How could God have allowed this to happen to us? I had tried to be a good person and raise my children that way — and this was my reward. I stopped going to church and swore I would never go again.

Into this turmoil came Terri Harris. Younger than me in years, in many ways she was actually older. Somewhat shy around other people, with me she was relaxed and at ease. She was steady and unflappable, with a great reservoir of common-sense wisdom. From the moment we met, the old saying about opposites attracting was true in my case, though heaven only knew what she saw in me with all my problems.

Yet Terri was the last thing I wanted in my life just then; it was no time to become involved in a serious relationship. Instinctively I sensed if we started dating it would get serious. We started — and it did.

Terri was the *only* good thing happening to me at that time. With my whole life unraveling, I was in no condition to run a newspaper — a fact which became apparent to the head office in Columbia. The general manager came to Myrtle Beach to have a "chat" with me. The upshot: while they appreciated my ten years of service, business was business, and things just weren't working out. They would keep me on the payroll for three months while I sought other employment.

At age 37, in the midst of a traumatic divorce, other employment was not that easy to find. At first I was optimistic; I had an impressive resume. But that soon became the problem: everywhere I looked I was told that I was overqualified. I lowered my sights and expectations; still nothing. I hit bottom one morning, when I happened to pass one of the paper's adult carriers on the street. His look was full of pity. No one at the newspaper was supposed to know that I had been terminated. But he knew. And if he knew, they all knew. That evening, after another day of fruitless job-searching, I just sat in total darkness in the motel room where I was living. It was one of the worst nights of my life.

Terri saw what was happening. She encouraged me to try employment agencies, even driving me to distant cities, as the company car was no longer at my disposal. The bank which had recently granted me a large mortgage to build a new home in Myrtle Beach, now refused me an $800 loan to buy an ancient VW, unless I produced a co-signer.

June 30th, 1974, was the date on my last paycheck. Most of it went to child support. About a week later, I finally got a call from one of the agencies. A representative of a national telephone directory service based in Tennessee wondered if I would be interested in selling yellow pages advertising. I assured him I would, and re-assured him in an interview a few days later.

He explained that it was a straight commission job, and that I would be responsible for my own traveling expenses. That was fine by me, I said; I knew I could sell. I tried not to show how scared I was, having never sold on commission. But I needed a job — any job. He promised to call in a week and let me know.

I thanked him for his time, thinking I would probably never hear from him again. But I did. He called the next weekend and offered me the job.

Now I *had* to get a car, and Terri offered to co-sign for me. I didn't like that, but my options were not exactly broad. The training program took a couple of weeks, and finally I was off on my new assignment. But after two days in the field, I had made no sales. Worse, one former account had decided not to renew which meant that the sum total of my commissions thus far was minus $35.

"I can't do this," I muttered over and over. This time, though, I was not alone. I telephoned Terri back in Myrtle Beach. She was convinced that all I needed was a little time and perseverance. In fact, she was so convinced that I got angry at myself for being such a quitter. The following morning I went out and started selling like a man possessed. And the next day I did the same. By late Friday, I had earned more than $500 in commissions.

The following week I made $800, and within six months I was one of the company's top five salesmen nationwide. What delight I took in going back to that bank manager, paying off the car loan, and arranging a loan for a new car. That car symbolized to me that I was out of that desperate period of trying to put my life back on track. Filled with new confidence, I asked Terri to marry me; in May, 1976, she became my wife.

A few months later I was up in North Carolina selling, when I noticed a small weekly newspaper in one of the restaurants. It was just a free-distribution advertising vehicle with some local community news, but it started an idea going. As soon as I got back to Myrtle Beach I told Terri about it. "You know, it's just the sort of thing I've always wanted to do; I could even write a weekly column in it that —"

"Are you crazy?" she cut me off.

"I can do it," I said defensively, "I've proved I can sell advertising and —"

"And now that you've finally got your life stabilized and are making good money, you want to risk everything on some hare-brained —"

"Hey, I've already been at the bottom so what's to fear? We can do it!" I was sure that, together, we could make it work.

But Terri remained skeptical — and scared. Finally I persuaded her to come with me to talk to the manager of a small weekly newspaper and printing plant about forty miles away. When she heard me talking knowledgeably to him in terms of column-inches and layouts and deadlines, she began to change her mind. Finally, she relented.

In February, 1977, I quit my job and laid the groundwork for a new weekly: *The Horry Shopper* (Horry being the county we lived in). After much trial and error, the first edition came off the press, and surprise: my weekly column turned out to be more than just a form of vanity publishing. In fact, in the first few weeks it was often the thing that shortstopped the newspaper on its way from the front lawn to the trash can.

People began to look forward to our little paper, stopping me on the street to tell me how much they had enjoyed my last column. Advertisers found their ads were producing results. As I'd anticipated, Terri and I made an excellent team, and by the end of the second year, we were in the black.

The year 1980 held several landmarks for us, the most important of which was the birth of our son Kennedy. Meanwhile our business continued to grow. We added a second paper and then a third and a fourth. In 1982, after taking a long look at our escalating printing costs, we decided to purchase a web-offset press to do our own printing. It plunged us back into the red, but I was confident we wouldn't be there for too long. We now had a combined circulation of over 55,000, covering a 60-mile radius from Myrtle Beach, with 35 people on the payroll. And even though we seemed to be perpetually cash poor, on paper we looked pretty good.

Certainly the wall behind my desk had a lot of plaques on it. I had joined several civic clubs and was president of the regional advertising publisher's association and on the board of the national. At 45, by all the conventional criteria, I had finally achieved success.

Life was good — better, in fact, than I had ever dared hope for. And then one Saturday morning, as we were working together in the yard, Terri mentioned that we ought to have our son who was now two years old, baptized in the church. Inwardly startled, I ignored her suggestion, hoping she would forget about it. But she persisted, and finally I drew the line: "Look, I'm not going back to church just to have Kennedy baptized. I don't believe in it, I think it's hypocritical, and I've had enough of church to last me a lifetime!"

Ignoring my anger she persevered. "Well, we should at least be in church for his sake. When he's older he can decide for himself," she said with a calmness that unnerved me.

I finally caved in. "All right, all right!" I exclaimed waving my hands in the air in frustration. "We'll go long enough to have him baptized, but that's all!"

About a mile from the house Terri found a Lutheran church with an excellent pre-school program. Judging it to be ideal for Kennedy, she decided we would go there, unaware that my family background was Lutheran. But first she had to meet the pastor. The following Friday as we were finishing dinner, the door-bell rang. It was Pastor William Wingard from St. Philip's Lutheran Church, and his wife; they just wanted to drop by for a quick visit — hopefully to entice us to join their church.

I was furious. We had a cardinal rule that no matter how much pressure we were under, we would never discuss business on the weekends, and if possible we would avoid doing anything at all on Friday evenings. It was a good rule and often seemed to be the only thing that kept us sane. Now, here was this unwanted interruption — and for religion of all things.

Bill Wingard walked into a hornet's nest that evening! He and his wife weren't in the door ten minutes before I announced bluntly that I wasn't interested in joining their church, now or ever. As far as I was concerned his visit was a waste of his time and mine. But I liked him in spite of myself and grudgingly admired his gracious persistence. In disbelief I soon heard myself agreeing to come "three or four times" until Kennedy was baptized.

"But that's it," I declared, "and don't think I'm going to change my mind."

Adding insult to injury, on our very first visit Terri insisted that I go with her to the adult Sunday School class before the service. And the next week, as well. Hardly anyone spoke to me, and I thought, well, nothing's changed: church was still where the hypocrites congregated.

But the third Sunday I spoke up during a class discussion, and afterwards a couple of people told me how much they'd enjoyed that week's column — and I thought, well, maybe I had been a little harsh on them.

Then two women in our class asked me if I would be willing to teach a few classes. How could I refuse? The ego wouldn't allow it. Before long, I was teaching regularly and joining this committee and that committee. When Pastor Wingard asked me if he could put my name forward for the church council, I agreed. To my surprise I was elected.

Very quietly, in my own way and time, I admitted that it was good to be back in church. And all because my wife wanted our son baptized. I smiled as I recalled the line from Scripture: "And a little child shall lead them."

And Sunday (could it have been only four days ago?), teaching Sunday School, was when I first heard of Medjugorje. . . .

As I drifted off to sleep, I seemed to hear the words again in my heart: *You are my son, and I am asking you to do my Son's will. . . .*

5

Write about Medjugorje. . .

I awoke with a start, my neck aching from lying in an awkward position on the couch. Squinting at my watch, I saw it was almost 6:00 a.m. Shaking my head, I went into the bedroom and began getting ready for work.

Soon Terri was up and about, preparing morning coffee and rousing the kids. I walked into the kitchen and began to help. "Terri, what am I going to do about this?"

She realized then that nothing had changed from the previous evening. I was still convinced I had received a personal message from the Virgin Mary. "Okay," she sighed, "so go write about it and be done with it."

I was pretty sure that was what I had to do, but I wanted her confirmation. But I also knew somehow that I would never 'be done with it.'

Arriving at work, I grabbed a cup of coffee and asked our receptionist, Denease, to hold all my calls; I did not want to be disturbed for *anything*. Locking the door to my office, I reviewed the notes I had made from the book and the videotape and cranked a fresh piece of paper into my typewriter.

Two hours later I was still staring at it. I wasn't at the point of panic — yet; there was still plenty of time — more than two days if I needed it. The problem was not what to write; it was just the opposite: there was too much to say. I didn't know where to begin. One thing was certain, though: I was not about to put in print that I had received a personal message from the Virgin Mary. The piece had to be scrupulously objective, or people would think I'd gone off the deep end. As sure as I was of having received that incredible message, I wasn't ready to risk my journalistic credibility by writing about it.

Thumbing through the Faricy book again, I began making more notes. There was no way I was going to get all of this in one column! After another hour went by, I forced myself to start by describing this little village named Medjugorje. I tore it out, balled it up, and threw it at the wastebasket. It missed.

I tried again, typing: "Do you believe in miracles?" After looking at it for a few moments I yanked it out, and sent it towards the wastebasket. It, too, missed. Now I was beginning to panic.

I'd occasionally had writer's block before but never like this! I sat there numbed by my inability to get anything down on paper. And then, once again, I felt a message within my heart, this one an admonishment: *Go pray more and study more.*

My heart leaped, but this time the shock was not as great. Instead, there was a quiet if hesitant acceptance that I was being gently led through the elementary steps of fulfilling the mission of writing about the events of Medjugorje. It would definitely take more than one column to tell the whole story. Meanwhile it was clear that the first one wouldn't be ready for next week's issue; there simply wasn't enough time.

I left the office and went into the production department, where our manager glanced up expectantly. "Look, Smitty," I said, "I'm not going to have a column for next week, so just put something else in its space."

He started to object, but I cut him off. "As a matter of fact, I probably won't have one for the next couple of weeks," and I left before he could comment.

Knowing there was no way I could concentrate on any other subject, I returned to my office and called Mary Jeffcoat, hoping that she might know where I could obtain more information on apparitions and their history. She gave me the name of Jim Stoffel who lived in North Myrtle Beach and who, as it happened, was leaving for Medjugorje with his wife Rosie on the first of November.

"Jim's got another book on Medjugorje, and I can get it for you if you'd like to see it," she added.

"Thanks, Mary, I'd really appreciate it."

I began to feel a bit better — and then, in obedience to the message I had just received, I bowed my head and began to pray aloud. "Lord, I don't really understand what's happening to me, or why, but I'll try. . . ."

It felt a bit awkward — but it also felt good. I was determined to accomplish what had been asked of me, and if it meant a few weeks of research, that was what I would do.

Mary dropped the new book by that evening, and I began reading it immediately. It was by Joseph Pelletier, a Catholic priest who had authored several books on Fatima. He narrated the original events at Medjugorje in detail, from the perspective of one who had investigated other appearances of the Virgin Mary. Totally engrossed, I finished it in two days.

Now, for background, I needed to find out more about apparitions in general. I looked in the telephone book for a Catholic book store and was surprised to find not one in all of South Carolina; in fact, the nearest was in Charlotte, North Carolina, about 200 miles away. As it happened, I did have to go to Charlotte on business in a few days. . . .

In the store I found a history of Marian apparitions, dating back to the sixteenth century. Also, I was pleased to find yet another book on Medjugorje, this one by a Father Svetozar Kraljevic, a Croatian priest directly involved in the Medjugorje apparitions.

I started reading the history and was amazed to learn that apparitions of the Virgin Mary had been occurring for more than 1900 years — in places that I had heard of but never paid any attention to. In Guadalupe, Mexico, in 1531, she had appeared to a 51-year-old Aztec Indian named Juan Diego; in 1858, she had appeared to a young French girl, Bernadette, in Lourdes; and then at the beginning of this century, to three very young children in Fatima, Portugal. And there were others — at Knock, Ireland, and Garabandal, Spain. . . .

I put the book down and shook my head. So, what was happening at Medjugorje was hardly new. But never, I noted, had she appeared this consistently for so long to so many different visionaries at the same time.

Father Svetozar Kraljevic's book was by far the best yet on the apparitions of Medjugorje. Much more than another recital of the details of the first days, he added a spirituality to them that came the closest yet to expressing the feelings I had in discovering this miracle. His writing was simple and direct. It made you stop and think and put into perspective what was happening in this remote little village. There was only a brief paragraph on the back cover about this Franciscan priest, but I immediately became attached to him.

Finally I sensed I was ready to write about Medjugorje. The research had taken the better part of November, but it was time well spent. Because of the depth of the story, I decided to do a four-part series and run them through the month of December, still hoping to tie it in with the Christmas season.

I hurried to the office, again instructing Denease to hold all interruptions. Cranking a piece of paper into my typewriter, I felt an urge to pray: "God, thank you for this," I murmured. "Whatever is to be done, please help me out."

The ideas came as I needed them, and my fingers flew over the keyboard, as I began the first article:

MIRACLE AT MEDJUGORJE
Part 1: The Apparitions
December 4, 1985

In the next four weeks of December, I am going to try to give as accurate an account as possible of an event allegedly occurring in a small nondescript village in the hills of central Yugoslavia. It is a supernatural religious event and is therefore bound to be viewed in a skeptical sense by many; in fact, that the area is heavily Catholic will add to the skepticism.

Obviously, if I personally did not believe there was something important happening there, I would not be writing about it. However, let me say from the outset, it is not an attempt to convert anyone to Catholicism, since I myself am not Catholic; it is also not an attempt to convert anyone to a belief in God. That is for the individual to determine, based on information and needs. I offer it simply as information timely to the Christmas season.

# # #

For the past four and a half years now, Medjugorje (pronounced Med-jew-*gor*-yay), a small village in the mountain area of central Yugoslavia, has attracted worldwide attention as the place where the mother of Jesus, the Virgin Mary, is reported to be appearing almost daily to six young teenagers. As I write this, the apparitions reportedly continue every day. Despite government attempts to discredit the apparitions and to make visits to the site difficult, millions have been and continue to come to the site to see for themselves what is happening. Yugoslavia is, of course, a communist country, which does not recognize any religion or the existence of God. Yet theirs is a heavily Catholic population that is grudgingly allowed to worship within their churches.

According to the children — called seers or visionaries — the message of the Blessed Virgin is simple and direct: she is appearing to the seers to tell the world of the urgency to return to the ways of God, to convert their lives to peace with God and with their fellow man. She is to give each seer 10 messages, or "secrets" of happenings that will occur in the near future. These messages will be visible signs to mankind that the apparitions at Medjugorje are real and that the conversion back to God must be started now. When she has stopped appearing to the youths — a time known only to them — a permanent sign will be left at Medjugorje. It will lead to many healings and conversions in the short time left before the messages will become reality.

The way to conversion is prayer and fasting, according to the seers. Since the apparitions began on June 24, 1981, the seers spend as many as six hours or more daily in prayer. They also fast up to three times a weeks on bread and water only.

The range in the age of the six young people at Medjugorje is noteworthy in view of the skepticism of such an occurrence. When the apparitions began, one was only ten years old, another was fifteen, three were sixteen,and one was seventeen. Four are girls, and two are boys.

Who are these young people to whom the Virgin Mary is allegedly appearing? They are all very normal, but different from each other in personality and, as I have noted, in age. With one exception, all of them are of average intelligence. The exception is Mirjana Dragicevic. She is the third oldest of the seers and attends college at the University of Sarajevo, where her family now lives.

Maria Pavlovic is the oldest of the group. She is of average height and thin and is the most serene and deeply spiritual of the seers. She plans on becoming a nun.

Vicka Ivankovic, the second oldest, also plans on becoming a nun. She has strong features, and her face is very expressive. She is the charmer of the group, although there is nothing "put-on" about her.

Ivanka Ivankovic, the youngest of the four girls is the only one of the group planning marriage. She is the prettiest of the girls and seems typical of today's teenagers, but is firmly religious.

Ivan Dragicevic, the older of the two boys, wants to become a priest. He is the most timid and retiring of the group and appears to be serious and pensive most of the time.

The youngest, and most lively, is thirteen-year-old Jakov Colo, who was only ten when the apparitions began. Like the others, he is quite normal.

The presence of this young, fidgety boy among the group of seers is very special in terms of authenticity of the apparitions. Comparing him to, say, our own children or brothers of this age, it would normally be highly improbable that he would go to church for two and three hours of prayer every single day, in winter and summer, in bad weather and good, and do this for well over four years, simply to make believe that he is seeing a holy apparition from God.

In fact, the age and character of all the seers and the consistency of the apparitions with them is strong evidence that something highly unusual is happening.

There is so much to tell about Medjugorje. Possibly the following excerpt, taken from a report that was sent to the Pope at the request of Mary, according to the youths, will summarize this segment best. A Catholic priest named Tomislav Vlasic, who has been involved in the apparitions almost from the very first, was asked by Mirjana to do this. Here is a portion of that report:

According to Mirjana, during the apparition on December 25, 1982, the Madonna confided the tenth and last secret to her, and she revealed the dates on which the various secrets will come to pass. The Blessed Virgin revealed many aspects of the future to Mirjana, many more up to now than to the other seers. For that reason, I relate now what Mirjana told me in a conversation on November 5, 1983. I shall summarize the essential things she said, without any literal quotations. Mirjana said: Before the visible sign is given to humanity, there will be three warnings to the world. The warnings will be warnings on the earth. Mirjana will witness them. Three days before one of these warnings, she will advise a priest of her choice. Mirjana's testimony will be a confirmation of the apparitions and an incentive for the conversion of the world. After these warnings, the visible sign will be given for all humanity at the place of the apparitions in Medjugorje. The sign will be given as the testimony of the apparitions and a call back to faith.

The ninth and tenth secrets are grave matters.

They are a chastisement for the sins of the world. The punishment is inevitable because we cannot expect the conversion of the entire world. The chastisement can be mitigated by prayers and penance. It cannot be suppressed. An evil which threatened the world, according to the seventh secret, had been eliminated through prayer and fasting, Mirjana said. For that reason the Blessed Virgin continues to ask for prayer and fasting: "You have forgotten that with prayer and fasting you can ward off wars, suspend natural laws."

After the first warning, the others will follow within a rather brief period of time. So it is that people will have time for conversion.

This time is a period of grace and conversion. After the visible sign, those who are still alive will have little time for conversion. For that reason, the Blessed Virgin calls for urgent conversion and reconciliation.

The invitation to prayer and penance is destined to ward off evil and war and above all to save souls.

According to Mirjana, we are close to the events predicted by the Blessed Virgin. Because of this, Mirjana says to mankind: "Convert yourselves as quickly as possible. Open your hearts to God."

Father Vlasic gave a little additional information about the secrets during a taped interview in August, 1983: "They (the seers) say that with the realization of the secrets entrusted to them by Our Lady, life in the world will change. Afterwards, men (mankind) will believe like in ancient times. What will change and how it will change, we will not know until the secrets are revealed."

These few words imply a lot about the extraordinary events at Medjugorje. As for its authenticity, that is for each of us in our own hearts to decide.

I leaned back and stretched. Two hours had passed — as long as I had originally sat paralyzed several weeks before, staring at an empty sheet of paper. It seemed like much less; in fact, I could not remember ever writing anything so effortlessly.

Taking it into the production department, I warned Smitty that this column and the next three were going to run longer than usual. And with that I closed up the front office and started for home.

*"Pray constantly and in this way,
I will give you the joy which
the Lord gives me. . . ."*

6

The Momentum Builds . . .

But now, as I began the drive home, negative thoughts of the effect of writing about such an unusual religious subject began to fill my head. What would this do to my journalistic credibility? Would I, in fact, even have any credibility? It amazed me that I could go from the euphoria of having finally finished the first column to complete uncertainty that I was doing the right thing by even writing it.

By the time I got home, I was sure it was a mistake. The peace and spiritual exhilaration from the message I had received had been overwhelmed by the reality of everyday living. I sat down with Terri and told her of my apprehension to publish what I had just spent the last month carefully and tirelessly researching.

As always, she had the right words. "Look: you wrote it objectively, and you really feel called to be doing this, so listen and do it. No one's going to laugh at you. It's a good story, and I like what you've done with it," she said, tapping the pages of manuscript I had brought home for her to proofread.

I decided to let it run. But in the three days before the presses would run on Monday evening, I almost changed my mind a dozen times. Once the papers were printed, there was no calling them back.

Meanwhile, teaching Sunday School, I stuck strictly to the Lutheran curriculum material. Not a word about Medjugorje. The Sunday after I had received the message, I told Becky Ginley that I was profoundly touched by what was going on there, but that was it; I did not go into detail.

Because of my close relationship with Pastor Wingard and our associate pastor, Dick Albert, I also discussed it with them — again leaving out the part about receiving a message from the Virgin Mary. Bill Wingard rejected it almost immediately as a "Catholic thing," citing Lutheran theology and the problems in the Catholic Church that inevitably led to the Reformation and the beginnings of Protestantism. And of course, "Mary worship" was mentioned; it would not be the last time I would hear it.

Pastor Albert, though extremely cautious, was also curious. He agreed to attend a lecture at the Catholic church in North Myrtle Beach to hear Jim and Rosie Stoffel who had just returned from their trip to Medjugorje. Becky Ginley, Mary Jeffcoat, Terri and I met him there just before the start of the lecture. Excited and pleased that he had come, I enthusiastically told him how I truly believed that the Virgin Mary was appearing there.

"Well, I'd love to believe it, too," he said, choosing his words carefully, "but to be honest, I would be more convinced if there was stronger evidence, say like pictures."

I was stunned when about half-way through the lecture, Jim passed around a picture that had been taken of the huge cement cross that stands on the mountain behind the church at Medjugorje. There, next to the cross was a blurred image of a figure, closely resembling a woman with a veil over her head, her hands folded in prayer! It was claimed that the picture had been taken of the cross by a pilgrim who when the film was developed, had found this mysterious picture among her prints. I watched as Pastor Albert looked at the picture. "Well," he said, "it's not very clear. . . ."

One thing was clear from my associate pastor's response: I was going to have a problem trying to make anyone believe that I had something even more astounding than pictures. If I told them that Mary had actually spoken to me and asked me to make the spreading of the message of Medjugorje my life's mission, who would believe me?

At work the following morning I felt positively ill worrying about it. And Tuesday morning was worse; I went immediately to the press room to get a copy of the just-printed edition of our Lake City newspaper. I turned to the column and read it; it sounded terribly religious, but it was too late to change anything. At least now it was out of my control: there was no longer anything I could do to alter the inevitable. At three o'clock the papers would be taken to the post office, for delivery the following day.

Wednesday, December 4, 1985, dawned bright and cheery — as if gently mocking the way I was feeling. "Well, Denease," I said on my way into my office, "brace yourself; the kooks will start calling any time now."

Sure enough, a few minutes later she came in and said, "All right, here's the first one, someone from Lake City," and she pointed to the phone on which the light was lit. "The guy is laughing, crying, I can't understand *what* he's saying! But he definitely insists on talking to you!"

"Great," I muttered.

"Get used to it, boss," she burst out laughing, "I think you're going to be getting a lot of them!"

She left, and taking a deep breath I reached for the phone. "Hello?"

"Is this Wayne Weible? The one who's written about Medjugorje?"

"Yes, it is."

"Well, Praise Jesus! I just thank God for you! God bless

you!" He went on in that vein while I stared at the receiver. Finally he paused for breath and slowed down. "Let me explain: My name is Scotti, Father Sylvester Scotti. I was one of a hundred American priests who went to Medjugorje in October, a year ago. I was so struck by what was happening there that when I returned home I went to all the major newspapers, television and radio stations in our part of South Carolina, but nobody would touch it. Nobody! And this morning I go out to my mailbox, and there's your little paper and your column, and there's Medjugorje." He started crying again. "Please, I'm sorry, but you just don't know what this has done for me!"

I didn't know what to say. I felt a surge of emotion welling up inside of me —

"Excuse me," he said, mustering control, "you probably think I'm crazy. I'm not, really; I'm just Italian!"

We both laughed at that. "No," I managed, "I don't think you're crazy. I'm a little overwhelmed with what you're telling me. I really didn't expect such a positive response. . . ."

And then we did talk, him mostly. He told me about how he and the priests had been present in the basement of the rectory when the Virgin Mary had appeared to the visionaries there and given them a special message for the priests. Father Scotti was definitely what was known as a Marian priest, that is, one entirely devoted to the Blessed Virgin. He had visited almost every shrine where she had reportedly appeared in the past five centuries. We agreed to meet in the next few days to talk further.

Hanging up, I went over and locked the door, then sat down at my desk and let the tears come. I realized that this was confirmation that the columns were definitely meant to be published. It was as though that still, small voice was speaking to me once again, saying: *You see?*

I was still choked up when I went into Terri's office to tell her what happened.

"What on earth's the matter?" she exclaimed, seeing my face.

"It's the column. I just got this call —" I had difficulty continuing, finally making a strong effort to control my emotions. I told her about Father Scotti. "I don't care what happens now," I concluded. "It was worth it!"

She just smiled. "That's wonderful!"

"Three more calls," Denease informed me when I returned to my office, "and they're asking for copies — what should I do?"

"Send them copies, for heaven's sake!" I grinned. "What's it going to cost us, an envelope with a stamp on it?"

More calls came in — congratulatory, curious, anxious to know if there would be a follow-up. When I went to the bank that afternoon the tellers began all talking at once, telling me how they loved what was happening in that little village.

"You know, we have no doubt that this is from God," one of them said.

"Are you Catholic?" I asked.

"Are you kidding? We're all Baptists!"

I laughed; this was beyond my wildest hopes. By the end of the day we had received more than a dozen calls — more than any of my columns had ever elicited. And then the letters started coming.

Normally I put off writing my column until the last possible moment which was Friday, but by Thursday I was so pumped and primed, I decided to write the second column a day early. This time I tried an outline and followed it — and then tore it out, balled it up, and threw it away.

Offering a quick prayer, I again asked for guidance —

and noticed that it didn't feel the least bit uncomfortable. I picked up Father Svetozar's book. People had been asking: what exactly was being said to the visionaries?

Well, why not simply tell them? Once again, my fingers flew over the keys. . . .

Part 2: Conversations with Mary, the Mother of Jesus. Dec. 11, 1985

This is the second in this very special, four-part series of columns I am doing for the Christmas season. The interest in the first part has been excellent and positive. Because of the nature of the subject, a supernatural religious event, I am going to restate several things from last week's column.

First, I personally feel something. . . important and meaningful to everyone, regardless of religious affiliation, is happening in Medjugorje. . .

Here are selected bits of conversations reported by the seers, of conversations with the Blessed Virgin Mary:

On the fourth evening of the apparitions, which began June 24, 1981, Ivanka asked the lady her name. "I am the Blessed Virgin Mary," was the reply. Later, Vicka said, "If you are Our Lady, stay with us. If you are not, be gone!" The lady smiled and remained.

Vicka asked: "Why have you come?" The reply: "I came because there are many good believers here. I want to be with you, to convert and reconcile everyone." Later on the same occasion, another seer, Marija, saw the lady on her way down from the hill where the apparitions first began. She stopped suddenly, ran to her left and dropped to her knees. There she says, "Our Lady was standing before a cross, with tears in her eyes. She repeated several times: "Peace, peace, peace, be reconciled with one another."

Many times during the apparitions, she has said, "Believe, as if you, too, see."

On June 29th, the children asked specifically for the healing of a two-and-a-half year-old boy who was mute and unable to walk. The seers asked the Virgin Mary to heal him. Jakov reported her response: "Let his parents believe that he will be healed." Later in the evening as the family of the boy was on their way home, they stopped at a restaurant. The mute little boy banged on the table and said, "I want a drink." Since then, he is now able to talk and walk. She has directed others to pray and fast and ask Jesus to be healed of their specific ailments or handicaps. Many have been healed, according to the reports of the people there.

Again, concerning healing Mary has told the seers: "I cannot heal; only God can. I need your prayers and sacrifices to help me."

Continuing: (speaking urgently on the need for conversion) "The only word I wish to say is 'conversion!' To the whole world. I am saying this to you to tell everybody. I ask only for conversion. Be ready for everything and be converted. Give up everything that goes against conversion."

On prayer and faith: "Let them (those in Medjugorje and the visitors; also those who hear about Medjugorje) believe as if they see; believe firmly. There are many believers who do not pray; faith cannot be alive without prayer."

When the children asked at the request of a priest if people should pray to Jesus or to Mary, her answer was: "Please pray to Jesus. I am His mother and I intercede for you with Him. But all prayer goes to

Jesus. I will help. I will pray, but everything does not depend only on me. It depends also on your strength, the strength of those who pray."

On why she has chosen to appear in Medjugorje: "I have chosen this parish in a special way. I want to protect you and guide you in love. And therefore, I ask for a total conversion of the parish so that the pilgrims can find a fountain of conversion here." At the time of this message, she also recommended a special passage from the Gospel of Matthew, chapter 6, verses 24 to 34.

During a special holy week in 1984, the Virgin Mary said to the parish through the young seer, Jelena: "Raise your hands and open your hearts. Now, in the moment of the resurrection, Jesus wants to give you a particular gift. It is this: You will undergo trials with great ease. We will be nearby and will show you the way out if you will accept us. Don't say that the Holy Year is now over and there is no more need to pray. On the contrary, reinforce your prayers, because the Holy Year is just one step forward." After this, Jelena reported that she saw the risen Jesus. Brilliant light radiated from His wounds onto the people. Jesus said, "Receive my graces and tell the whole world there will be happiness only through Me."

A final note on this part of the articles. Today, the entire parish of Medjugorje, with, of course a very few exceptions, attends church services daily. These services usually last for more than three hours. The greatest miracle of Medjugorje that is proven fact, is the total conversion of the community that was already faithful by today's standards.

This time I was ready for the response. Everywhere I went — the supermarket, the gas station, the Rotarians — people were talking about the columns. And now a great many of them were asking for copies — of the first column, if they hadn't seen it, or of both, so that they could pass them on. I spent most of the week about two inches off the ground.

*"Live the fasting — with it you will give me
joy for the fulfillment of all
of God's plans. . . ."*

7

And Continues. . .

This time there was no thought of waiting till Friday
to begin the third article in the series; I could hardly wait
till Thursday! I was getting a lot of how-and-why questions
now, and I decided to let the visionaries answer for
themselves. One of the strongest elements in Father
Svetozar's book were interviews with them, conducted by
the author and another priest, Tomislav Vlasic. In this
third column I would feature two which together did a
superb job of answering many of the questions I was
receiving.

Part 3: Interviews with the Seers
Dec. 18, 1985

It hardly seems possible that two weeks have passed
since I began running this very special series of
columns concerning reports of the Blessed Virgin
Mary, the Mother of God, appearing to a group of
young people in Yugoslavia.

While it is by far one of the most difficult subjects
I have attempted to write about, it is also the most
satisfying from the standpoint of having done
something worthwhile. Professionally, I want readers
to see it as objective and informational; personally,

I want it to inspire everyone who reads it to strengthen their relationship with God and fellow man. That is the purpose of running it during the celebration of Christmas.

This week, interviews with two of the young people are featured. The answers given were taken direct from a tape recording of the conversations with them. Parts of the interviews were excluded at my discretion so that I could run as much of them as possible. (Excerpts taken from *The Apparitions of Our Lady at Medjugorje*, by Svetozar Kraljevic, O.F.M.)

Father Vlasic: Mirjana, we have not seen each other for some time, and I would like you to tell me about the apparitions of the Blessed Virgin Mary, and especially the events that are connected with you.

M: I have seen the Blessed Virgin Mary for eighteen months now, and feel I know her very well. I feel she loves me with her motherly love, and so I have been able to ask her about anything I would like to know. I've asked her to explain some things about Heaven, Purgatory, and Hell that were not clear to me. For example, I asked her how God can be so unmerciful as to throw people into Hell, to suffer forever. I thought: If a person commits a crime and goes to jail, he stays there for a while and then is forgiven — but to Hell, forever? She told me that souls who go to Hell have ceased thinking favorably of God — have cursed Him, more and more. So they've already become a part of Hell, and choose not to be delivered from it.

Then she told me that there are levels in Purgatory: levels close to Hell and higher and higher toward Heaven. Most people, she said, think many souls are released from Purgatory into Heaven on All Saints'

Day, but most souls are taken into Heaven on Christmas Day.

V: Did you ask why God allows Hell?

M: No, I did not. But afterward I had a discussion with my aunt, who told me how merciful God is. So I said I would ask the Madonna how God could . . . .

V: According to what you've said, then; It's as simple as this: people who oppose God on earth just continue their existence after death, and oppose God in Hell?

M: Really, I thought if a person goes to Hell. . . . Don't people pray for their salvation? Could God be so unmerciful as not to hear their prayers? Then the Madonna explained it to me. People in Hell do not pray at all; instead, they blame God for everything. In effect, they become one with that Hell and they get used to it. They rage against God, and they suffer, but they always refuse to pray to God.

V: To ask Him for salvation?

M: In Hell, they hate Him even more.

V: As for Purgatory, you say that souls who pray frequently are sometimes allowed to communicate, at least by messages, with people on earth, and that they receive the benefits of prayers said on earth?

M: Yes. Prayers that are said on earth for souls who have not prayed for their salvation are applied to souls in Purgatory who pray for their salvation.

V: Did the Madonna tell you whether many people go to Hell today?

M: I asked her about that recently, and she said that, today, most people go to Purgatory, the next greatest number go to Hell, and only a few go directly to Heaven.

V: Only a few go to Heaven?

M: Yes. Only a few — the least number — go to Heaven.

V: Did you ask about the conditions for a person to enter Heaven?

M: No, I didn't; but, we can probably say what they are. God is not looking for great believers but simply for those who respect their faith and live peacefully, without malice, meanness, falsehood.

V: This is your interpretation, your understanding?

M: Yes. After I talked to the Madonna, I came to that conclusion: No one has to perform miracles or do great penance; merely live a simple, peaceful life.

V: Well, besides Heaven, Hell and Purgatory, is there any else new recently?

M: The Madonna told me that I should tell the people that many in our time judge their faith by their priests. If a priest is not holy, they conclude that there is no God. She said, "You do not go to church to judge the priest, to examine his personal life. You go to church to pray and to hear the Word of God from the priest." This must be explained to the people, because many turn away from the faith because of priests.

Today, as it was a long time ago, the Virgin told me, God and the devil conversed, and the devil said that people believe in God only when life is good for them. When things turn bad, they cease to believe in God. Then people blame God or act as if He does not exist. God, therefore, allowed the devil one century in which to exercise an extended power over the world, and the devil chose the twentieth century. Today, as we can see all around us, everyone is dissatisfied; they cannot abide each other. Examples are the number of divorces and abortions. All this, the Madonna said, is the work of the devil.

V: This behavior of people — they're under the

influence of the devil. But the devil does not have to be in them?

M: No, no. The devil is not in them, but they're under the influence of the devil, although he enters into some of them.

To prevent this, at least to some extent, the Madonna said we need communal prayer, family prayer. She stressed the need for family prayer most of all. Also, every family should have at least one sacred object in the house, and houses should be blessed regularly.

She also emphasized the failings of religious people, especially in small villages — for example, here in Medjugorje, where there is separation from Serbians (i.e., Serbian Orthodox) and Moslems. This separation is not good. The Madonna always stresses that there is but one God, and that people have enforced unnatural separation. One cannot truly believe, be a true Christian, if he does not respect other religions as well. You do not really believe in God if you make fun of other religions.

V: What, then, is the role of Jesus Christ, if the Moslem religion is a good religion?

M: We did not discuss that. She merely explained, and deplored, the lack of religious unity, "especially in the villages." She said that everybody's religion should be respected, and, of course, one's own.

V: Tell me where the devil is especially active today. Did she tell you anything about this? Through whom or what does he manifest himself the most?

M: Most of all through people of weak character, who are divided within themselves. Such people are everywhere, and they are the easiest for the devil to enter. But he also enters the lives of strong believers — sisters, for example. He would rather "convert" real believers than nonbelievers. How can I explain this? You saw what happened to me. He tries to bring as many believers as possible to himself.

V: Can we suppose, then, that one of you might say that three secrets would be revealed before the great sign appears; then the rest of the secrets will be revealed, one by one? Is there anything to that?

M: Nothing like that, but something like this. First, some secrets will be revealed — just a few. Then the people will be convinced that the Madonna was here. Then they will understand the sign. When Jakov said that the mayor will be the first one to run to the hill, he meant that generally people of the highest social class. They will understand the sign as a place of occasion to convert. They will run to the hill and pray, and they will be forgiven. When I asked the Madonna about unbelievers, she said "They should be prayed for, and they should pray." But when I asked again recently, she said, "Let them convert while there is time." She did not say they should be prayed for.

V: You can say nothing specifically until the moment the Madonna says you can?

M: Yes.

V: What does the Madonna say? Can we prepare ourselves for what will happen?

M: Yes prepare! The Madonna said people should prepare themselves spiritually, be ready, and not panic; be reconciled in their souls. They should be ready for the worst, to die tomorrow. They should accept God now so that they will not be afraid. They should accept God, and everything else. No one accepts death easily, but they can be at peace in their souls if they are believers. If they are committed to God, He will accept them.

V: This means total conversion and surrender to God?

M: Yes.

V: After these ten secrets, after these eighteen months of apparitions, what do you tell the people that they should do? What do you say to priests, to the Pope and bishops, without revealing the secrets? What does the Madonna want us to do?

M: First, I would like to tell you how it was for me at the end, and the—

V: All right.

M: Two days before Christmas, the Madonna told me Christmas Day would be the last time she would appear to me. (I didn't quite believe this.) On Christmas Day, she stayed with me for forty-five minutes and we talked about many things. We summarized everything that had been said between us. On behalf of many people, I asked what they should do. Then she gave me a very precious gift: she said she would appear to me on my birthday every year for the rest of my life. Also, independently of the sign — and anything else — she said she will appear to me when something very difficult happens — not some everyday difficulty, but something quite grievous. Then, she will come to help me. But now, I have to live without her physical presence, without her daily, personal visits. I say to all people: Convert! — the same as she said. "Convert while there is time!" Do not abandon God and your faith. Abandon everything else, but not that!

V: What is the greatest danger to mankind? What does it come from?

M: From godlessness. Nobody believes — hardly anybody. For example, the Madonna told me that the faith in Germany, Switzerland, and Austria is very weak. The people in those countries model themselves on their priests, and if the priests are not good examples, the people fall away and believe there is no God. When I was in Askona I heard of a priest to whom a rich man had left money to build a home for old people, but instead, the priest built a hotel. Now all the people in that city have turned their backs on the faith, because how could a priest not fulfill the last wish of a dying man and, instead, build a hotel and make money for himself? Nevertheless, people must understand that they shouldn't scrutinize a priest's private life, but listen to what he says through God — God's word.

V: Before we finish this interview, is there anything you would like to add?

M: She said some things that are for me personally. She advised me on various matters. Then she said: "Go in God's peace!"

V: Did she talk to you about the other visionaries and further apparitions?

M: She told me I am — well, more mature than the others and therefore I must help them, spend time with them and talk with them. This will make things easier for them and for me. We are to understand each other and stay together — united.

V: She did not mention further developments or apparitions, either individually or to all of you as a group?

M: I think that when each individual learns the tenth secret, she will cease appearing to that person.

Father Svetozar interviews Ivanka Ivankovic

Father Svetozar: Ivanka, you and Mirjana were taking a walk together that day. Why were you walking together?

I: We regularly walked together in that area. We had been at my house; then we decided to take our walk.

S: Who was with you, besides Mirjana?

I: At first, just Mirjana and myself. When we returned to my house, Milka, Marija's sister, asked us to go with her to get the sheep and bring them home.

S: So the two of you went with Milka to get the sheep?

I: The first time, Mirjana and I were walking alone, and as we were returning to the village I happened to look toward the hill — and I saw the figure of the Madonna, bright and shining. I said to Mirjana: "Look, the Madonna!" Mirjana dismissed what I said with a wave of her hand as if I'd been joking, and she said: "It's not very likely that the Madonna would appear to us." So we continued to walk toward the village. Mirjana did not even look where I pointed to the hill. When we got to Milka's house, Milka said: "Help me get the sheep and bring them home." So we turned around and started walking back to the fields. This time, all three of us saw the Madonna. We knelt down and prayed; then we got the sheep and chased them home. Later, Vicka and Ivan and the other Ivan joined us.

S: On that first day, you saw the Madonna twice?

I: Yes. The first time when Mirjana and I were walking back to the village, and the second time when we went with Milka to get the sheep.

S: Who saw the Madonna first?

I: I did.

S: What did you say when you saw her?

I: I said: "Look, Mirjana, the Madonna!"

S: Then what did you do? Where did you go?

I: We went to Milka's. We stopped in front of her house and she asked us to help her get the sheep. Then the three of us went to get the sheep to bring them home. When we passed the hill, I saw the Madonna again, this time holding the baby Jesus in her hands. Mirjana and Milka also looked, and they too saw the Madonna.

S: What did seeing the Madonna mean to you?

I: It meant everything in the world!

S: When you talk with the Madonna in your visions, we cannot hear you speak.

I: We speak out loud, the same as now.

S: Let me put it this way. Do you speak with the Madonna mentally — that is she understands what you think — or do you speak to her in a low voice, a whisper, so we cannot hear you? Or is your conversation miraculous — beyond our power to hear and understand?

I: I speak with her normally, the same as I'm speaking now. Also, I hear her voice and words in the normal way, as well as what the others say.

S: In your visions, have you ever asked favors for anybody?

I: I have, in the beginning, I asked a favor for little Daniel.

S: What did the Madonna say?

I: She said the same thing she always says: Strong faith and prayer will help.

S: What do you mean, "strong faith and prayer"? For what?

I: To believe and pray for a healing.

S: Did you ever ask for anybody in your family who has passed away?

I: Yes. I asked for my father not long ago, and she said the same thing.

S: What did Our Lady say?

I: She said my mother is with her, and that I should obey and not worry.

S: You were saddened by your mother's death, and because of that the Madonna came to comfort you.

I: I don't know; but I don't think so. We asked her why, of all people, she appeared to us. She said she does not always seek out the best people.

S: To whom are the Madonna's messages sent?

I: To the whole world.

S: What are the messages?

I: Peace, conversion, fasting, penance, prayer.

S: Which is the most important?

I: Peace.

S: Why peace?

I: When everyone in the world is at peace, everything is possible.

S: You mentioned prayer. Tell me honestly, how do you pray?

I: When I get up in the morning I pray seven Our Fathers and the Credo. At noon, I pray the Angelus. In the evening, I pray seven Our Fathers and the Credo, and sometimes the rosary. When we are all home together, we pray an evening prayer.

S: It is known that the Madonna recommended that all of you enter a convent.

I: She told us it is her wish that we enter a convent — but only those who have such a wish. She does not want anyone to disgrace the faith and the Church.

S: I believe that everyone is free to choose, and you are free as well. Have you decided what you will do in this connection?

I: To tell you the truth, as I feel right now, I do not want to enter the convent. I can live a Christian life, the same as a nun, raising—

S: Bearing in mind what you know about the future, tell me if the Madonna of Medjugorje will reconcile the world even more.

I: I think she will.

S: Will the "great sign" help in achieving this?

I: Yes, when the time comes. More believers will come to church.

S: Will the sign appear very soon, or later?

I: It will appear at the proper time.

S: Ivanka, are you in any way fearful of being able to do what the Madonna expects of you in this life?

I: Why should I be afraid when God is with me? God gives me whatever strength I need.

S: You speak to the people of the Madonna's messages, but some do not believe you. In that case, what do you do?

I: I pray for them, that God will enlighten them.

S: Can you do anything else?

I: I will go on trying to persuade them. They will be convinced, once they—

S: I believe that, but in the meantime people become nervous. It is difficult to wait for that day. What should people do?

I: Pray that God will give us the strength to endure.

S: There are those who are opposed to the Madonna. What would you tell them?

I: I'd tell them: Convert! There is a God. That is it!

S: Can those who oppose the Madonna frustrate her plans in the world?

I: You mean the great sign?

S: Yes.

I: No. All their armaments and explosives could not destroy it.

S: Can they do harm to the souls of the people

and to the Madonna's plans for the people?

I: No.

S: Does that mean the Madonna is stronger than they?

I: Normally she is. It is Jesus who decides — God. Not the Madonna.

S: Tell me about this.

I: I think that God has sent her here. When we asked her for a sign, I think she asked Jesus and He gave her a sign. Then she promised to give us a sign.

S: That means she cannot act independently on her own. She must do the will of God, as she always has.

I: I believe so.

S: It is important that people of good faith, regardless of denomination, not be turned against each other. But tell me more about this. What did the Madonna say about this?

I: The Madonna said that religions are separated in the earth, but the people of all religions are accepted by her Son.

S: Does that mean that all people go to Heaven?

I: It depends on what they deserve.

S: Yes, but many have never heard about Jesus.

I: Jesus knows all about that; I don't. The Madonna said, basically, religions are similar; but many people have separated themselves, because of religion, and become enemies of each other.

S: I thank you, Ivanka, for this conversation and testimony!

I groaned as I pulled the last page out of the typewriter — the eighth! Smitty was going to have a fit!

He did. "What did you do, write a book?" he shouted,

looking at the pages in my hand. "That's going to run more than a whole page!" To Smitty, my column was one big headache. He would rather have no news copy at all, just ads.

"Well, then let it," I answered, smiling. "Look, I got it done a day early; you should be happy. Lay it out, and let me worry about it."

"Well, what if we get an ad at the last minute?" Normally our policy was to take out the column, if necessary, to make room for the paying customers.

"No," I replied, "not this time. It runs as is."

I turned to leave, then remembered something: we had received more than forty requests for copies. "Oh, and Smitty? Leave room for a little blurb telling people that if they request copies, they're going to have to send us a self-addressed, stamped envelope. I'll give you the copy tomorrow."

Leaving him shaking his head and muttering, I went happily out into the night.

8

Father Scotti

I was not in my office to take the calls Wednesday morning. I was on my way to the town of Lake City, 60 miles away, to pay a visit to Father Sylvester Scotti.

After the second column had come out, he had called again, wanting to know when I was going to come by to see him. As I had planned to wrap up the four-part series on Medjugorje with interviews of local residents who had actually made the long trip to Yugoslavia, I readily agreed to include his story. Besides, I was curious to meet this not-so-crazy Italian priest.

Not being good at directions, I had a little trouble finding his house. Actually, it was more like it found me: I drove around the streets of his neighborhood, trying to make sense of the notes I had scribbled down over the phone. Then all at once I looked up, and it was right there.

As I walked up the front steps, the door suddenly swung open, and I was greeted by a great bear of a man, beaming, heavy-set, in his fifties, with thick glasses and unkempt hair. He was wearing an old shirt and pants and scruffy shoes — exactly what I had expected him to look like, based on our original phone conversation.

When I reached the door, he grabbed me and hugged me like we'd known each other for years and said, "I've got the coffee pot on; let's talk." And so we did.

I learned that my host was pastor of two tiny mission churches in Kingstree and Lake City. "It's the Siberia of this diocese," he explained, pouring me some more coffee, "but I don't mind. It gives me more time to pray. I think I've been assigned here because they don't know what else to do with me. They think I'm a bit — unconventional."

I was soon to discover just how unconventional. He had already told me how much his pilgrimage to Medjugorje had meant to him. Now I began my tape recorder and started asking questions. Time flew, and changing tapes for the second time, I suddenly realized I had been there for more than three hours of almost non-stop conversation.

I had just begun to tell him how I had heard of Medjugorje, when all at once he held up his hand for me to stop. Then looking steadily at me, he proceeded to speak in tongues. I knew just enough about the gifts of the Holy Spirit and Charismatics to know what was happening. While I had no idea what he was saying, I didn't feel at all alarmed by it or threatened, just a little uncomfortable. He wasn't shouting, but speaking in soft, melodic tones.

Part of me was wondering: what have you gotten yourself into? But the other part was content to just listen and wait. After a couple of minutes he stopped, and we looked at each other. "I hope you're not embarrassed," he said.

"No," I assured him. "A little surprised, but not embarrassed."

"Good. Because that was a message for you, from Mary. She says: you are her son. And she is asking you to write about this, but more than that: to contribute your life to it, to completely consecrate yourself to spreading the message of Medjugorje."

He stopped. My mouth was open, and my eyes were

widening. And then in a stammering voice, scarcely able to find the words, I told him about the message I had originally received — of which his was an almost verbatim confirmation. I could feel my scalp tightening even as I spoke; this was getting a little frightening.

Encouraged, Father Scotti continued, "The sense I get is that you're going to go far beyond South Carolina with this message, or even this country, for that matter. You will be involved in broadcasting —"

"Oh, come on, Father!" I interjected. "I'm a newspaper publisher; I do a column, more for my own ego than anything else. I'm not into TV or radio."

"Hey," he laughed that big Italian laugh of his, "I'm only repeating what I think she's telling you!" And then he had compassion. "Look, I know that's a whole lot for you. Just keep praying and remain open to what is being asked of you — and don't worry about it."

How could I *not* worry about it? All of this was beyond anything I had ever imagined. A few weeks ago, I would hardly have mentioned the name of Jesus outside of my church. Now, I had been told everything in the message — by a stranger.

I looked at my watch; it was after four. "It's getting late; I've really got to go," I said. "Can we get together again in a couple of weeks?"

"Of course!" he grinned, showing me to the door.

"You know," I smiled, as we said good-bye, "I've never been around anyone who spoke in tongues before. The funny thing is, it wasn't offensive to me. I mean, as a Protestant and a journalist, it's just that — well, nothing about any of this has rubbed me the wrong way. But I'm not so sure about your message. . . ."

He just smiled and said, "You'll see."

It was late when I got back to the office, but I went straight to my typewriter. I wanted to get down everything Father Scotti had told me while it was still fresh. I worked away for about an hour and a half, and as I finished I thought that if I could see Jim Stoffel in the morning, I could have this column done tomorrow. That was important, as we were leaving for Charleston, West Virginia, for Christmas with Terri's family.

Jim seemed the logical choice of the other local who had been to Medjugorje. He and his wife Rosie had been extremely struck by it, and that had come through in the talk he had given. Besides, there was something special about the two of them; Terri and I had liked them instantly and had talked of getting together in the future. Together, the two interviews would make the perfect wrap-up for the series. Yawning, I switched out the light and headed for home.

But the following morning I awoke with an ache in my head and nausea in my stomach — and realized that I was not going to escape the flu bug, after all. A couple of weeks before, it had hit Terri but had passed over me — or so I had thought. No such luck. And now I had no choice but to postpone the last column until after Christmas; there was no way I could interview Jim and write the column in this condition.

I had recovered enough by the time we left for West Virginia not to ruin everyone else's Christmas. Actually, it had been an extremely good Christmas so far — in fact, because of Medjugorje it had been just about the best I'd ever known. For the first time I felt the full impact of God's gift to us of His Son. And this same Mary, who had accepted the motherhood of our Lord without question, was now asking me to take an active part in bringing others back to a full acknowledgment of that gift. I could not think about it without tears.

There was one other special gift that came a little early. One evening I was mopping the kitchen floor for Terri, when she had her bout with the flu. The phone rang, and I tiptoed across the still-wet floor to answer it. It was George McMath, head of Atlantic Publications, a company that owned a chain of 29 weekly newspapers and other publications, one of which was located in Myrtle Beach. We made small talk for a few moments, then he came to the purpose of his late call. Would we be interested in selling our four newspapers?

I went into a state of shock. For more than two years we had been trying to sell the papers. After nine years of deadlines, personnel problems, and financial crises, we were both stressed out. Terri wanted to stay home and spend time with our children; I wanted to free-lance as an advertising consultant and at last spend some time on the golf course and tennis courts. But the right offer simply never came. Until now.

And then I remembered what the Blessed Virgin had said to me: *You will no longer be in this business . . . .*

I tried to maintain some composure, as we sketched out how the transaction might work. It looked like the right changeover date might be April 1 — the ninth anniversary of the beginning of our first paper.

I hung up and walked slowly into the den. "Terri, we've just sold the papers," I murmured with a dazed smile. "The message — it's coming true. . . ."

She looked at me as if she didn't know whether to laugh, scream, or cry. "Well," she said after a long pause, "If it's true, that's great — but I'll believe it when we sign the papers."

Yes, I thought, looking out at the passing West Virginia scenery, this has already been one very special Christmas.

We arrived at Terri's mother's home in time to help set up the nativity scene in the living room. It was an old one that had been in the family for a long time. The stable was sturdy, not flimsy or tacky like some of the modern ones, and the figurines were ceramic, not plaster. All at once as I placed the kneeling figure of Mary beside the manger, my eyes filled. "Hail, Mary, full of grace," I whispered, nestling her in the straw.

We returned to Myrtle Beach a couple of days before New Year's — just in time for me to suffer a severe relapse of the flu. After recovering for the second time, I got together with Jim Stoffel, did the interview, and wrote the last column on the events of Medjugorje.

Part 4: Interviews with Local Residents
Who Have Been to Medjugorje
January 15, 1986

I sincerely apologize to all of you for not having this article in last week's edition, but unfortunately the flu bug won out and I was totally out of it for almost a full week. This is the final part of a four-part series begun back in the first week of December. It is in the form of statements from two people who live in this area who have actually been to Medjugorje to witness first-hand the events happening there.

Rather than doing a question-answer type of interview, I have chosen to do them in statement form for the sake of brevity and easier reading.

The interviewees are Jim Stoffel, who resides in North Myrtle Beach, and Reverend Sylvester Scotti, pastor of St. Philip's Catholic Church in Lake City.

Jim Stoffel is a golf pro at Carolina Shores Golf Club in North Myrtle Beach. He and his wife, Rosie, have been living here since 1972. They were joined by Hal and Peggy Todd, also of North Myrtle Beach, in a trip to Medjugorje in November, 1985. I use the comments of Jim that were given at a meeting at his church . . . after they had returned. Again, because of the limited amount of space I can devote to this, I use only his comments, even though the others had much to say about the trip. Perhaps at a later time, we can do more on this.

Father Scotti has been the priest at St. Philip's Catholic Church for the past two and a half years. He has been in the priesthood for 14 years. I went to Lake City and sat with him one morning talking about his experiences in Medjugorje.

We'll begin with the comments of Jim Stoffel:

"We had heard about the events at Medjugorje two years ago through a friend who had heard someone speaking about it at Greenville, S.C. Naturally, we got interested and started looking into it. We got some books. There were about six out at the time.

"I had read about apparitions at Lourdes and Fatima, but the big thing here was that this was happening now — here today — in our time. We got hold of information about going there and went in November, 1985.

"My personal feeling is that everything that is happening in Medjugorje is authentic. There is really and truly something supernatural going on there.

"The purpose of the visits by the Virgin Mary is to relate to the seers 10 messages for the world. She has also told the children that it is important to pray, fast and reconcile oneself with God. After the apparitions cease, the 10 messages, or things, will begin to happen. Numbers seven, nine and ten are grave chastisements for the world because of the sins. I might add that the seventh message has been done away with because of the response of the people to the Blessed Virgin's urgent request for prayer and fasting and reconciliation. She says that the ninth and tenth things will happen, but they can be lessened with more prayer and fasting. I guess that is what the whole thing is about.

"I really don't think it's meant to scare, because her message is nothing more than what is in the Gospels that we all have every day and every week. The Lord is using the Holy Mother as a means of making the whole thing more emphatic.

"It truly is a unique experience over there. It's just a little village (Medjugorje) that really is now a very holy place. It's almost indescribable, frankly. The message we would like to get across is that this is really the work of the Holy Spirit to bring the Gospel of Jesus Christ to the world through the Virgin Mary. People have gotten so far away from God, and this is a very urgent call to turn back to Him. I guess to sum up what she is trying to say is that people need to have peace within themselves, and that this can come through prayer, conversion, and of course communion. I'm not trying to transform anyone to Catholicism, nor is that the purpose of the message of Medjugorje. It is a personal commitment for everyone in the world.

"This parish or community in Medjugorje only has 400 families, yet the church of St. James (where the Virgin Mary is reportedly appearing-Ed. Note) holds roughly 2,000 or more. Nobody knows why it was built so large. She is trying to mold the perfect parish here and she has succeeded. Six miles away from here and you're right back in the 'real world.'

"As I said, the Blessed Virgin is very happy with the people of the church here. She usually appears at about 5:45 p.m. (the time difference is seven hours ahead of our time-Ed. Note) in the evening and the apparitions last about three-four minutes now. They used to last 20-30 minutes. After the apparitions, Mass is held and then the kids stay in the church for a while longer, staying about three hours daily. They also spend up to four hours a day in prayer and fast three times a week. If you've never tried fasting, you should. It's very difficult for just one day. The people are just so nice and gracious, very friendly and warm. They're really just very simple people.

"The Virgin Mary has messages for the western world too. We seem to think we're better than the rest of the world. She talks about too much drugs and far too much television, which takes up so much of our time. We waste an awful lot of time that could be spent on better things. Also, we have too many religions in the United States; too many cults and worship of false gods, this sort of thing. Another thing: we have advanced far ahead of the rest of the world in technology and we seem to think we have done it on our own — that is, without the help of God. It's man's technology, so to speak. If you really want a perfect description of the way people of the western world are living today, you need only to pick up your Bible and read the first chapter of Romans, verses 18 through 32. It's amazing that something written so many centuries ago can so perfectly fit our lifestyle today."

Father Sylvester Scotti:

"In October of 1984, I went to Rome for a meeting of priests from all over the world. Just prior to leaving, we were asked if we wanted to make a pilgrimage or side trip to Medjugorje, Yugoslavia, a place where reportedly, the Blessed Virgin Mary was appearing to six young people on a daily basis.

"I had heard vague reports about Medjugorje, originally through a local newspaper where a story appeared about a priest from that parish being arrested for stirring up trouble. Yugoslavia is, of course, a Communist country, and while they allow church services, they do so only as long as it does not interfere with the daily goings-on there. The article stated that the priest had been arrested for taking part in lies about supernatural things occurring there.

"Later, from other priests and my own research, I learned more of the events taking place there, so, of course, I was excited about an opportunity to go there myself with this group of priests.

"There were 110 of us (priests) that went there after the trip to Rome. This was the largest group of priests ever to visit the site of the reported apparitions. In order to get there, we had to go through a town called Mostar, some short distance from Medjugorje, and 'pretended' we were tourists. It went so far as all of us buying bathing suits to convince the authorities that we were there to enjoy the recreational interests of the area. Finally, we ended up going to a small town between Mostar and Medjugorje. It was very bad accommodations from what one is accustomed to. That is, not really bad, but very primitive from where we stay in our country. Such things as outside plumbing and such.

"Our group finally went to Medjugorje and as I stated, it was the largest group of priests ever assembled there at one time. We were taken to the basement of the church rectory, because there were so many of us. We were going to meet with the children (seers) after the apparition. It was hot and stuffy and very crowded. Soon one of the nuns there at the church who works closely with the children came into the room and announced that the Blessed

Virgin had told the children that she would appear
to them in the basement where we were because she
had a very special message for us.

"What can I say? We were absolutely enthralled
that she would appear to the children there. Shortly,
the children came into the room and stood just on
the other side of the table where I was standing with
a fellow priest who was a good friend. They began
their prayers and shortly thereafter fell to their knees,
which was an indication that the Holy Mother had
appeared. We looked at the line of where the
children's eyes were looking, and it was directly over
our heads!

"After the apparition, the children wrote something
down on paper and the nun who could speak English
translated it to us. The Blessed Virgin's message was
directly to us: 'Thank you for coming when I called
you. Those of you who love me have been specially
called.'

"Well, you can imagine how we felt. We all prayed
and then went upstairs into the church for Mass. I
could hardly believe what happened next. Several of
the seers, the children, began vesting (dressing) us
for the Mass, me and my friend! What a blessing!
Then during the Mass, they were right there next
to us and we were holding hands with them and
praying. I cannot describe to you what this meant
to me.

"I have to tell you of two 'miracles' that happened
while we were there. On the way to Medjugorje on
the bus, we were all talking and praying about what
was taking place there. The sky was totally clear and
cloudless. Later, someone noticed up in the sky two
small clouds shaped in the form of a cross. I tell
you the sky was completely clear except for this cross

of clouds. Later, it turned into a perfect shape of a dove.

"After the trip to Medjugorje and when we were back in Dubrovnik, we stopped at this beautiful church there for Mass and prayer. All of us were sick. I mean bad sick with the flu and colds and the kind of scratchy throat you get when you catch it. We were praying in this beautiful church and when the prayers were over and we were preparing to leave, a young Canadian stood up and said: 'Brothers, I have to tell you this. I was praying here with you and certainly not praying for something as unimportant as a little flu or cold. But suddenly, I felt this warmth come over me and all of a sudden my sore throat, all my symptoms of the flu are gone! I'm completely well.' We continued to pray for awhile after that.

"You asked me about reaction after I returned to Lake City. Well, naturally, I was filled with the wonder of all this and I went to all the media in the area and in Columbia. The result? Absolute blank stares and nothing. But that is all right. I personally feel that the events taking place there are real and I thank God for that."

This is the final part of our series about the events of the reported apparitions of the Blessed Virgin Mary in Medjugorje, Yugoslavia. I don't know what else I can tell you except that I will be happy to continue sending back copies of the articles to anyone who may have missed them and would like to read about them. Just send a self-addressed stamped envelope to: Weible Columns, P.O.Box 2647, Myrtle Beach, S.C. 29578

And that, I thought typing the zip code with flourish, was that. I had carried out my assignment; it was finished.

Now I would go on and live the message as best I was able, but the main part of my work was done.

Or so I thought.

9

I Believe. . .

A few days later, I had stopped at the bank and was discussing the apparitions with one of the tellers. She expressed her sadness that the columns were finished, stating that she had wanted them to go on forever, because she had been so touched by the events of Medjugorje.

I told her that I had related about all that could be written about them. "Yes, but you never really gave us your own opinion," she countered. "We know what others think, but what do you really think?"

I looked at her, taken back. In the interest of maintaining journalistic credibility, I had bent over backwards to remain objective. I had wanted the readers to draw their own conclusions and not be influenced by what had so dramatically affected me. Had I gone too far?

It gave me something to think about. And the more I thought, the more I saw how much professional pride had influenced that decision. After all, a column was supposed to be a vehicle of personal opinion; that was its whole point. But for this series I had treated it as a news medium.

So apparently I had not written the last column, after all. There would have to be one more — a final summary. There was only one problem: how far should I go in expressing how I felt about Medjugorje? I still was not ready to tell anyone about receiving a personal message from this heavenly visitor.

When I got back to my office, I locked myself in. I had always thought more clearly on a typewriter, so I put in a sheet and started to describe my feelings. I told myself that I was just thinking out loud, as it were, not intending it to be the column. But at the same time I had a hunch that the gist of it might be there when I got done. . . .

Personal Thoughts on Medjugorje
Feb. 5, 1986

I had made a half-hearted promise to myself not to write about the events in Medjugorje for a while. But I find that I can't do that — at least not until I've had a chance to speak on the subject from a personal standpoint.

Medjugorje can be taken several ways. There are the curious people who like anything that is out of the ordinary just for the sake of curiosity; there are the non-believers who scoff at such nonsense that is outside of the accepted see-touch category; and there are the believers. They look for signs and reasons to strengthen their faith. Sometimes they victimize themselves by trying to believe in too much.

Medjugorje can lead one into any of these, and maybe more. After all, you're looking at an event that claims something far out of the ordinary. We are told that the Blessed Virgin Mary, the Mother of Jesus, is appearing to a group of young people in a remote village located in a Communist country. We are told that this has been happening since June 24, 1981 — and is continuing up to and including this very day. And we are told that it is urgent that we reconcile with God, as quickly as possible, because of the world-wide decline of faith.

If I were to be categorized within the ways given above, it would be among the curious, for that is the reason I first became interested in this unique event. I was told about it in a casual conversation and, with interest piqued, I looked into it. My feeling was that it would make a good column for Christmas. As it developed, it somehow evolved into a four-part series that went far beyond my regular column space. It became the most important thing I had done in the way of writing. At least that was the way I felt about it. Why, I did not know at the time.

Now I think I know why.

The real miracle of Medjugorje is the conversion of the people who live there. It is also the conversion of those who hear about it and renew, convert, reconcile, or whatever you want to call it. It is discovery or the rediscovery of faith as it is truly meant to be. A simple reunification with God and what He wants of us.

Every day, requests come in to the office for copies of the four parts. So far, more than 135 have been received. This entails people sending in a stamped, self-addressed envelope, something most people will not do unless it is very, very important. I have received numerous telephone calls and just about everywhere I go, people want to talk about Medjugorje.

Almost everyone who has written, phoned or talked to me about Medjugorje feels that something is happening there that is not to be explained by the usual scientific methods. Most accept it for what it is. Others have told me it has changed their lives. If even one feels this way, the series was worthwhile.

I personally believe that the Virgin Mary is

appearing in Medjugorje. I believe in it so strongly that I plan to go there sometime this year. I cannot explain the exhilaration this one event has put into my life. I believe in it so strongly that I plan to continue investigating it, reading about it and talking to people who have been there.

It is also my hope that I can receive permission to reprint in segments one of the books on Medjugorje. It is the most-up-to-date and complete, running through May, 1985.

I've always tried to write exactly what I feel or believe. That, to me, is what a writer is supposed to do. This is a little odd for me, but it is something I felt I had to do.

Have a good week!

That really did sum it up; it also committed me in print to going there myself — something I desperately wanted to do, yet seemed to be postponing for one reason or another. The Virgin Mary's message to me had said this would become my life's mission — *if* I accepted it. In researching the various books on Medjugorje, I had noticed that she never told anyone that they had to do something; it was always a request. Even the visionaries themselves had stated that she had asked — not told — them to enter the religious life as priests and nuns. Ivanka and Mirjana had indicated that they planned to marry and raise families. The Blessed Virgin then said that was their choice, and she would respect it. I knew what she was asking of me, yet I seemed to be accepting only the writings and the commitment to live a better life — and ignoring the call to make Medjugorje my life's mission.

In the last two months many things had occurred that seemed to be part of the spiritual growth that would be necessary for that task, although I did not recognize them as such at the time. For one, I discovered the rosary. A lady from the local Catholic church had called requesting copies of the columns. She told me that she ran the gift shop at the church and was calling for a group of nuns stationed there. "We can't thank you enough for writing about Our Lady at Medjugorje," she said. "The sisters and I have a gift for you, if you'll come by the church this Saturday at 5:00 p.m. We want to show our appreciation for what you've done. Just ask for Mrs. Alford."

Deeply touched, I agreed to go by, although I was a bit uncomfortable, having never been in a Catholic church before. The gift shop was just off the lobby, and I met her there. "Just call me 'Taxi'," she said, "That's what everyone calls me." She held out her hand. "Here, I want you to have this rosary. It comes from Fatima."

I looked at the string of wooden beads. "Well, uh, thank you. My wife will like that."

"No, no, it's for you! Would you like one for her also?"

"Oh, no. It's just that — well, what do I do with it?"

She began to laugh. "That's right, you're a Protestant and don't know what a rosary is. It's a prayer! A crown of roses to lay at Christ's feet — that's what the name means. Here's a little booklet that will show you what to do. You know, you really ought to find out more about us Catholics and what we believe," she smiled. "Say! Why don't you come to Mass with me? It starts in a few minutes."

"Well, I don't know; I've got to —"

"Oh, come on, it won't hurt!" she laughed. "And it won't be long."

So I attended my first Catholic Mass. I was nervous in the beginning but surprised to find out how similar it was to our own Lutheran service. Indeed, with the exception of a few words, the liturgy was almost the same. The main difference was in the celebration of Holy Communion, or the Eucharist, as they called it. I loved the whole service,

and by the time it ended I felt at home. That is, until
I was greeted by the pastor. I had known him for at least
nine years, as we were both members of a local civic club.
As we were chatting in the lobby of his church, one of
his parishioners mentioned that I was the author of the
articles on Medjugorje, "Where Our Blessed Mother has
been appearing for more than fours years now," she added.

Suddenly my friend backed away, waving his hands and
exclaiming, "No, no, no! Don't get involved in that kind
of fantasy! You're a journalist, Wayne; you should know
these things are not real — just fairy tales or a case of
over-active imaginations!"

We stood there in shocked silence. Finally, one of the
ladies asked, "Father, you don't believe in the apparitions
of Medjugorje? You don't believe that Our Lady is appearing there?"

"Of course not!" he exclaimed. "I don't believe in
apparitions of any kind. We don't need apparitions of the
Blessed Virgin Mary or anyone else; we simply need to
keep our eyes on Jesus. That's all!"

I was stunned; I had just received the first negative
reaction to the articles — and from a Catholic priest! After
a few more moments of forced conversation, I thanked
Taxi for the gift of the rosary and excused myself.

I had difficulty dismissing the priest's negative response
and somehow sensed that it would not be the last. Naively
I had assumed that every Catholic simply accepted apparitions as part of their Church; I would later discover
that there was as much controversy over the Virgin Mary
and apparitions among Catholics, including priests and
nuns, as existed in other denominations.

Meanwhile, I made an effort to learn about the rosary.
To me, it wasn't Catholic; it was just a beautiful prayer.
But when I first tried to pray it, I couldn't maintain
concentration long enough to realize the beauty of its

meaning. After all, prior to learning about Medjugorje, my cumulative prayer life might have amounted to five minutes a week. This prayer, if done correctly and from the heart, took at least twenty minutes.

It was while recovering from my relapse with the flu that I began to grasp its full beauty and power. I discovered that it was a prayer composed of meditations and lines straight from the Bible, focusing on the life of Jesus. It was, in fact, like a biography of Jesus' life. I determined to pray it daily — not because of Medjugorje, or especially for Mary; rather, it was for myself. I had never known a deeper feeling of having talked with God.

And then came my second visit with Father Sylvester Scotti. The fourth column had run, and Father Scotti had seen his interview. He called me shortly afterwards, grateful but sounding uncharacteristically grave. He wanted me to come see him as soon as possible.

I was glad he'd called; I'd wanted to get together with him again. I also felt he might be able to advise me what to read next. "How about this afternoon?" I asked, hoping that he would be free.

"Well — I've got a dinner engagement this evening, but I could see you before that."

I assured him I would be there in about an hour.

When I arrived, there was something different about him. He was as glad to see me as before, but he seemed to be more serious this time, and more than a little preoccupied. The coffee pot was on, and we talked for a little more than two hours. Finally, he reminded me that he had an engagement that evening, and there wasn't much time left for us to spend together. "I've got some books I want you to have," he said, practically clearing several shelves by his desk.

Most of them were on Mary — the history of her role in the Church, the story of priests and others who had been devoted to her. Several were on the early Church. Soon we had filled a large box. I assured him I would bring them back as soon as I had read them.

"Keep them," he insisted, dismissing the idea of their return with a wave of his hand. "You know, he added wistfully, "I've given my whole life to Mary. Every vacation I had, I would go to Fatima or to Lourdes or to Knock — the different places where she appeared." He paused for a moment. "I guess I've branded myself as something of an oddball," he sighed, "but it's been worth it. And of course Medjugorje capped them all."

He looked at his watch. "I've got to get ready — but look, there's one more thing I have to give you before you go. Wait here, and I'll get it."

He returned with a packing crate about a foot wide and three feet long. In it was a statue of Mary. "This is a very special statue," he explained. "I took it to Rome, and the Pope blessed it. It was a crazy thing to do, but when we went to Medjugorje, I took it there, too." He paused and looked in my eyes. "I want you to take it home and keep it for a couple of weeks."

"Father Scotti, I can't accept this! I might break it or something." I could just picture Terri, as I walked in the house with a three-foot statue of the Virgin Mary. She was already concerned about my 'obsession with Medjugorje,' as she put it.

"No," he said with such solemnity that there was no arguing, "you must take it. Tonight. Just keep it for the next few weeks."

I sighed and reluctantly agreed, and we carried the crate and cartons of books out to my car. When I finally closed the trunk lid he seemed immensely relieved, as if he had discharged some burdensome obligation. "Now," he smiled, "you've been given all this; put it to good use!"

"I will," I smiled. "Look, I've got to go out of town next

week on business, but let's get together when I get back
— how about a week from Monday?"

"Fine," he agreed absently, and I made a mental note
to call and remind him.

"God go with you, Wayne," he said quietly, as I got
in my car.

"You, too," I said cheerily through the open window.
"See you a week from Monday."

On the way home I tried to figure out how to introduce
the statue of Mary into our home. There was just no easy
way to do this. Terri was concerned that I was going
overboard; this could well confirm it. But luckily when
I got home she was in the kitchen, fixing dinner. The
laundry room was right off the garage, so I brought the
crate in there and unpacked it.

The statue was plaster, delicately hand-painted, and I
thought it was one of the most beautiful things I had ever
seen! Carefully, I lifted it out of its crate and tiptoed with
it past the kitchen and into our bedroom, where I set
it up on the low bureau. Then I called Terri and Kennedy
to come into the bedroom.

I stood in the doorway to watch their expressions.
Kennedy was puzzled; Terri frowned, put her hands on
her hips, and turned to me.

"Isn't it beautiful?" I asked her, hoping to de-fuse what
I saw in her eyes.

"No it isn't," she said slowly shaking her head. "I can't
believe how far you've gone with this Mary business! Where
did you get this?"

"Father Scotti told me to take it home and keep it for
a couple of weeks."

"You know, you really worry me! All I hear from you
is Mary! Where is Jesus in all this?"

Shaken by her response, I stammered, "Terri, I'm
praying to Jesus. I'm closer to Him than I ever was before.

In fact I'm praying more than I've ever prayed — and it's all because of her. She's pointing me to Him, and I'm not putting her in His place, believe me!"

She just shook her head. Nothing I said had registered. "I'll take it out of here," I sighed resignedly, "and put it in the living room."

"No, leave it there. Don't worry about it; for two weeks I can live with it."

The following Monday I left on my business trip, and when I called home that night as I always did on the road, Terri sounded a little strange. I asked her if there was anything the matter, but she assured me that everything was fine. When I got home Thursday evening, and we'd gotten the kids to bed, I found out what it was.

"There's something I have to tell you," she said quietly. "Jim Stoffel called Monday. Father Scotti died that morning of a sudden heart attack. I didn't want to tell you on the phone, while you were traveling."

I sat there, dazed at the news, then went to the bedroom. I closed the door and sat on the end of the bed, gazing at the statue of Mary. Tears rolled down my cheeks. Then all of a sudden, it was as though I could hear Father Scotti's laughter, and I felt a surge of joy. Somehow, I found it impossible to be sad. It was as though I knew he had received what he had wanted for so long: a place in heaven.

I came back out to Terri and told her what I felt. "I know he's in heaven right now, and he's very, very happy." I shook my head. "This is the strangest feeling!"

"Jim Stoffel knew you'd be upset, and he —"

"But I'm not upset; not like he thinks. I'm just happy for Father Scotti. I can't really explain it." I frowned. "I don't know what to do about the statue, though; I think he said he had a sister somewhere — or maybe he meant for me to keep it."

"I hate to tell you this," Terri interrupted, "but Jim said

the statue didn't belong to Father Scotti; it belonged to the diocese, and it has to be returned, because it is loaned around to different churches. He said, if you'll drop it by tomorrow morning, he'll take it from there."

It broke my heart, but I finally said okay.

Later that evening, as I thought about my two visits with Father Scotti, I realized how much he had given me in so short a time — far beyond the books and the statue. Moreover, I was convinced that somehow he knew he was going to die and had given them to me deliberately. (This was later confirmed by his sister, whom I met on a speaking tour in Florida.)

The following morning, as I gently laid the statue back in its crate, I said to Terri, "Well, I guess you'll be happy to see this go."

"No," she said, her voice breaking, "it's beautiful." And there were tears in her eyes.

10

Come and See

I had to go to Medjugorje — and soon. Not to prove
it was real; the last column had put me on record that
in my opinion it was. I wanted to go and experience the
spirituality there myself. The sale of the newspapers would
be finalized in early April; I would go as soon afterwards
as possible.

The last column had also done much to free me from
the bondage of desiring to be thought well of by others.
I no longer worried about journalistic credibility. Within
me now was at least an elementary understanding of
what the Virgin Mary was referring to when she called
for conversion of the heart. And needless to say, her
request of me to become an active participant in the
spreading of the message of Medjugorje was never far
from mind.

Meanwhile, fresh information on Medjugorje was
continuing to come in, and I realized that I needed to
write one more column updating the situation before
I made any more plans for my trip.

This is getting almost easy, I thought, as I typed in
the headline and the date. I began by restating the basic
story and then continued:

Update on Medjugorje March 5, 1986

The total number of reported apparitions is now close to 2,000. Never in the history of Marian apparitions has such a condition existed. At an early point during these appearances, the heavenly visitor promised to reveal 10 secrets, or messages, to each of the six young people. . . . the seers say that only four of the revelations are common to all mankind; the others have to do with the individual visionaries or the Medjugorje community.

. . . The main message given by the Blessed Virgin Mary has been made clear. It has been repeated many times over the course of the apparitions: conversion with God, repentance, increased faith, fasting, prayer, and peace refers to the individual and is a peace that is known only by those who have discovered the true meaning of a personal relationship with God.

Regular readers of The News & Shopper were able to read a four-part series on the events at Medjugorje which ran in December and early January. This article is an update on what is happening with the six youths who have been involved with the apparitions.

At present, only four seers have the regular daily apparitions wherever they may be. They are Vicka, Marija, Ivan and Jakov. Two others, Mirjana and Ivanka, do not see the Blessed Virgin daily any longer. They have already received ten secrets each, Mirjana on Christmas day, 1982, and Ivanka on May 6, 1985. Since then they have stopped seeing her on a regular daily basis. The Virgin Mary promised to Ivanka that she would visit her on the anniversaries of the first apparition, and to Mirjana she promised to appear to her on her birthdays as long as she lives, and also in difficult moments of her life. In an interview, Mirjana was asked why Mary promised to appear and offer help in her difficult moments, but she is not coming in such a way to help the rest of us in our difficulties. Mirjana said, "I am not speaking of the ordinary problems of my life. My difficult moments stem from the secrets concerning the future of the world, which Our Lady revealed to me. At times, I hardly can cope with it when I seriously think of it. In those moments, Our Lady appears and gives me the strength and courage to go on with my life."

Both Mirjana and Ivanka received from the Blessed Virgin, a piece of material which looks like paper, but it is not paper, like cloth, but it is not cloth. On this parchment, all ten secrets are written, with the dates, even the minutes. Each of these two seers is only able to read her own secrets.

The paper, or the cloth, or whatever it may be called, cannot be destroyed even by fire. Each of these two seers is told by Mary to select a priest to whom they will give that material on which the secrets are written ten days before the secrets are to happen. The priest, in turn, with the help of the Madonna, will be able to read the message of each secret and will announce it three days before it happens. He will describe the full nature of the secret, its time and even minute, and the place. The priest will then return the paper to the seer from whom he received it.

The priest will not be able to read all ten secrets at once, but just one by one when the time comes for it to be announced.

Mirjana has revealed the name of the priest she selected. According to Mirjana, Our Lady was pleased with her choice of the priest, who, she said, is a good priest.

Mirjana told of an incident connected with her selection of the priest. "When I chose the priest who would announce the secrets," Mirjana said, "I revealed his name to Father Tomislav Vlasic, O.F.M., (who at that time was the spiritual director of the seers). When he heard the name of my choice, Father Vlasic said: 'He is far away from Medjugorje, and you should choose someone who is close to the place.' My answer to him was that Our Lady would take care of it." A short time after that, to be exact, in August, 1984, Bishop Zanic had Father Vlasic removed from Medjugorje and had him replaced with the priest whom Mirjana selected to announce the secrets.

The irony here is that Bishop Zanic is not a believer in the apparitions, and has done everything he possibly can to prevent them from continuing.

The fact that Mirjana has already selected the priest who would announce the secrets indicates that the time for the first one to happen is approaching. Other secrets, with short intervals, will then follow.

Vicka, the oldest of the seers, has received only eight secrets. She completed writing the notes of the Blessed Virgin's life on this earth, as dictated to her by her. For the last two years she has been suffering from severe pains in the head caused by a water bubble situated between the small and the large brain. Doctors in Zagreb, Croatia, avoid surgery because of the delicate position. She suffers much, especially in the afternoons. Often she goes into a coma; however, she always comes out of it before the time of the daily apparition, which occurs in her small and simple room.

Vicka's friends, and the friends of Medjugorje who are trying to help her, offered all financial assistance for her travel, medical, and hospital expenses if she would be willing to come to the United States or London or Switzerland for surgery. When people try to convince her, her simple answer was no. Asking her why, she said, "Our Lady told me that God sent me this illness for a special purpose, and I accepted it!" Has Our Lady ever told you that one day she would cure you, she was asked? "No, and I did not ask her to do so!"

This girl in the prime of her life, coming from a financially poor family, is being offered such royal treatment for her physical health, but she refuses all because of the supernatural motives. Who can possibly accuse her of fraud, of lies, of deception?

Vicka's life is full of God's spirit, which radiates on her face even when she suffers excruciating pains.

Marija, who already received nine secrets, and is receiving from Our Lady messages for the parishioners of Medjugorje every Thursday, gives the impression of a saintly girl.

Ivan, who did not succeed in two seminaries, for various reasons, still hopes to become a priest one day.

Jakov, the youngest of all, is growing and maturing fast, but he is still full of restlessness. During interviews, he tries to speed up questions so he can go play. When posed a serious question, though, he immediately turns into a thinking young man and gives some very sober answers.

All six seers are well aware of the fact that they are misunderstood, criticized, and even condemned by those who should "respect and protect them," as the renowned theologian Hans Urs von Balthasar said.

They are also convinced of the fact that the Blessed Virgin Mary appears to them and uses them as the instruments of the heavenly messages to mankind.

That should do it, I thought, winding the last page out of my typewriter. And now I turned all my attention to getting ready for my trip.

Through Jim Stoffel I had gotten in touch with the Center for Peace group in Boston, whose sole objective was to help spread the message of Medjugorje, through distributing books and literature and organizing pilgrimages. Jim had gone with them on their initial trip in November. And when I learned that they had another scheduled for April 30th, leaving from New York, I signed on. As our children were too young to leave them for that long, Terri would have to stay home. That was fine with her, and as the departure date approached, she became less than enthusiastic about my going.

Another who was hardly encouraging was my pastor, Bill Wingard. We had several heated discussions in the privacy of his office, invariably centering around his concern that in my enthusiasm for Mary, I was losing sight of the centrality of Christ.

"All I hear from you is Mary!" he would exclaim.

"Then you're not really hearing, because I keep saying Jesus, and you hear only Mary. Look, Bill," I pleaded, "she's only pointing me to Him!"

But the discussions invariably deteriorated into theological debates, with him critiquing my columns and the books I had loaned him, for Lutheran-based doctrinal error. I became increasingly depressed — and sad, for we had grown to be good friends.

Gradually I became aware that others in the church were "just waiting for Wayne to get through this thing," and when it became apparent that I was not about to, the Sunday School teaching assignments were rotated — and I found myself no longer teaching a class.

What I was not aware of was the effect all of this was having on me. With the sale of the papers nearly completed, and the prospect of a regular income assured by the fact that our press would continue to print them, I had begun to think of the future. Once again I ignored the part of Mary's message about my no longer being in newspaper work; in fact, part of the arrangement with the new owners of the papers was that I would continue to write my column, for which I would even be paid a nominal fee. It was easy to rationalize continuing: more articles would obviously have to be written on Medjugorje after I returned. In the meantime, I turned out a couple of columns as they had once been, concerned with matters of routine local interest.

Increasingly my thoughts of the future revolved around the possibility of going into partnership with a former employee of our newspapers who now owned an advertising agency. Since I had extensive work experience in that field, I would be a free-lance advertising consultant.

Such was the tenor of my thinking one April morning in my office, with my chair tilted back and my mind about six months ahead. Suddenly I once again felt a strong, clear message from Mary within my heart: *If you don't want to do this, someone else will.*

I sat bolt upright, practically falling out of my chair. My heart leaped, and I jumped up, exclaiming: "Yes, I do want to do this!"

Feeling a little foolish then, I wondered if maybe my imagination wasn't working overtime. But I quickly discarded that thought; however gently the admonition had come, I knew its source — and its meaning. From that moment on I gave no further thought to going into advertising and focused all my attention on getting ready for the trip to Medjugorje.

Five days before I was due to leave, headlines blared the meltdown of the Russian nuclear power plant at Chernobyl. A huge radioactive cloud had been released and was passing over southern Europe — and Yugoslavia. On top of that there was a fresh outbreak of terrorism against Americans in Europe, and Munich, where we were scheduled to make a plane change was one of the most dangerous places of all.

"Frankly, I can't think of a worse possible time for you to go!" Terri confronted me from behind her desk. My wife was as valuable a business partner as I could ask for. Whenever I got carried away or sidetracked, she would bring me back quickly with a sharp dose of reality right between the eyes. The truth would hurt the ego and pride, but more often than not she would be right.

Today her concern was not with the business. "That cloud's headed straight down there, and you're flying right into it! That's just plain stupid!" She paused, but I said nothing. "And it's a Communist country; you can't tell what they're capable of." I bit my lip. "And I don't think it's right for you to leave right in the middle of the transition of turning the papers over to the new management, especially after you agreed to stay on as a consultant for the next two months."

I did not point out that the transition was going smoothly, and that I had made ample provision with the owners for my being gone for nine days. I kept silent, knowing that Terri needed to vent these things, even though she knew that they weren't going to change my mind.

The 30th arrived, and she drove me to the airport. "Don't worry," I laughed, as we parted, "I'm not going to come home glowing in the dark! And I'm not going to wind up languishing in some Communist prison, either; I'll probably be home before my postcards will!"

She put on her bravest smile as I turned and waved, but she wasn't fooling either of us.

At Kennedy Airport I went to the assigned gathering room. The name tag on the broadly smiling woman who sat behind the registration desk announced that she was Rose Finnegan from Boston. When I told her who I was, she stood up and gave me a big hug, crying, "God bless you, Wayne! You're the Lutheran who's going with us!"

Several heads nearby turned to see the token Protestant. Pinning a name tag on me, she stood back to admire her handiwork. I kept the plastic smile on my face. As a rule I detested name tags and never wore them at functions if I could possibly get away with it; this one I would have to wear for the next eight days.

I had several books on Medjugorje with me; taking a seat away from the others I prepared to immerse myself in one. But as I took it out of the travel bag they had given me, my eye fell on their name on the bag. I tried to recall what Jim Stoffel had told me about the Center for Peace.

It began with John Hill, an extremely successful businessman in Concord, Massachusetts. Everything he accomplished, he earned, having come up through the school of hard knocks as a child. Actually, he was something of an entrepreneur, being involved in several things simultaneously, including a factory which reproduced antique wrought-iron gas street lamps and benches.

John had a strong independent streak in him. When a long-time friend gave him a videotape on Medjugorje, he viewed it and was convinced that this was a message of peace for the world. Something from the past seemed to click inside of him, touching him more deeply than anything had in years. A nominal Catholic who except for weddings and funerals had not been in a church since childhood, he found one and began to pray.

I smiled to recall his story — which was so similar to my own. It seemed as if Mary was recruiting a most unlikely cast of new apostles. I smiled again; when the visionaries had asked her why she had picked them, she had smiled and replied, "I do not always choose the best people. . . ."

Feeling that God had spoken, John and his friend started the Center for Peace, setting up an office in the gas-light factory and bringing in volunteers. In a sense they were true pioneers, working out travel arrangements and accommodations in a place totally foreign to international travel. By now, of course, a good working routine had been established, but in the beginning they were truly pathfinding. Ironically, John himself had never been to Medjugorje; he was convinced his job was to stay home and get others there. I looked forward to the day I would be able to meet this man who had done so much to spread the word but who had no desire to go there himself.

They were announcing our flight, I realized, getting up and joining the line. Everyone was excited; we were on the verge of leaving on the adventure of a lifetime. There were about 70 of us, a good mix of men and women, young and old.

On the plane I found myself seated next to a young woman named Maureen Thompson from Philadelphia. She was open and friendly, and we soon were exchanging stories of how we had become involved in Medjugorje.

I was fast discovering that everyone on this trip had a unique story of how they happened to be there. Gradually I would realize that this was a common thread on all pilgrimages.

I had noticed Maureen before boarding, and for some reason had thought she was a nun. She was wearing a dress much like a uniform, and with acceptance of modern dress by some orders today, I had assumed that to be the reason she was not wearing a habit. It turned out that she was in her final year of study to be a nurse. She had heard about Medjugorje and yearned to go there, even though it was financially impossible. Her father, a Philadelphia policeman with four other children, was hard pressed just to send his kids to school.

Nevertheless, Maureen wrote the Center for Peace for information for future reference. She had told God in prayer how much she would like to go, but when she found out that the trip would cost around $1,300 that seemed to finish it. It was a nice dream. . . .

And then came a letter from the university where she was about to receive her Bachelor's degree in nursing. To her utter dumbfoundment she had overpaid her tuition for the past four years, and they had enclosed a refund check for more than five hundred dollars! That same week she heard from the IRS: she had made a miscalculation on the previous year's income tax, and they were refunding her a little over $500!

When she told her parents of this extraordinary joint windfall, they made up the difference.

"Even so, I shouldn't be here now, because I'm supposed to be taking my finals this week," she laughed. "But after what happened with the money, I realized it was the Blessed Mother who was calling me to Medjugorje. So I applied for special permission to take the exams when I get home, and it was granted!"

It was an amazing story — and the first time I had heard anyone refer to the Virgin Mary as "The Blessed Mother." In fact, this was my first real encounter with someone so Catholic. Right then and there, Maureen Thompson became my "Catholic Connection" for the remainder of the pilgrimage. I was surprised when she later confided that she, too, had had struggles in her faith.

I told her my story then (leaving out the part about the message from Mary). She was as excited for me as I was for her; in fact, we were both so keyed up, we forgot about sleeping and spent the next nine hours talking — which I would learn was also fairly common on trips to Medjugorje. Somewhere in the course of those nine hours, I said to her, "Maureen, this may sound crazy, but — we're going to know each other for the rest of our lives."

She looked at me and smiled. "Yes, I know."

Someone a few rows ahead of us raised his window shade, and I was startled to see that the sun was well up in the heavens, as we began our descent.

*"Pray, pray, pray. In prayer you will come
to know the greatest joy and the way
out of every situation that
has no way out. . . ."*

11

The Village

As the plane began to bank to our side, preparing for its final approach to the airport at Dubrovnik, the view of the Hercegovina Mountains of central Yugoslavia was spectacular. We were beginning to feel a little turbulence for the first time on the trip, but in the excitement of knowing how close we were, no one seemed to mind. In a few minutes, we would be landing and boarding the buses for the final leg of our journey.

From my research I had learned that the first Croats had migrated to the Dalmatian Coast in the 6th century, in the wake of the receding Roman occupation. They were a farming people who had come southwest from the region that would be later known as the Ukraine, and with them came Franciscan missionary priests. Also into that country came the Serbs whose religious orientation was Eastern Orthodox — a mix that proved exceedingly volatile in medieval times. The recurring clashes between the Eastern and Roman Catholic faiths were eventually quelled by the invading Turks who imposed Islam on all the peoples whose lands they occupied. By the 16th century they controlled most of the Balkan peninsula and held it for the next three centuries. The Balkans' reputation for bloody turmoil would be well justified.

As Father Svetozar, a Croat who was born and raised in Bosnia-Hercegovina, would later describe it: "When the Turks came to my parish in 1525, the Franciscans were there. There were two churches, twelve priests. Seven escaped; the remaining five were executed and thrown into the River Neretva. The Christians fled the region and went into hiding. For three hundred years there was nothing. Maybe once or twice a year priests would come secretly to where the Christians were, to celebrate the Mass, baptize the children, teach them a little — to keep the faith alive. Whenever the Turks would discover such a gathering, they would kill them all.

"When I was little, my mother used to go every year to one of those places, to pay homage in prayer. She would sit me nearby, while she walked on her knees around the place in prayer. When I think of that now, I realize that in her life and commitment was the whole history of our people. It is a history of our faith, of the struggle for the survival of that faith, which did not end until the Turks departed."

There was something else that Father Svetozar would have to say about his people's history: "Those years of persecution and suffering were also a time of grace, a time of purification and even revival. In those days if you wanted to believe, you had to suffer for it. There was a price on faith, and it wasn't cheap. It wasn't easy. Yet it was — is, and will be — a blessing for the Church. For from the earliest times, the examples of the Christian martyrs have always been a source of great inspiration, guidance and leadership."

Yugoslavia (literally "State of the South Slavs") was made up of Serbs, Croats, Slovenes, Montenegrins, Macedonians, Muslims, and Bosnians, and emerged after World War I, a weak, disunited conglomerate of quarreling factions. As the nearby Russian Revolution gained momentum, so

did the influence of the Communist Party in Yugoslavia
— though never to the extent of the political parties of
the Serbs or Croats. King Alexander reigned as a dictator,
maintaining an uneasy peace until his assassination in
1934, and his son carried on until 1941.

Then came the Nazis. The Yugoslavian army proved
no match for them, and in a few weeks the Axis Powers
were dividing up the spoils — Germany taking the lion's
share and leaving Dalmatia and Montenegro to the
Italians.

The first partisan resistance broke out in Bosnia-
Hercegovina, the region in which Medjugorje was located.
But even in the presence of a common enemy, Serbs and
Croats could not give up fighting one another. Meanwhile,
the influence of the Communist partisans under the
leadership of Josep Tito, a protege of Karl Marx who had
strong-armed his way to the top of the Red insurgency,
continued to grow. As the Germans gradually fell back
before the advancing Red Army, in each town that was
liberated the installed provisional government was
Communist. Nonetheless, when the partisans were finally
able to throw off the yoke of the Nazi conqueror, there
was still hope for the restoration of the constitutional
monarchy which was in exile in England. But Communist
control proved absolute. In a nationwide plebiscite, Tito's
People's Front was elected unanimously — not too
surprising since no political opposition was allowed.

At that point my reflection was interrupted by a sudden
increase in turbulence. Dubrovnik had only one runway
long enough to accommodate Trans-Atlantic jets, and there
was a strong wind apparently blowing directly across it.
As the big plane bucked and crabbed in sideways, trying
to line up with it, I glanced around — at white knuckles
and white faces and more than a few airsickness bags
out and ready. Those who weren't too frightened to think

of it, were praying as hard as they knew how. If there were any non-believers on board when we took off, there weren't any by the time the wheels slammed down on the runway. Feeble applause rattled around the cabin; we were clapping out of relief at being alive.

Noting the red flag over the primitive terminal building towards which we were now taxiing, the reality of being in a Communist country suddenly sank in. How ironic, I thought, that the Lord would choose to send the Blessed Virgin to a country under a totalitarian and atheistic regime.

In 1948 there had been a surge of hope when their leader Tito broke with Stalin, and initially the majority of Yugoslavs embraced him for saving them from Russian domination. But gradually they had come to see how little his brand of Communism differed from the Soviets'. In truth, they could perceive no difference whatever between the quality of life on their side of the Iron Curtain and that in neighboring Hungary, Rumania, or Bulgaria.

Nor could I. When the plane landed, and they rolled out the steps, there was a military guard observing us, a submachine gun cradled at his waist. I had been surprised at the vast number of military aircraft — helicopters, troop transports, and the like — until I realized that the primary function of every Yugoslavian airport was military. As we were waiting to disembark, we were warned not to take any pictures, unless we wanted our cameras confiscated.

None of the officials smiled as they inspected our passports or baggage; no one seemed to care at all if we enjoyed our stay in their country. And anyone carrying rosaries or other religious objects had been advised to keep them well out of sight; the Communists did not want religious objects brought into their country and would hold them at the airport until the owner's departure.

The pall of our welcome was soon dispelled as our bus wound its way up the spectacular coast. The reception by our spiritual guide, Sister Margaret Catherine Sims, could not have been warmer. Associated with the Center for Peace, she had spent the previous two months in Medjugorje. The drive took three and a half hours, yet as tired as we were, we enjoyed every mile. The blue Adriatic, the clusters of centuries-old houses clinging to pine-covered cliffs, the little towns nestled in beautiful coves — every turn produced another picture-postcard view. Our cameras were out now and clicking constantly.

We would be staying with Croatian families in a town called Citluk, a little over three miles from Medjugorje. Talk about language barriers! No one spoke English; anything we needed would have to be communicated by sign language. After meeting our host families and unpacking our bags, we hurried back to the bus, for it was fast approaching 6:40, the time at which the apparition customarily appeared.

About half of us were on board when a woman at the front of the bus suddenly shouted, "Oh my God, look at the sun!" As I looked where she was pointing I could not believe what I saw: the sun, still an hour from sunset, had a corona around it. It was as if there were some kind of eclipse going on which enabled us to look right at it. But instead of the dark silhouette of the moon, there seemed to be a white disc in the middle of it. Incredibly, we could stare unblinking at the sun. And what we could see of it behind the disc seemed to be spinning. Also, the corona around it was throwing off different colors. It was absolutely stunning.

"I can't believe this!" I whispered to Maureen who was sitting next me, not taking my eyes off the sun. "What I am doing is impossible! I am looking right into the sun, and I should be doing permanent damage to my retinas.

Yet I sense no danger. In fact, I feel like I could go on staring at it as long as I care to." I shook my head in disbelief.

"And look," Maureen said, "it's happening to everyone. I mean, all of us are seeing it!"

Needless to say, by the time we got everyone back on board and got underway, we were too late for the apparition. No matter; we were all so elated to have witnessed the phenomenon of the sun so soon.

We were still two miles away when we caught sight of our first landmark, Mt. Krizevac ("Cross Mountain") towering in the distance. I could make out the cross on top of it and was surprised that it seemed so small. Somehow I had gotten the idea that it would dominate the entire valley. As we crossed the little bridge into Medjugorje, a cry of joy went up: there was St. James with its twin spires, just as we had seen in countless pictures and videos. We were actually here!

The bus came to a halt right at the edge of the grove of trees in front of the church; we rushed out to where a large crowd had gathered outside the adjacent rectory. The apparition inside was over, but the crowd lingered on — and we wanted to be a part of it. Just then a door opened and Marija, the young visionary who always seemed so quiet and reserved, appeared. Accompanied by a priest, she headed for the back of the church. As she crossed the lawn, the crowd surged after her, those closest to her shouting to her and asking for prayers, or just trying to touch her. All at once I was reminded of the crowd that used to follow Arnold Palmer around the Masters' Golf Tournament at Augusta, Georgia. I remembered in particular the face of an old man who had excitedly walked beside the golfer and gotten his autograph. He was as happy as a kid, and his face positively glowed — just as the faces of those accompanying Marija now were glowing.

They went in the back door to the sacristy and the crowd left and went around to the front of the church, for the Croatian Mass would be beginning soon. But for some reason Maureen and I lingered. "Look, look!" She nudged me and pointed up to the window of the sacristy. I looked — and saw Marija, helping the priest into his vestments as he prepared for Mass. A feeling of humble thanks for the privilege of witnessing this moment filled me — until the bell tolling for Mass broke our reverie.

Hurrying around front, we found the church packed. Every pew was filled, and people were standing in the aisles, crammed in as tightly as they could fit. The service began with a Croatian hymn, and the church fairly roared with it! The only thing I could think to compare it to, was a Baptist church in full revival!

I managed to work my way forward down the left aisle until further progress was impossible. The singing of that incredibly beautiful hymn resonated in me to the bone. Many people, I noticed, had tears streaming down their faces. But I was too stunned to cry. By this time, after the sun and the cross and observing Marija helping with the preparations for Mass, all my senses were on overload. All I could think was: this was so much more than I expected! None of the tapes, none of the books, not even Father Scotti, had prepared me for this.

And then as I stood there, I felt a tugging on my right sleeve. I looked down; an old Croatian woman who had to be at least in her seventies, was motioning for me to take her seat. Horrified, I shook my head. But this woman with the gray hair and careworn, sun-browned face insisted. Again I refused, smiling and gesturing for her to stay there. Finally, she took me by the arm and literally forced me to take the space. It took me a moment to realize that she was being obedient to the "Blessed

Mother," who had asked the villagers of Medjugorje to give to the pilgrims as her Son would give.

I did as the old woman in the black babushka and black dress bade me. I sat down in her place, and she stood up in the aisle.

And now I felt the tears on my cheeks.

*"Rejoice in the Lord always. I will say again:
rejoice! Let your gentleness of spirit
be known to all men. . . ."*

12

Birdsong at Midnight

That evening, back at the hotel in Citluk where we took our meals together, we shared our experiences. I was too excited to eat as I told of the old Croatian woman getting up to give me her seat. Others were awed at the huge throngs of people packed into the church, many standing for the full two hours-plus the service lasted. All of us were struck by the pure reverence in that service; there was no other way to describe it.

After the evening meal we went to our different accommodations, but nobody wanted to go to bed. By this time we had been up for thirty hours straight; still, we would rather talk than sleep. Finally we did sleep, and the next thing I knew, it was 4:30 in the morning — and I was wide awake. Deciding to take a walk around Citluk, I got dressed and went outside, where to my surprise it was already half light. The sun was not up yet, but it seemed much brighter out than I remembered it being before sun-up back home. In fact, this far before dawn in South Carolina, it would be plain dark.

After awhile the others were up, and after a quick breakfast of bread and coffee or tea, our bus took us to Medjugorje. When we got there, we walked everywhere, even taking the twenty-minute footpath over to Podbrdo, the hill where the apparition first appeared. On our way, an old Croatian woman, holding a basket of fruit, offered us some as we passed and a glass of wine. One of our group tried to give her some money, but she wouldn't take it. This, too, happened to others — and it kept on happening wherever we went. Sometimes a little boy or girl would be standing there alongside their grandmother, helping. . . . It was a scene I would remember as long as I lived.

The next three days became a blur. We went to the English Mass in the morning and the Croatian Mass in the evening; I had never thought it possible that I would spend so much time in church — and love every minute of it. We joined the crowd outside the rectory at the time of the apparition; we wandered and explored every nook and cranny of Medjugorje.

Monday evening the group was back at the hotel in Citluk, just sitting down to supper, when Sister Margaret came rushing in. "I know this is short notice," she announced breathlessly, "but during the apparition this evening the Blessed Mother told the visionaries that she would appear to them tonight on Podbrdo." She paused to catch her breath. "I've got the bus outside, and if any of you want to come, we've got to leave right now!"

Soup spoons clattered down, chairs scraped back. It was like a stampede as we hurried out into the night and onto the bus. When we got to the hill, I was momentarily disappointed for there were already many buses ahead of us. I had assumed we were the only ones to know about this special apparition.

We joined the stream of pilgrims groping their way up the steep, rocky path in the dark of the moonless night. No flashlights were allowed, for the Communists had banned public gatherings on the hill. It was so dark, you could hardly see the silhouette of the person in front of you, yet no one slipped or complained. We seemed to find just the right spots to place our feet as we made our way up the hill. There were millions of stars out, their beauty adding to the drama even if they provided little illumination.

We reached the top of the hill and were able to find an unoccupied bit of space which I sensed was fairly close to the visionaries. From the murmur of the crowd as they prayed, there was a large turnout. Sister Margaret had warned us not to take any flash pictures, and even as we crouched in the dark waiting, other guides were repeating the warning in French and Italian, as well as English. But in every crowd there were always a few who felt that the rules did not apply to them. They took their flash pictures anyway, sending a clear signal to the valley below, if anyone happened to be looking in our direction.

In one group someone began to lead a Rosary prayer in German, and the rest of us quietly joined in the response. We were scarcely murmuring, but together we made a low rumble that spread over the hillside. When it ended, the ensuing silence was highly charged, and we barely breathed, listening to it. And then someone started another Rosary.

Around eleven (it was impossible to be certain, for there was no way to see my watch), the apparition came, and everything became absolutely still. Near us, I could hear the visionaries praying in Croatian. They would stop, then pray again, and I sensed that Mary was praying with them. Then they would speak softly to her, sometimes in turn, sometimes together.

At length, one of the visionaries softly exclaimed, "Ode," which meant "she's gone," and someone else made an announcement in Croatian which was subsequently translated into Italian and then into English. Ivan had recommended us (whatever that meant) to the Blessed

Mother who was pleased that we had come up the hill. The gist of her message to us that night was to go home and pray together as a family, because if we would pray together, then we would grow holy together, and she could present us as a beautiful flower that unfolds for her Son Jesus. She also blessed all who had come to the hill on this special night.

There were whispers of quiet joy at that, and people got to their feet in the pitch dark and began making their way down the rocky path. There were so many that the going was slow, but that was all right; someone started softly singing "Ave, Maria," and we joined in. The singing was everywhere — above us in the night air, swirling around us, seeping inside of us. I didn't care if we ever got off that hill.

Then, standing in the road waiting to get on the bus and listening to the others still singing as they came down, someone exclaimed, "My God, listen to the birds singing!"

"Yeah," I replied, "It's beautiful."

"Don't you understand? Birds don't sing at night!"

Sure enough, it sounded like every songbird in the valley was singing at full cry, as if it were greeting the coming dawn, instead of midnight. And they kept it up until we were all on the bus and driving away.

No one spoke at first as the bus threaded its way along the street that was so narrow that there was barely room for it. Each of us was savoring the tiny miracle we had just experienced. We had actually been there for an apparition — and the Mother of God had blessed us. And then, to descend the hill wreathed in song and discover the sounds of thousands of birds singing at midnight — truly the miracle of God's presence was here!

The silence was broken by a heavy-set woman sitting across the aisle from me. "I'm so disappointed!" she exclaimed. "I didn't see anything!"

I looked at her, incredulous. "What did you expect to see? Didn't you realize that you were there during an appearance of the Blessed Virgin Mary right at the spot where she first came? You were there!"

"Yes, but some people said they saw flashes of light. And I didn't see a thing!"

I winced and said nothing more. In the few days we had been there, I had heard similar comments from people wanting to see the miracle of the sun, or to have their rosaries turn golden in color. The signs and wonders were indeed the goal of many, and when they didn't happen personally to them, they felt cheated. They didn't seem to realize that the real phenomenon was the miraculous change in those who came here and those who lived here. Lives were dramatically changed to loving God and fellow man, but that was not as instantaneously spectacular as the sun spinning. I would later come to understand that conversion took different courses, but inevitably it became the centerpiece of a pilgrimage to Medjugorje. One day this lady would realize the grace of what she had experienced on the hill.

It was 12:30 a.m. by the time we reached our hotel. Tempted as I was to stay up talking with the others, I went to bed. I would get precious little sleep as it was, for I had decided to get up early enough to walk to Medjugorje from Citluk and climb Mt. Krizevac in time to be at the summit for sunrise. Not knowing precisely when that was, I nonetheless counted on waking up early enough to complete the five and a half miles before dawn.

Several others had expressed an interest in joining me, but when it was finally settled, Maureen and Bernie Hanley, one of the volunteers from the Center for Peace who was helping with this trip, decided they would go with me. I arranged with Bernie to meet him at the little bridge just down from the road where we were staying. Maureen was quartered several rooms away from mine in the same home.

When I awoke, I fumbled for my flashlight, holding it next to my watch; it was a little before 4:00 a.m. Dressing quickly I knocked softly on Maureen's door, then went to the main room to wait for her. In a little while she came out, looking pale and tired. "I don't feel too good; I really want to go, but I don't think I should." She paused. "Could we go tomorrow?"

"Maureen, I've got to go today even if you can't. But if you want, we'll go tomorrow, too."

Outside, the moonless night was still black as I started up the road to Medjugorje. So enthralled was I by the crispness of air and the millions of stars that I continued on past the bridge, forgetting all about meeting Bernie.

There were no birds singing this night, and the thought struck me that I was the only creature stirring on the whole plateau — no birds, no cows, nothing. My way was illuminated only by the light of the stars. Settling into a steady pace, I pulled out my rosary and began to pray. After awhile I could make out the outline of Mt. Krizevac looming in the distance. Our group had still to make the pilgrimage up Mt. Krizevac doing the Stations of the Cross, yet I had already developed a deep fondness for the mountain, regarding it as the gentle guardian of the village.

As I looked now at its barely discernable outline, I noted light emanating from its peak. Probably an airplane beacon, I thought absently — and then it struck me that no airplane beacon I'd ever seen emitted light like that. It was neither a beam nor a strobe; it was much softer than that.

As I watched fascinated, the light seemed to be pulsating on an irregular basis, rising and falling in a gentle motion. I could not go on. I stopped and stared at it, wondering at its strange beauty. And then in my heart I heard the words: *This is for you.*

I was overwhelmed. All I felt was immense peace and happiness and gratitude. Then I took a long breath and praying the rosary as reverently as I ever had, I started forward. As I walked, my eyes kept going back to the mountain top; the light was still there, ebbing and renewing. After twenty minutes or so I was almost embarrassed: okay, I thought, that's enough; I see it, and there's no doubt that it's there.

It lasted all the way to the church and only faded when the first light began to line the horizon behind Podbrdo to the east. I was so exhilarated that when I reached the mountain and started up its rocky path, I stopped and prayed at each of the 14 Stations of the Cross, another beautiful tradition I had discovered in my reading. As I prayed, I let this new spirit of God's love fill my heart with the magnitude of the sacrifice which Christ had made.

At the top was a massive cement cross which the villagers had erected in 1933 to commemorate the nineteen-hundredth anniversary of the Crucifixion. It was a crude, powerful structure, and gazing up at it as the rising sun began to catch the top of the vertical, all I could think of was the enormous amount of work that had gone into the building of it. For there was no road up here, only that difficult, craggy path. Everything had to have been carried up on the backs of the villagers — women as well as men. It said something about the devotion of the people in this valley — and why God might have chosen it.

Taking off my pack I sat down on a boulder at the base of the cross and watched the edge of daylight creep across the floor of the valley. Back home in America, I could never have sat still this long, not doing or even thinking anything. Medjugorje was working tremendous changes in me, in more ways than one. I felt as if I was now bathing in that beautiful light that had been given to me as a special gift of the Blessed Virgin. And I remembered reading in one of the Medjugorje books that she said she prayed to her Son each morning at the foot of this magnificent cross.

With my arms around my knees I sat there and watched the valley slowly coming to life. This surely had to be the edge of heaven.

My reverie was broken by the crunch of approaching footsteps on the small stones at the top of the mountain. It was Bernie. "Hey, why didn't you wait for me? I thought maybe you overslept, so I came on alone."

"Bernie, I'm sorry! I was so taken by the morning, I just plain forgot you."

From my pack I pulled out a loaf of what had become my favorite — and many times the only — food in Medjugorje, some homemade bread. I had also brought some juice, and now I offered to share my makeshift breakfast with him. Bernie was a tall, lean, older man who was also a runner. He had made the trip to Medjugorje several times and climbed Krizevac often.

As I ate, I decided to share my experience with him, but with caution; the old journalistic training kept me from being completely open. "Bernie, as you were walking, did you — see a light up here?"

"No, why?"

"Because, well. . . I did."

I then went on to describe to him what had happened, suddenly having to fight back emotion as it all came together in my mind. Bernie smiled and said, "That is a very special blessing. I've heard of it before. Usually, one of the villagers will see it and start door-to-door to tell others."

My eyes filled, and I excused myself and went to the other side of the mountain. I didn't pray consciously; I just sort of locked my heart right up into heaven.

After awhile — I don't know how long; it might have

been hours — Maureen found me, as she and the rest of our group had made the climb after the English Mass.

"How was it?" she beamed.

"What?" I looked up, startled.

"The sunrise! Was it beautiful?"

"Yes," I nodded, "but I saw something else that was even more beautiful," and I told her of the light. "Listen, Maureen, forgive me but I've got to go down now. I just can't be around people. I'll see you at the church in a little while."

"I understand," she nodded, and I left the mountain top and slowly made my way back down.

One thing I knew very clearly now: I was going to write a book about Medjugorje. I had always felt I would write a book one day, but the subject and the exact time in my life when I would begin were unknowns. They weren't unknowns any longer.

The way from the mountain to St. James became a path that wound through a vineyard and then through an old cemetery in a grove of cedars about a quarter-mile behind the church. When I reached it, the grove was deserted and perfectly still; not even the suggestion of a breeze moved through the tops of the towering evergreens. A shaft of sunlight picked out a cluster of white lilies planted at the foot of an ancient tombstone. I stopped and stood motionless in the dappled shade, melding into the stillness of that timeless place.

Then, from the very depths of my being, I thanked God for bringing me here, for my assignment, for — everything.

13

Edge of Heaven

Sister Margaret had scheduled a meeting at the church at 2:00 for "a special treat." No one knew what it was, and we speculated that perhaps she had arranged for one of the visionaries to come and speak to us. Now, sitting in the warm sun with my back against the side of the church while I waited for the others, I suddenly grinned at the thought of writing a book about Medjugorje.

A book — one that would be different from the dozen or so already on the market. Almost all of them had been authored by Catholic priests and dealt mainly with the early days. Little had been said about the process of conversion that occurred to so many of the ordinary people who visited here. I wanted to write about the tremendous spiritual transformation that had struck this luke-warm Protestant. And the important message coming from God to this tiny, remote village somehow had to be spread to the millions of people who would never have the opportunity to come here. It also had to be told to those who needed to come, so that they, too, would return to become apostles in spreading its urgent message.

Also, I was a Protestant. That would add to the impact of personal conversion. I shook my head, realizing that I no longer thought of myself as Protestant or the whole

Medjugorje phenomenon as Catholic. I was simply a child of God, living at the edge of heaven.

Several members of our group now arrived at the church, and I got up to join them. Inside, they had set up chairs for our group at the front. As we went forward, passing French and Italian pilgrims scattered in the back, their heads bowed in silent prayer, I realized that we were the only Americans in Medjugorje at that time. In fact, except for a few Irish pilgrims, we were the only English-speaking group in the church.

The door to the sacristy opened, and out came Marija, Vicka and Ivan. But I hardly saw them; my gaze was fixed on the brown-robed priest leading the way. Slight of frame and thin of hair, with steady gray eyes, he was immediately recognizable from one of the videos: this was Father Svetozar, whose book on Medjugorje had meant more to me than all the others. I hurried over to where Sr. Margaret was sitting. "Sister, I've got to meet that man!"

"Don't worry, you will," she said calmly, looking at me with a knowing smile. I returned to my seat somewhat confused by her statement, but also very happy.

With Father Svet translating, the visionaries gave a brief account of the events of June, 1981. Then they answered the inevitable questions from the group: What did she look like? What was she wearing? What color was her hair?

As I listened, I marveled at the patience of these young people who by now must have heard these same inane questions ten thousand times or more. Yet I could not detect the slightest hint of weariness or boredom in their answers — and that had to be the grace that came with their fulfilling their call.

It was a call I did not envy. Outside of Vicka's house the groups were often lined up in the road, waiting their turn to hear her and ask her questions. The Philippinos would take 20 minutes, then the Italians, then the Germans, and so on. It went on that way all day long, yet she never complained: she was merely doing what the Gospa had asked of her.

And so was I — but until now somewhat less willingly. Silently I hoped that the commitment to write the book would spur me on to heeding the whole of the message that Mary had given me.

When the talk was over, I tried to get to Father Svet but was swamped by people pushing past me from all sides of the church. Apparently word had spread that Father Svet was here with the visionaries, and the church had quickly filled. The next thing I knew, he was surrounded by people, many of them villagers, and was reaching out over them with his hands to bless them. He reminded me of a Presidential candidate back home, and these people were thrilled; he was like a movie star to them.

When it finally subsided and I had a chance, I grabbed his hand and held on. "Father, I'm an American journalist, and I just want you to know how much your book has meant to me. You write with your heart and soul, and I'm so happy to meet you!"

"Wait for me," he whispered, gripping my hand, "please." And with that he turned back to the crowd of well-wishers. I stood there, numb. What did he want with me? When the last had been greeted, he motioned for me to accompany him into the sacristy, the small room adjacent to the altar where the priests robed and prepared to celebrate the Mass. I followed, feeling that I was treading on hallowed ground.

Scarcely had I gone through the doorway than a family of three Croatians barged in, beseeching Father Svet to pray for a young girl member of their family who was in trouble — at least that was what I was able to surmise. When he had finished with them, and they had departed, he closed the door and turned to me, placing his hands on my shoulders and looking directly into my eyes. "Wayne,I have a special favor to ask of you: I have completed the manuscript for my second book on Medjugorje, and I need an American or English writer to help me with the editing. Could you possibly stay for ten or fifteen more days to help me? Or come back?"

I was bowled over; it was like Michelangelo asking a house painter to assist him. "Father, me? How could I possibly help — ?"

"No," he cut me off, "you're the one. Trust me; I know," and he fixed me with his gaze.

I explained to him that I was married and had two small children at home and that I was fortunate to even be here, much less stay an extended time. "But," I added, "it would be an honor to work with you. I will go home and try to work it out."

At length he sighed and said, "Well, I will await word from you. If nothing else, maybe you can help me from America. Sister Margaret will take my manuscript home and make you a copy at the Center for Peace. If it is meant to be, you can return with it next month, and if not, possibly you can return it with corrections through the Center for Peace when they come back to Medjugorje."

"Yes," I replied, "maybe I can. At least, I can try."

He gave me a hug and said, "God go with you, Wayne."

I floated down the aisle of the church which was empty now, save for a few people praying, and went to find Sister Margaret. In my heart I felt it would be impossible to come back, but nevertheless, I was thrilled that he would even ask me. When I found her I asked dazedly, "Do you know what he asked me to do?"

"Yes," she laughed, "I know."

"Well, would you mind telling me what you know that I don't know?"

"I told Svet that there was an American writer with this group, and he was very happy."

"What makes him think I can do it?"

"Well," she shrugged, "if he says you can, you probably can."

I sensed there was more to it than she was telling me, but just then Maureen and a bunch of our group came up all excited, wanting to know the details of why Father Svet had wanted to talk to me, and there was no opportunity to pursue it further with Sr. Margaret. I made a mental note to see her later and find out more about this deeply spiritual priest and his new book.

Some of our group, having heard about the light I had seen on the mountain that morning, had asked me to go back up with them early the next morning, so that night I went to bed early, reminding them that four o'clock would be the latest we could leave if we wanted to see the sunrise.

The next morning, two of them actually made it — Maureen and a young man named Paul. "Hey, Wayne," he said as we started walking, "how far away were you when you first saw that light?"

"A couple of miles."

"Well, had you crossed the bridge into Medjugorje, or what? And what exactly did it look like?"

I walked on as if I hadn't heard him, and suggested we pray the rosary as we walked. Paul was easily excitable and anxious to see any phenomena connected with Medjugorje. His intentions were good, but this was not the time or place for running conversation. It was a time for quiet meditation with God. I was glad when Maureen began the first prayers of the rosary.

We would see no light this morning. Maureen and Paul were disappointed, but I was not surprised. I knew that yesterday's experience had been especially for me — one more incontrovertible piece of evidence of the mission I was being asked to undertake.

When we reached the mountain, Maureen decided she wanted to make sure we were at the top in time for the sunrise, so she quickened the pace as we began the ascent. Well, there was no way I was going to let her outpace me, and I started off right after her, leaving Paul lumbering behind and calling, "Hey, where are you guys going so fast?"

We got to the first Station of the Cross and gasped our way through a prayer, then Maureen was off like a gazelle again, with me right behind her. We did four stations that way, until Paul, looking like he was about to die, pleaded, "What are you guys doing?"

Maureen shrugged. "I'm doing this as a special penance, but that doesn't mean you have to."

"Me, too," I added, determined to stay with her. The sky behind Podbrdo was so light now that the sun would be up at any moment, and we wanted to be to the summit for that. Dripping with perspiration we made it — and it was worth it. Less than a minute after finishing our prayers at the last station, the entire mountaintop was suddenly transformed into a daylight flood of gold and diamonds. Alone at the foot of the cross Maureen and I were speechless. We savored the moment, and then a few minutes later Paul arrived, too out of breath to talk.

The three of us sat around talking, drinking fruit juice, and sharing a loaf of homemade bread I had picked up at the store in Citluk. As I looked around I was dismayed at the amount of discarded litter on the mountain top. I picked up an empty Coca-Cola bottle, then a candy wrapper and someone's half-finished box lunch and took them over to the trash pit that had been dug over to the side of the summit. Everything was covered with the wetness of the new morning, and I wiped the drops of dew on the side of my pants after discarding the pieces I had picked up.

Suddenly, I noticed what appeared to be a picture lying on top of the pile. I climbed into the pit and picked it up. It was a picture of Jesus, about four inches by five inches in size. Strangely, it was perfectly dry, when everything else on the trash pile was soaked with dew. No one was on the mountain when we reached the top, nor had anyone passed us coming down, so the picture had to have been there at least during the night. "Maureen," I called, "come over here. I don't believe this!" I showed her the picture. "It's bone dry," I murmured.

"Oh, I want it, I want it!" she exclaimed, clasping it to her, and missing the point that it was completely dry.

Well, that killed me because I wanted it, too — but then I remembered the gift I'd been given the day before, of being permitted to see the light. Perhaps this was her gift.

"Where did it come from?" I wondered. Turning it over, we found nothing on the back but a handwritten date: 18th June, 1986. "Must be European," I observed, "since the day is first, instead of the month. But why just the date? And why a date six weeks from now?" Maureen just shook her head and then happily pocketed the picture, after showing it to Paul. We started back down a little later, to make the morning Mass. The mysterious picture with its future date on the back was forgotten.

With each of us conscious that this would be our last day in Medjugorje, everything seemed remarkably clear, every feeling acute. Gradually I became aware of how much I did not want to leave. Which was crazy! I missed Terri and the kids and was dying to see them. But in the Mass later that morning I found my emotions running high. "O God," I whispered, "this is my last full day here!" My heart was breaking, for despite Father Svet's request and

my own desire to work with him, I never really thought
it would be possible for me to return.

The rest of the day passed quickly — too quickly.
Everywhere I looked, I saw something else that I wanted
to remember always. The sun sank lower over the
mountains to the west, and all too soon it was time to
go to the church for the evening rosary before the Croatian
Mass. As we entered, my eyes fell on the confessionals
at the back of the church. There were three on either
side, and in front of each was a small sign: Hvrotski
(Croatian), Deutsche, English, Francais. . . .

As usual, the pews were crammed, but in the last pew
on the right hand side the people made room for me
and insisted that I join them. The prayers began, but my
mind was not on the rosary; I was thinking about
confession. All day long — in fact, for the last several
days — I had thought about going to confession. As a
Protestant this was new to me. We Lutherans had it publicly
as part of our litany, but I was overwhelmed at the large
number of pilgrims I had seen lining up inside and outside
of the church to go through this special sacrament. And
several people in our group had been asking me if I
intended to go. As the cumulative impact of Medjugorje
mounted, many pilgrims felt compelled to cleanse their
souls through confession — some for the first time in
years. By this act they would seal their Medjugorje experience in their hearts for the rest of their lives.

I wanted to do that, too — but I was a Protestant. Would
it be all right for me to go through this special sacrament?
I asked Sister Margaret, and she didn't know; I was the
first Protestant she had ever brought here. On the one
hand it was for Catholics, but on the other hand how
could anyone refuse someone desiring to formally repent?
I also asked Maureen and she encouraged me to go. "But,"
she added, "whatever you do, don't go to Father Arcadius,

that priest with the white beard and fierce eyes. I went to him and he's tough on Catholics, not exactly what a Protestant needs for his first confession!" she said with a twinkle.

In the end the decision was mine, so I decided that I would wait until I got home. If I still felt as strongly about it, I would ask my Lutheran pastor to hear my confession. I tried to concentrate on the rosary, but as the time for the Croatian Mass drew closer, I was increasingly torn apart inside at the thought that it would be my last.

At length I could stand it no longer. I got up from the pew and started out of the church. As I passed the Italian confessional for some reason I glanced down at the sign and then into the eyes of the large, round priest who was standing there. "Italiano?" he whispered.

"No, English," I replied and started to leave. But he had misunderstood my intent, and beaming he took me by the shoulder and fairly shoved me into the booth on the other side of him, where the little sign said English. Shocked, I suddenly found myself going to confession whether I wanted to or not!

When I dropped to my knees on the hard wood I realized how badly they hurt; I had been doing a lot of kneeling that week — for the first time in my life. I glanced at the screened window and saw the profile of a white-bearded priest whom I recognized as the hermit monk who traveled around to shrines like Lourdes and Fatima, helping out by hearing confessions. It was the same Father Arcadius that Maureen had warned me about! Well, it was a little late now.

"Yes, my son?" said the priest softly.

All I could remember was the response I had seen in a movie somewhere. "Bless me, Father, for I have sinned."

He waited, and I waited; I didn't know what to say next.

Finally I blurted out: "I want to make confession, but I don't know how. I've never done this before. I'm a Protestant."

"You're what?" the priest's head jerked around.

"I'm a Protestant, Father," I mumbled. My knees were killing me now, and sweat was pouring off me. All I wanted to do was get up and run.

He looked at me intently and then said, "Well — I will hear your confession, but I am not permitted to give absolution to non-Catholics."

"Fine, Father, it doesn't matter." I hadn't the foggiest idea what he was talking about.

There was another pause. "Well," he said, "go ahead."

"Father — I don't know what to do."

He shook his head, paused for a moment, then said, "I will go through the Ten Commandments, and you — simply answer yes or no."

I thought to myself, I don't believe this is happening!

He started in, going through them one by one. I was relieved when he got to Thou Shalt Not Kill, and I could finally answer no.

When he finished, he said, "When you get back to the States, if you want to go to confession you should go to your own pastor."

"Thank you, Father," I said, getting to my feet and exiting the confessional as quick as possible.

Outside, my legs were shaking, and I quickly hailed a taxi to Citluk. When we got there, I got out and walked up the little dirt path to where we were staying — and kept walking. I was deeply shaken, but I also realized that I actually felt tremendous — cleansed — deep down, like never before. Then I began thinking about what had just happened. And I started laughing. That poor priest! I'm not sure which of us was the more shaken.

I went back to the room and took a shower and packed, because this was the last night, and I wanted to have a little free time in the early morning. I had made up my mind to go once more to Medjugorje — not to the mountain this time, but to have some time alone in the church before the seven o'clock Mass, right after which we would be leaving for Dubrovnik.

I went to bed before the others got back, and as I waited for sleep, I thought how glad I was that I had gone to confession. It didn't make me Catholic — or non-Catholic, for that matter. It did do for me what it had done for others: it sealed my Medjugorje experience.

And then I realized something else: I hadn't thought a whole lot about Mary since I had come, even though she had been appearing every day. I was almost ashamed of that, since it was she who had brought me here to begin with. Yet I sensed she didn't mind. She preferred to recede into the background and point people to her Son. In my case she had certainly succeeded: after this week my relationship with God was more real and immediate than it had ever been before. It was personal, close, and intimate, and I sensed it would continue to be when I got home. I found myself murmuring from time to time, "I love you, Jesus," or "Thank you, Jesus." My prayer life would never be the same; in fact, my entire life would never be the same — which was the whole point of Medjugorje.

The next morning as I walked the now-familiar road, the early morning air, crisp and clear, seemed to crystallize all the events of the past week. To me there was a discernible, spiritual progression to them. Certainly I had seen the gradual transformation in others: the large complaining woman on the bus had softened and calmed down; priests who had come here with an almost callous indifference were almost glowing by week's end.

As for me, I just kept saying, "Lord Jesus, I just don't think I can walk away from this. I'm here on the edge of heaven and I don't really want to go back home." And then my heart would yearn for Terri and Kennedy and Rebecca, and I would wish that I could just transport them here.

When I got to the church, it was empty — the first time I had ever seen it that way. Not too surprising, I thought; I was at least an hour early for Mass. I went up to the front pew and slipped in — and almost immediately began to feel the emotion welling up inside of me. You can't do this, I told myself, but the tears wouldn't stop. "Jesus," I whispered, "I know we have to leave now, but I just can't. . . ."

Time seemed to evaporate, and suddenly Maureen and several others from our group slipped in beside me. "You sneaky thing," she whispered with a smile, "why didn't you let us know you were coming early?"

"I just had to be alone for a few minutes," I answered, glancing at her and then quickly turning away. I simply couldn't control the tears. The English service was smaller and more intimate than the evening one. There was a tender presence of God there during the communion that I would never forget. When it was over, I hurried out; I simply had to get away from everyone. There was half an hour left before our bus would come to take us to Dubrovnik — and our pilgrimage would be over.

I walked quickly around the outside of the church to the back, where no one could see me. The sun was well up now, and there was not a cloud in the sky. I dropped to my knees and began to sob uncontrollably. "Lord God, please — don't take me away from here!" I became a little boy — that child of God that we had been hearing about all week. Words were beyond me; all I could say over and over was, "Jesus — Jesus — Jesus."

Gradually I became aware of a great peace settling over me, and the assurance that I would never leave Medjugorje spiritually. But it was time to go home — and live every day what I had experienced here. Finally I got to my feet and glanced up at Mt. Krizevac for one last mental photograph of the symbol of this beautiful little village. I looked again — and stared: there was no cross!

I blinked and squinted, turned away and turned back — still no cross. Shocked, I dug my camera out of my pack and looked through the viewfinder: nothing. I took a couple of pictures for evidence, as I had already snapped some of the mountain — and the cross — from approximately the same location. Slowly I made my way to the front of the church, where I found Maureen and another pilgrim from our group, Bob Veasey, who had become a good friend. "Look," I said quietly, pointing at the mountain.

"We know!" Bob grinned. "We don't see it, either!"

For ten or fifteen minutes we gazed at the mountain top, and then it was time to board our bus. Funny thing: when we were in our seats and taking a last look at Mt. Krizevac, the cross was back again and clearly visible.

Turning to Bob I said softly, "That's the most beautiful good-bye we could possibly have."

*"Totally commit yourself to Him — so that
you will comprehend and burn
with God's love. . . ."*

14

Home, Sweet Home

As our plane gathered speed down the Dubrovnik
runway early Friday morning, I could not get over the
transformation of our group since our arrival eight days
before. Medjugorje had profoundly affected each of us
individually; but it had affected us as a group, as well.
We had shared this extraordinary experience, and that
sharing had produced a bonding that would last a lifetime.

I had a new understanding of what it meant to be a
pilgrim — to share experiences and impressions with
others from all different backgrounds who were placed
with you for a period of time. In the natural we might
never have become friends — but we were not in the
natural; we were in the supernatural. Somehow I knew
that these friendships would always be strong, even if we
didn't see each other for years. As soon as the seatbelt
sign was off, little groups clustered in the aisles, talking
about their plans and arranging get-togethers when they
got home.

Maureen would soon be heading for a little town on
the Texas-Mexican border to work for a year in a birthing
clinic for the poor. There would be little pay — just room
and board and a stipend for necessities, but plenty of long
hours and extremely difficult work. I was impressed that

she would make such a commitment, more so because it had been made long before she knew she would be going to Medjugorje — back when, as she put it, she was not a very good Catholic. Yet, this young nurse-to-be loved God enough to give the first year of her professional life in service to others. She was engaged, but they had decided to wait until her year of volunteer work was finished. She agreed to stop by Myrtle Beach with her fiance Fred, on their way to Texas, to visit Terri and me.

It was a happy time for all of us — but in the back of my mind was a nagging concern that I knew I would have to resolve. For there was more to the Father Svet episode than Sister Margaret had let on. I had not had any time alone with her to find out the details. But now that we were on the way home, I decided to just ask her. Fortunately there was an empty seat next to her, and asking if I might join her for a moment, I came right to the point: "Sister, how could Father Svetozar, after spending just a few minutes with me, be so sure I would be the one to help him with his manuscript? He didn't know me from Adam."

She looked at me for a moment and smiled, "All right, I'll tell you: About two months before this trip, I visited Father Svet at his monastery up in Konjic. He asked me to read his manuscript, and I did. Then he wanted to know what I thought of it. I told him I thought it was great. But he wasn't sure; he desperately wanted someone who could handle the English language to help him with the phrasing and editing — someone he could work with face to face. He asked me if I would do it."

She smiled at the recollection. "I told him I wasn't qualified, and that even if I was, I did not have the time. When I got home my schedule was already completely full until the moment I returned. So, he asked me if I knew anyone who would be able to assist him. When I said no, he said he didn't know what he was going to do, that he had to have someone to help him soon. I suggested we pray about it. You know," she smiled again, "I'm a firm believer in prayer."

I nodded. "What did you pray?"

She paused for a moment. "That in the next Center for Peace group to come over — this group — there would be an American writer or journalist, what have you."

I stared at her. "That's incredible!" I exclaimed, feeling that one more step of the spiritual journey which Mary had asked me to undertake, had been made. Recalling my near-obsession, in spite of Terri's vehement objection, that I come to Medjugorje in May, the thought suddenly struck me: "That means I'll definitely be returning —"

"Well," she gently reminded me, "don't forget you've still got to get over the hurdle of going home and talking to Terri."

My euphoria vanished. I had assumed since this little miracle of my coming in May had occurred through her prayers, it was almost destined that I would return to work with Father Svetozar. Now I wasn't sure. "What do I do? I've just got to come back now."

"Do exactly what I did," she replied in that blunt, New York way of hers. "Go pray about it."

Feeling a bit sheepish that after eight days in Medjugorje I still had to be reminded to pray, I thanked her and assured her I would.

Back in my seat I shut my eyes and prayed silently: Lord, if You mean for me to come back, — and I really dare not even think I'm going to — then when I tell Terri about it, if she objects in the slightest, I'll know that it's not Your will. I'm just going to leave it that way — and Lord, I added, I'm praying that the answer is yes. Amen. It was a discomforting thought to put it on the line like that, but what was done, was done.

We landed at Kennedy and deplaned — into the bustle of a busy airport, the noise and organized chaos of New York City, with people in a frenzy to get here, there, everywhere. We were back in the world, and it was a jolt — which was sharpened when we went outside, where people were yelling for cabs, and cabbies were yelling at one another.

After our group's good-byes and promises to stay in touch, I had some time before my flight to Myrtle Beach, so I went to a phone to call Terri. There was so much to say. In all our years of marriage this was the first time we had been apart this long without at least being able to call. I couldn't wait to hear her voice! And yet — when I finished dialing and started thinking about what I was going to say, I choked up. I couldn't do it! Hanging up the receiver before it could ring, I shook my head; it would have to wait till I got home.

I went into the washroom to clean up and try to look presentable — and was startled by the tanned face looking back at me from the mirror. I was hollowed-eyed, but it was more than a ten-hour flight without sleep, and more than the weight I'd lost skipping meals. The eyes seemed somehow older.

When the next flight landed at our home airport, I had been traveling more than 16 hours — yet I still did not have my emotions under control. Normally I would be one of the first up and waiting in the aisle; this night I was happy to let the others go ahead. Sitting there, trying to compose myself so that I could handle the reunion with Terri like a mature adult, I wound up being the last one off the plane.

As I came through the door of the airport, there she was, absolutely beautiful! There was a startled expression on her face when she first saw me, then she smiled and held out her arms. The moment I was in them, the tears came. I just couldn't help it. The combination of coming home and the full impact of those eight days in that holy little village were just too much.

She hugged me and kept asking, "What's the matter?"

But I couldn't answer. "Please," I finally managed, "just get the van. I need to go home."

We drove in silence. When we pulled into our driveway, it was so good to be home! But — I still felt this terrible longing to be back in Medjugorje. And now the cumulative effect of the mental, physical, and emotional fatigue of the past eight days began to catch up with me, and I collapsed into the lounger.

"You want anything?" Terri asked.

I just shook my head, and she came around in front of me and scrutinized me. "You look terrible," she said with a smile, "but you look good. I can't believe you've lost all that weight."

She went on trying to make small talk, and I tried to smile a couple of times and make replies. Then deciding to just get to it, I started to tell her what had happened and how it had affected me. Frequently I had to pause, unable to continue.

We talked for two hours — and scarcely scratched the surface. Finally, around 11:00 I went to bed. But even though I had been up for nearly two days, I could only sleep for about four hours. I got up and went into the living room and prayed, then went outside and walked around in the warm night for awhile. I longed for the beautiful Croatian language in song and prayer that I had become so accustomed to hearing each evening. The eight days in Medjugorje now seemed like a lifetime, and I was terribly homesick for the village and its people.

Finally, I made myself go back to bed and slept until the kids burst in and started jumping all over me. I felt good.

"You've slept long enough!" they yelled, "It's time to get up!"

We rumpused around for awhile; then I shooed them out and showered, shaved and dressed. Throughout that day I did very little; it was all I could do just to unpack my suitcase and sort things out. But we talked — a little at a time. And we hugged a lot.

The next day was Sunday, and it was time to go to church. I started getting ready and then stopped, telling Terri that I didn't think I was up to going. I wasn't ready to face people just yet, especially our pastors. I recalled the rebuff, the refusal to accept anything out of line with Lutheran belief. As far as they were concerned, apparitions of the Blessed Virgin Mary were way out of that line. Yet, I had been there. For me, its authenticity was no longer a question; I was convinced that it was the most important event occurring in the world at the time.

"Come on," urged Terri, "you'll be all right."

As luck would have it, no sooner did we pull into the church parking lot than one of my friends spotted me. He greeted me and told me how glad he was to see me again, and then added, " Boy, I'll bet you're glad to be back here in the good old USA!"

I just stared at him with a funny smile and said nothing. I was not glad to be back in the good old USA. I wanted in the worst way to leave right then and catch the next plane to Yugoslavia. Terri assured him that I would be all right, and that I was just suffering from jetlag.

Getting out of the van, I whispered to Terri that we ought to just go home; I had no desire to go inside. But she just squeezed my arm and said it would be okay.

So we went in, and when people would ask about my trip, I would smile and make a few comments, saying it was fine and so forth, struggling to keep my composure.

Terri would trail along behind, cleaning up the mess, making excuses for my strange behavior.

We sat in the back, and I rediscovered how much I loved our Lutheran liturgy — which was closer to the Catholic Mass than I had realized. But nothing could compare to St. James — the joy, the thunderous response of the people, the soul-stirring singing — I just closed my eyes and pretended I was back in Medjugorje.

As we left, Pastor Wingard greeted us warmly at the door, and again I was overcome; having seen Bill occasionally moved to tears in the pulpit, I knew he would understand. I simply told him that it had been a deep, deep spiritual trip, and that sometime very soon I wanted to sit down with him and talk about it.

"That's great," he said, "I look forward to it."

It had gone better than I had expected. But it was good to get back to the house and to be alone with my memories.

The next day the jetlag really did catch up with me. I didn't even try to go into the office, but napped whenever the mood hit me — which seemed to be practically every time I turned around. Several times during the day I told Terri that there was something important I had to discuss with her — and then I would doze off again. Finally, around 10:30 that evening, I asked her to turn off the TV; we had to talk.

Keeping my emotions as calm as I possibly could, I told her about the incident with Father Svet and handed her his first book which she had read. "I still have a hard time believing it," I concluded, "but he's asked me to come back over there for ten days or a couple of weeks, to help him get the next one ready."

Without looking at me or saying anything she began to thumb through the blue book. I sat there in agony — for 30 seconds — 40 seconds. . . .

Then she looked up and with a slight smile said, "Well,

if Mary wants you to go back and do this, I guess I have to say yes. But who do you think you're kidding? It won't be ten days; it'll be more like three weeks."

I could not believe what I was hearing! I reached over and hugged her, and told her that I loved her very much. "Well," she said, shaking her head and smiling, "I don't know if I'm being conned or not, but —"

"Terri," I cut her off, "you're not being conned! If you want to change your mind —"

"No, no, I understand," she sighed. "When do you have to go back?"

"In the middle of June," I replied, trying not to sound exuberant.

We talked about it for another hour, and then as we were going to bed she said, "You know, I don't have the slightest idea in the world why I'm agreeing to this; it's ridiculous!" But seeing my expression she added, "Don't worry about it; it has to be done."

I went to bed a very happy man.

*"I call you to be an example to everyone,
especially in prayer and
witnessing. . . ."*

15

Telling The Story

Tuesday morning I awoke in a state of euphoria. I was going back to Medjugorje! I lay in the bed for a few moments letting it sink in. And finally feeling like something approaching normal, I was anxious to get to work. It would be good to gather my thoughts while they were fresh; I figured it would take at least two columns to tell about the trip.

There was, however, a tiny cloud on the horizon. Yesterday I had remembered that this morning I was scheduled to be the breakfast speaker at one of the local civic clubs. It was too late to get a substitute, and except for the feeling that it was supposed to be about my trip to Yugoslavia, I had no idea what I was going to talk about.

Nor was it any clearer by the time I arrived at the motel where we met every Tuesday morning. At least I was on time, I thought, entering the conference dining room. The clock on the wall said exactly 7:30. Glancing around, I noted that there were forty or fifty men there already — not a bad turn-out for the beginning of summer.

Normally I would join one of the tables towards the back, but this morning I had to sit at the head table by the podium, next to the club president. We chatted lightly, and I didn't eat much. Public speaking had never been easy for me — a necessary evil, as far as I was concerned. No matter what the occasion or the size of the audience, I always seemed to feel ill, sweaty-palmed, and incapable of following my notes properly. It was definitely not my favorite thing to do, especially in front of business peers.

And now I was going to talk to them about Medjugorje, about something —religious.

I tried to organize what I was going to say, even scratching out a few notes on a napkin. But the next thing I knew, we had finished with club business, and the president was announcing me. Gripping the podium to keep my hands from shaking, I plunged in.: "Look, I know you people; we're members of this club, and I've worked with a lot of you. I don't know how I'm going to tell you what I'm going to tell you today, because it isn't what I planned to talk about." I paused and took a deep breath. "But if I can say it to you, I can say it to anyone."

With that I proceeded to tell them about the apparitions of Medjugorje — what was happening there, and how it had begun. "I was there," I said. "I've met these people, I've been in that church, I've felt what happened." For the first time in my life I began to talk publicly about Jesus Christ — and suddenly there was no more embarrassment, no fear, no sweaty palms. And no stopping me; I went on for nearly forty minutes, twice the normal length. And all the while I was calm and quiet, as the words just poured out of me.

Normally, people who had early appointments would get up and leave before the speaker was finished, and some Tuesdays it seemed as if a lot of people had early appointments. Those who didn't would be fixing themselves another cup of coffee or sneaking a look at the morning paper. This morning, no one left; no one even moved.

Finally I got to the end. I just knew it was time to stop, and I did. "I don't know why I've done this," I told them, "because normally I would never say the things I've said to you. All I can say is, this has affected my life so profoundly that I'll never be the same, and I can only leave you with that."

There was silence, and then — they began to applaud. And it struck me: my God, what have I said? Now I did feel embarrassment, like when I turned in the first column on Medjugorje to production. As before, the thought struck me: if only I could pull those words back! But of course it was too late.

The president got up and mumbled something about this being one of the most unique programs we'd ever had. And then he dismissed us, much to my relief. Some of the men came up to speak to me, and I would never forget the first one. He looked at me and said, "Well, that took more guts than I'll ever have." He paused. "But it was beautiful. You touched me, I'll tell you that," and he turned and walked away.

Others made positive comments, and a couple of men even invited me to come and speak to their churches. When it was over, I walked out of that place in a daze. I got in my car and just sat there for a moment. Then I drove to work, my heart overflowing with gratitude.

By the time I reached the office I was jubilant. I didn't even bother with the week's worth of correspondence which Denease had carefully stacked on my desk. I went straight to the typewriter and started in on my next column, the seventh in the Medjugorje series. Talk about easy, it was like writing a letter to an old and interested friend.

A Visit to Medjugorje
May 13, 1986

I ran into an old friend at the airport a couple of weeks ago. I was waiting to leave on a nine-day trip to Medjugorje, Yugoslavia. The usual light chatter ensued and in the course of that, I asked him where he was going. He told me he was heading for a few days in Cancun, Mexico, for a business meeting and some relaxation. Then, the inevitable: "Where are you going?"

"Uh, Yugoslavia," I said hesitantly. "I'm going to Yugoslavia."

The look on his face said it all, but he asked anyway. "Why in the world are you going to Yugoslavia?"

After spending nearly two weeks there, I can understand why someone would question a trip to Yugoslavia. It's communist, mountainous, and hard to get around in, and they don't exactly welcome visitors — especially Americans — with open arms and smiles.

But I didn't go there as a tourist. Anyone who has read this column regularly over the past six months knows why I went to Medjugorje.

For almost five years now, this small village has attracted world-wide attention as the place where the Blessed Virgin Mary, the Mother of Jesus, is reportedly appearing daily to six young people in this remote mountain village. Despite government attempts to make visiting the site difficult, millions have been and continue to come from around the world to see for themselves what is happening.

It has become the number one tourist attraction in Yugoslavia. For this reason, while the government continues harassment of the locals and the visitors, they grudgingly "accommodate" the influx of people because of the economic gain. Guest houses are being hastily built, but they are built by the individual landowners, not large construction companies. Progress is slow. There are scattered vendors of food and souvenirs. But the ratio to the number of people there is minute. There are no bathroom facilities, nothing to make the visiting pilgrim's stay comfortable. Yet, thousands come weekly.

The believability of such an event in today's technical world is difficult. However, to go there and be there for an extended period of time leaves little doubt that something definitely beyond technical or scientific explanation is taking place.

The multitude of religious beliefs and cults in the world today, the generally apathetic attitude of church-goers, and the divided opinions even within the Catholic Church lends credence to the skepticism of this supernatural phenomenon. Yet my own involvement and the circumstances that brought it about have me convinced that this is an authentic call for peace and a return to the ways of God for the whole people of the world; and I am also convinced that the Mother of Jesus, Mary, is the messenger.

I believed this before I went to Medjugorje. I came home with no doubt at all.

I kept asking, why me? I'm a journalist and journalists demand hard, cold, substantiated facts and evidence. I'm not Catholic and know very little about the Catholic Church's reverence for the Virgin Mary. My own Lutheran beliefs virtually ignore Mary beyond her role as mother of our Lord.

My interest in learning more about the events of Medjugorje was simply curiosity: I thought it might make an interesting Christmas column. That "curiosity" turned into four very long columns during the entire month of December. Since that time, over 250 requests that required a self-addressed, stamped envelope have been received for back-copies of the articles. They continue to come in.

That curiosity now has me wanting to spend the rest of my life spreading the message of Medjugorje to any and everyone who will listen. I intend to do just that.

What I saw and what I felt is not easily put into words. It will be difficult for others to accept it or believe it. Yet, I was there, and I know what I saw and what I felt. I saw the sun dance and move and whirl and pale so that I could look directly at it with the naked eye. That is impossible, but I saw it. It was the same sun you and I see every day.

I also saw a huge, 14-ton cement cross mounted high on a mountain that stands behind the church at Medjugorje totally disappear on a cloudless, bright morning. This same cross was observed by me early in the black of morning to glow and shine as though it was covered with lights. That also is impossible. There is no electricity on that mountain, but I saw it.

There was more, but the point is, there is no explanation for these phenomena. They usually occur at the time the Blessed Virgin is appearing to the children. Some see them. Some do not. Others saw them at times when I did not.

The most important phenomenon at Medjugorje is not the supernatural occurrences, however. It is the almost unanimous commitment to the messages delivered by Mary to the villagers. This village is the closest thing there is to a perfect community of love and adherence to the ways of God.

This community, while simple, rural, backward and lacking in material gain, was in many ways no different than our own communities, prior to the beginning of the apparitions in June, 1981. They had their share of trouble with drunkenness, cheating, greed, fighting. They went to church, but not enough to fill the pews every Sunday.

Today, these ways are non-existent. The church is filled daily, not just on Sunday. Devotion to God is the main course of their lives. This is the real miracle, the real message of Medjugorje. That is what is stressed to the visiting pilgrims.

One of the young people who sees Mary daily has said that the highlight of her day is not the apparition of the Mother of Jesus, but rather the attending of church. This is what the Blessed Virgin wants of all of us.

So, where to from here? Next week will probably be my last column on this subject. . . . I will also be glad to speak to any group and show the video. Most important, though, I will make every effort to adhere to the message of Medjugorje. May it live forever in all of us.

Two weeks later, the eighth and last Medjugorje column came just as easily:

A Final Word on Medjugorje
May 28, 1986

Two weeks ago, I returned from a nine-day trip to Medjugorje, Yugoslavia, a small rural mountain village where the Virgin Mary, the Mother of Jesus, is reported to be appearing to a group of six young people. The apparitions as they are called have been occurring since June 24, 1981, a period of almost five years. Last December, I did a series of four columns on this supernatural religious event, and followed that with several follow-up reports earlier this year. This will be the final column I will do about Medjugorje. . . .

This final column on Medjugorje concerns several of the most recent messages given by Mary. Permit me if you will, though, to divert briefly to tell you about one of the people who went to Medjugorje with our Center for Peace tour group.

Frank Fiamingo, Jr., is a paraplegic. He has lived in a wheelchair for 19 of his 33 years. His story of coming to Medjugorje is very special to me.

Frank's parents, Frank, Sr. and Yolanda live here on the Grand Strand, in Surfside Beach. You only have to spend a few minutes with Frank, Sr. to know he is one of the happiest, most optimistic persons you'll ever meet. Yolanda is quiet and always seems to be in control. Both are devoted to their church and family and it shows.

What makes their going to Medjugorje extra special for me was the fact that they found out about it through the columns I had done in December. They then called Frank, Jr. who lives in Columbus, Ohio and decided they would all go as part of the same tour group I was with.

I asked Frank, who is a research scientist at the medical school at Ohio State University, why he had decided to come to Medjugorje, and if he thought he might find a cure there.

He thought very carefully before answering. "I guess I came here for the same reason you and the others in this group came for. I wanted to find out more about what is happening here. I came for my own personal reasons and for spiritual nourishment."

He paused, and then continued, "But to answer your other question, no, I didn't come here expecting a physical cure."

I think it would be safe to say that Frank found those things he went to Medjugorje seeking. He was greeted warmly by Vicka, one of the young people who sees the Virgin Mary daily. She posed with him and his family for pictures and said prayers with them. He later was invited into the room where the apparitions occur and was present for one of them.

Frank Fiamingo, Jr. left Medjugorje the same way he arrived: in a wheelchair, but I think it would also be safe to say, he left as happy, as complete and as fulfilled as any of us in the group.

Every Monday and Thursday, the Virgin Mary gives messages to the children that are meant for the whole parish of Medjugorje and the whole world as well. She addresses all people as "Dear Children." Every message is ended with: "Thank you for your response to my call."

March 6, Thursday evening: "Dear Children, today I am calling you to open yourselves more to God, so that He can work through you. For as much as you open yourselves, you will receive the fruits from it. I wish to call you again to prayer."

March 27, Thursday evening: "Dear Children, I wish to thank you for your sacrifices. And, now, I invite you to the greatest sacrifice. The sacrifice of love. Without love, you are not able to accept me or my Son. Without love you cannot witness your impressions to others. That is why I invite you to begin to love the love in your hearts."

April 7, Monday evening: "Dear Children, now, you are preoccupied about material things. In the material, you lost everything that God wants to grant to you. I am inviting you, dear children, to pray for the gifts of the Holy Spirit that you need now in order that you may witness my presence here and everything I am giving you. Dear Children, abandon yourselves to me so that I can lead you totally. Do not be so preoccupied about the material things of the world."

The message of May 5, Monday evening, was very special. Almost everyone in our group was present when it was received.

We got word at 9:45 p.m. that evening. One of the seers said that Mary had invited some of the pilgrims to Medjugorje to come up on the Hill of the Apparitions for a special apparition with the children. It was pitch black, yet we were able to make our way up a steep, rocky path to the top of the hill where the visions had first occurred.

In the moment that Mary appeared, she was happy and content and said to the children, "Praise Jesus." Then, she prayed over us and blessed us. Later when one of the seers "recommended" us to her, she blessed us again. Her message that evening was as follows: "Dear Children, I would like to collaborate with you and at first I would like you to be apostles of the messages of peace, conciliation, prayer, fasting and penance. I encourage everyone to live these messages for the changing of your lives."

Afterwards, she said she was very happy that all of us were there. She then left in a shining light of the cross.

I can only end this the way Mary ends her appearances with the young seers: "Go in God's Peace."

With the last of the Medjugorje columns now behind me, I turned my attention to the preparations for my return. As I began to edit Father Svet's manuscript, I found it was going to be a difficult task because of the tremendous differences between Croatian and English. As much as I admired this man and his first book, in reality there was a tremendous amount of editing to be done on the next. Terri had also read portions of the manuscript and was deeply impressed by it — for which I was grateful, as she was now enthusiastic about my going.

Almost before we knew it, it was June 15th, the day of my departure.

"Around every oasis of peace is a desert where Satan is lurking — only by prayer are you able to overcome every influence of Satan. . . ."

16

Return

It was different to be flying to Dubrovnik on my own. With no other pilgrims with whom to share expectations and exchange stories, the nine-hour, night flight seemed about twice as long as it had before. Then we landed, and I felt even more alone when the unsmiling uniformed woman in the Passport Control booth took my passport and then held it — for fully two minutes, slowly flipping through it, before tossing it back to me. No explanation; she just wanted me to know who was in control.

I acted as nonchalant as possible and went to find my bag. My stomach was tied in knots. This was definitely different from the first trip; there was no one to tell me where to go or what to do, no friendly bus full of pilgrims to take me to Medjugorje, no accommodations reserved for me when I got there. There was not even a road map at the car rental booth. The travel agency which handled my business flights had reserved a Renault for me, and as soon as I got used to the gear-shift lever extending out of the dashboard, I was ready to go.

In response to my plea, the rental agent reluctantly loaned me his only map, on my promise to bring it back. I turned the little red car out of the airport parking lot with only the vaguest idea of where I was to go, but filled with a sense of excitement.

I stopped to give a ride to a young hitchhiker, hoping that he could direct me to the right road to Medjugorje which I knew was about 90 miles away. He spoke little English, but he did point me in the right direction and said that since there were few roads between Dubrovnik and the area where I was going, it would not be difficult to find the village.

I began to enjoy the spectacular drive up the Adriatic Coast, winding in and out of tiny villages clinging to the sides of rocky cliffs. The sun-drenched coastline fairly sparkled. Even the crazy drivers whizzing around me on blind curves didn't bother me; I was going back — to the edge of heaven.

Medjugorje was not on the well-worn map the agent had loaned me. But Mostar was, and that city, I knew, was only about 20 miles from Medjugorje. Approximately an hour of driving along the coastline led me to the turn-off leading to that area. The closer I got, the more excited I became. Finally, about two and a half hours after leaving the airport, the landscape began to look familiar.

Citluk at last! I drove straight to the home where our group had stayed and arranged for a room with my surprised hostess who remembered me. But it would be available for only three days. Just then I remembered a man whom I had met there in May who ran a small business of his own and was building a tourist rooming house. He had asked me to check with him if I ever returned and was in need of a room. I made a mental note to look him up the next day.

Anxious now to reach the church and once again feel the peace and security of the village and its people, I unloaded my bags quickly and headed the car down the familiar road to Medjugorje. When Mt. Krizevac came into view, my heart leapt and I literally yelled out a grateful thanks to God for bringing me back.

My happiness abruptly ceased when I rounded the next curve and spotted the white police car with the blue light on the top and the word Milicia in big blue letters on the side. The police were known to stop drivers just for the sake of harassing them. At that moment I would not have minded being in the middle of a big tour group instead of on a solo mission; but they didn't bother me, and I drove on with a sigh of relief. Crossing the little bridge, I caught my first glimpse of St. James' twin spires. I was back!

Parking in the front of the church, I all but ran inside and knelt immediately in a back pew. Words could not express what I felt — how good it was to be back among these people, to hear the sounds of Medjugorje, to see faces that I remembered from the first trip and be again among those so privileged to come here on pilgrimage. As a group of older women dressed in black with black kerchiefs on their heads circled the statue of Mary on their knees, praying fervently, all the holiness and intense devotion that personified the general conversion of the village now filled my heart to over-flowing.

It was a little after four, and already the church as usual was beginning to fill, in anticipation of the prayers and Mass that began at six each evening. As pilgrims filed into the pews, I marveled anew at the incredible transformation of this tiny rural village by a supernatural happening which had brought the world to worship here. So many churches across America were begging for people to come, and here they come two hours early just to be inside. . . .

My reverie was interrupted by the sight of Father Tomislav Pervan, pastor of St. James, casually strolling up the middle aisle of the church. Father Svet had instructed me to get in touch with him through Father Pervan when I arrived, indicating that it would be the best — and safest — way to contact him in Konjic.

Reflecting back on a phone conversation I'd had with Father Svet after Terri had consented to my returning to work with him, I recalled that it had been a guarded conversation. In fact, it had taken me a few moments to catch on. The monk at the monastery in Konjic who had answered my call spoke no English, and I wasn't sure he had understood me.

After a long wait, Father Svet came on the line.

"Father Svetozar?" I asked.

"Yes, who is this?"

"This is Wayne Weible, calling from the United States — do you remember me?"

"Ah, yes, Wayne, from the Center for Peace! How are you?" There was a hesitancy in his voice, as if he wasn't comfortable with the conversation or its purpose.

"I'm fine, Father. I'm calling to let you know that I will be returning to Medjugorje in June to help you with your book. I'll be arriving — "

"No, no!" he quickly cut me off, adding, "I understand you are returning with a group of pilgrims — that is good. That is very good!"

There was an awkward moment of silence, and then all at once, I realized what was going on. Yugoslavia was a Communist country, and Father Svet was a tremendously popular and influential figure. (As was Father Jozo, the pastor of St. James who had spent 18 months in prison at hard labor.) Father Svet had been closely watched and constantly harassed by the Government, ever since some comments he had made years before while stationed in the States — comments which they had construed as being anti-Government. The telephones of such people were likely to be tapped.

"Yes," I replied trying to sound casual, "I'll be coming with the Center to work on my book. I look forward to seeing you again. . ."

Now, kneeling in St. James, it seemed providential that less than ten minutes after my arrival, I would see Father Pervan. slipping into the aisle, I introduced myself to this thick, strong-faced Franciscan priest with the somber glint in his brown eyes. I told him that I was here to work with Father Svet on his new book and asked him if he would call him, to let him know I was here.

"Come with me," was all he said. I followed him to the rectory, past the apparition room, just inside the door leading to the living quarters where he motioned me to a chair while he used the phone. Saying a few words in Croatian he waited, then handed me the telephone.

"Father Svet?"

"Yes, who is this?"

"Wayne Weible — from the Center for Peace. How are you?"

There was silence; then, "Ah, Wayne, it is good to hear from you."

I told him that I was here for three weeks to work on my book. "Yes, that is wonderful! I will be there tonight, and we can talk after the Mass."

Telling him that would be fine, I hung up and thanked Father Pervan for his assistance. He shrugged, smiled, and walked me to the rectory door. On the way out, I paused a moment outside "the room" — that little space where millions of people from all over the world wanted to be when the Blessed Virgin Mary appeared to the young Croatian visionaries. In another hour, it would be the scene of much pleading, pushing, arguing and earnest prayer, as it was every evening. This, I imagined, was as close as I'd ever get to it.

It was near 4:30, which meant I had about four hours before Father Svet arrived. Aching with fatigue, but exhilarated at being here and having so quickly arranged a meeting with my Franciscan friend, I started walking through the village — with the odd feeling that I could actually inhale its sights, sounds, and mystique. As I looked around it struck me that Medjugorje, by all outward appearances was about the most unlikely place where an event like this would occur. So simple and rural, even now it was unrushed by the events engulfing it. I paused along a pathway to allow a woman with a small herd of goats to pass by. She smiled and nodded to me, speaking a few words of what I took to be a greeting. Her acceptance of me, a stranger in her land, was typical of the majority of the villagers who had gone on with their lives, outwardly unaffected by the constant presence of a increasing number of pilgrims.

Yet the influx of so many foreigners had indeed had a drastic impact on daily living in Medjugorje and the surrounding area. There was money now — a great deal of it by local standards, and all of the foreign currency was a good deal harder and more durable than the Yugoslavian dinar.

And there were more cafes now. And the narrow, roughly-paved (or not paved at all) roads and footpaths which tied the five communities of Medjugorje together were better suited for walking, herding animals, and as playgrounds for small children — than for the steady stream of cars and huge tour buses which dominated them.

For all this, the people seemed to have a peace within themselves and a strong tolerance for the ever-increasing disruption. Some did struggle with it and resented the changes it had wrought; others welcomed it strictly for its commercial impact. But most went out of their way to be polite and helpful to the pilgrims, as this shepherd woman had. In a region noted for the incessant feuding among its inhabitants, this one change in the people of Medjugorje stood out like a beacon in the night, attesting to the authenticity of the apparitions.

As I strolled the streets, construction was underway everywhere. Ironically, the Government, which for the first five years viewed the apparitions with suspicion and hostility, was now working at a furious pace to capitalize on them. And capitalize was the right word: indifferent to the distinction between pilgrims and tourists, they only had eyes for the capital they brought with them. Yet despite the accommodations springing up, there were still surprisingly few full restaurants and almost no public bathroom facilities.

Meanwhile, the majority of the pilgrims continued to stay in the homes of the villagers, many of whom were adding rooms to their stark, cinder-block homes. It was a slow, tedious process. They had to wait until they were financially able to buy the construction materials — when they were available — then work late into the evenings and weekends to build the additions. Everyone helped, from the smallest child to the live-in grandparents.

I stopped at a small snack shop for a cup of the thick, strong coffee that was a trademark of the area, a tradition left by the long dominance of the Moslems. There may not have been enough bathrooms, but these little eateries and the ever-present souvenir stands seemed to be everywhere, selling everything from plastic Madonnas to pizzas and encroaching more and more on the church's grounds. Most of them were operated by Communist party members or Moslem Gypsies, both anxious to do business with the throngs of Christian pilgrims. The local priests, frustrated in their attempts to keep commercialism from overpowering the intent of the apparitions, discouraged people from buying from the stands. But it was the Government that had allowed them to settle on the church property and around it.

Commercialism was only one aspect of the ongoing skirmish between the Franciscan priests and government officials since the apparitions began. For most of the first five years, they harassed and badgered priests, visionaries, villagers and pilgrims alike. Early pilgrims were often stopped on the road just outside Medjugorje (where I had passed the police car) for a random luggage search. If it was discovered that religious materials were being "smuggled" into the area, the ensuing interrogation could take hours. Helicopters from Mostar often over-flew the area to keep an eye on things, swinging low over the church during services.

In the wake of the economic boom, the Government had been forced to moderate its hard-line stance somewhat, but it was still uncomfortable with the basic situation — as any Communist regime whose official religion was atheism would be. And adding a fresh twist to the irony of the "Red Madonna" as they referred to her: Medjugorje had now become the #1 tourist attraction in Yugoslavia.

I arrived back at the church in time for the evening Mass. The weather was so beautiful that instead of trying to go in, I settled on the edge of the front steps of the church where many of the Croatian families now congregated, since the church was overcrowded. It was wonderful to hear once again the singing and the tolling bells. The deep peace of the service and the warm summer breezes seemed to wash away all fatigue. Truly this was the edge of heaven.

During the homily, I noticed Father Pervan strolling among the throngs of people outside of the church. I smiled, recalling what I had read about him. He had arrived at St. James soon after the apparitions had begun and was highly skeptical of their authenticity. He demanded an immediate and thorough interrogation of these children, even to the point of suggesting exorcism. Shortly after Father Jozo was arrested, a surprised Tomislav Pervan found himself assigned as the new pastor of St. James, and thus in charge of the daily apparitions.

It was not long before their consistency and sincerity thoroughly convinced him of their innocence and that something extraordinary was occurring. Without his belief, and strong, steady leadership, it was doubtful that Medjugorje would have evolved into the powerful spiritual mecca it had become.

In a video I had seen during my early research, Father Pervan had described the changes in the village: "There is a line that can be drawn at the date of June 24, 1981. There was a Medjugorje before that, and a Medjugorje after that; before, it was just another village in the area; after Our Lady started appearing, it began to change, and the people began to truly live the Gospel life. They might be compared to the disciples of Jesus and the Resurrection; before the Resurrection, they were ordinary disciples; after the Resurrection, they were enlightened disciples."

It seemed that all of the Franciscan priests at St. James and many priests from surrounding villages were enlightened by the Blessed Virgin's appearances. Called by God to be stewards of what He was doing at Medjugorje, as a group they themselves had grown in maturity and spirituality. And as the fame of the apparitions spread, they responded with remarkable wisdom and competence to the increased demands being placed upon them. This was typified by Father Pervan's stroll through the crowds, denying himself the enjoyment of administering the Eucharist inside, so that he could be out here with this portion of the flock.

After Mass, I waited around the rectory for Father Svet, anxious to get started — and to get to bed, for my body was now numb from lack of sleep. An hour passed and still no Svet. Finally, Father Pervan came down the rectory steps, and I asked him if he had heard from or seen Father Svet, thinking maybe I had missed him. "He will come soon," he answered, hardly stopping as he made his way toward the church.

At a little past 10 o'clock, a small white VW pulled into the rectory parking lot. Father Svet got out, embraced me, and ushered me to a nearby pile of boards as we exchanged greetings.

"I want you to tell me everything about your family, your involvement in the apparitions, and yourself," he said in that soft voice that immediately put one at ease in his presence. "We have plenty of time now."

The thought that I had been awake and moving for more than 38 hours straight flashed through my mind, but it was quickly forgotten as we sat down on the lumber, and I began to recount my story, my life — everything. Afterwards, he told me about himself, and before long, it was midnight. Then came the killer:

"Wayne, my friend, how very much I appreciate your coming such a long distance to help me with my manuscript. But, I must tell you, I will not be able to return to Medjugorje to work with you until after the anniversary (of the apparitions). I hope you will be able to work alone now and also enjoy the peace of Medjugorje until I return. . . ."

I was stunned. "Of course, Father," I heard myself saying, "I'm grateful for the opportunity to work with you and

for just being here again." But, I was thinking, what am
I going to do for the next nine days?

Planning to meet the following noon to discuss the work
I had already done on the manuscript, we said goodnight.
I drove the three miles back to Citluk in a fog, through
which one thought kept coming to me: now that I was
here, this deeply spiritual but somewhat unorganized priest
really didn't know what to do with me . . . .

1

1. Father Slavko Barbaric prays in the choir loft of St. James, shortly before the apparition of the Blessed Virgin Mary.

2. Visionary Ivan Dragicevic kneels in the choir loft during the apparition.

2

St. James Church, Medjugorje.

1. *Visionary Vicka Ivankovic, in the living room of her home.*

2. *Vicka chats with author Wayne Weible on her terrace.*

3. *Rita Klaus, completely healed of Multiple Sclerosis, stands on the front steps of the Ephrata Retreat House.*

1. Father Jozo Zovko, pastor of St. James Church, prays in front of his church. Soon after this photograph was taken, he was imprisoned for refusing to curtail the visionaries.

2. Father Svetozar Kraljevic with Terri Weible outside of St. James.

3. Visionary Ivanka Ivankovic on the day of her wedding to her husband Reijko. Flanking them are Visionaries Mirjana Dragicevic (left) and Vicka.

1. Visionary Marija Pavlovic, receiving an apparition in Birmingham during her trip to America. (On the left is Kathleen, Marija's American companion and interpreter.)

2. Ivan and Visionary Jacov Colo (right center) during an early apparition in the rectory.

1. The exact spot on Podbrdo where the apparition first appeared is marked by the plain wooden cross on the right, composed of tree branches.

2. Milka Pavlovic, Marija's younger sister.

1

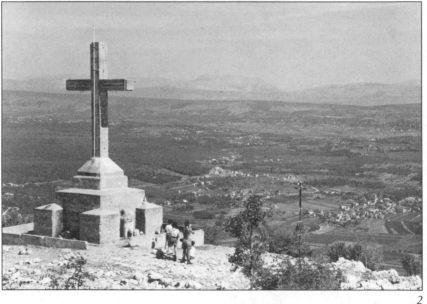

2

1. Innerlocutionary Jelena Vasilj (right) with Tanya (center) and Jelena's little sister, Ivana.

2. The cross on Mt. Krizevac, overlooking the village of Medjugorje.

1. Father Svet speaks to a group of pilgrims in the cedar grove cemetery behind St. James.

2. Crowds throng in the courtyard outside the rectory at the time of the apparition.

*"Take seriously the messages I am giving
you — I have remained this long to
help you put them into
practice. . . ."*

17

A Time of Learning

I woke up the next morning about nine, greeted by
dazzling sunlight, warm temperatures, and gentle breezes.
It was absolutely beautiful — almost enough to counter-
act the mood I was in. It was good to be back; I loved
the simple living here and open commitment to God. And
it was a relief to be able to shelve, at least temporarily,
all the worries of the surrounding world. Yet I felt guilty
— I had returned under the assumption I would be working
with Father Svet, only to discover there was nothing to
do for the next nine days. I sighed and decided I would
keep busy editing the manuscript until he returned.

The feeling of having "nothing to do" quickly dissipated,
as the day began to unfold. I located the man who had
offered me a room if I returned to Medjugorje. His name
was Primo, and he ran a small cleaner and laundry business
in Citluk. Since his tourist project was not yet completed,
he invited me to stay in his home as his guest. When
I shook my head, insisting on paying, ·he reluctantly
accepted, on the condition that I give it to his son whose
room I would be using.

That done, it was time to get to the rectory for my meeting
with Father Svet. He had said noon, but having learned
that time was "flexible" with this enigmatic priest, I arrived

about 45 minutes early. Finding a small bench to the right of the steps leading into the rectory, I made myself comfortable and for the next half hour buried myself in the editing of Svet's manuscript. Suddenly my train of thought was broken as I heard a young woman's voice with an English accent ask, "What are you writing?"

I looked up to see a blond teen-age girl perched at the other end of the bench, staring at me. "I'm working on a book about Medjugorje. Are you from England?"

"Of course not!" she laughed. "Haven't you ever talked with anyone from Australia? But you're from America, aren't you?"

"You're right," I smiled sheepishly, "I guess we Americans do sort of stick out."

"My name's Tanya; what's yours?"

"Wayne."

She laughed again. "I'm going to call you John Wayne, after the movie star!"

Charmed by this Australian teen-ager, I listened beguiled to a non-stop stream of conversation, intermingled with questions about my work and why I was here. She hardly paused long enough for me to give a complete answer before popping another question or revealing some new, startlingly personal detail of her life.

She was sixteen, and had been in Medjugorje for almost two months under the care of Father Slavko Barbaric, one of the spiritual advisors for the visionaries. In typical teen-age fashion, Tanya told about how she had suffered from acute drug addiction since she was 13, which had resulted in seven trips to the hospital for long periods of recovery. That was why she was here. Rather than return to the hospital after her last bout with drugs, she had begged her mother to let her come to Medjugorje, where Father Slavko, who had a degree in psychology and had set up a counseling program for troubled youths, had agreed to care for her.

Once she had begun, Tanya seemed compelled to pour out her entire life's history, talking as rapidly as possible and pausing only occasionally to gauge the shock value of intimate family detail. I was taken back, but I tried not to let it show. Her parents were separated. Her mother — who was Croatian, as it happened — lived on a small island off the Adriatic coast near Split, and operated a tourist resort, while her father, whom she had not seen in over a year, lived and worked in Australia.

Having spent a great deal of time in Yugoslavia, Tanya spoke fluent Croatian. She had been in the apparition room during the apparitions many times, knew the visionaries, and felt that she was being healed of her drug addiction and related emotional problems by staying in Medjugorje for such a long time.

Her rapid-fire delivery was briefly interrupted when another young woman joined us. "Oh, this is my friend, Kathleen; she's also an American," Tanya explained. "We room together, and she looks after me and helps Father Slavko. And this," she turned to Kathleen, "is my new American friend, John Wayne. He's a writer!"

There was hesitancy on Kathleen's part; she seemed to be sizing me up before saying too much. But after a few minutes, she relaxed and began to relate a little of her background and how she had come to Medjugorje. I noticed that she was barefoot but before I could ask why, Tanya blurted out that Kathleen was on a nine-day fast of bread and water, and was going barefoot as a special penance. That was going a bit far, I thought to myself. On my previous trip I had met several people whom I loosely classified as eccentric, fanatical, or just plain crazy. My initial reaction was to put Kathleen somewhere in that group. As if to confirm it, she acted a little spacey and had long straight hair that reached down to the small of her back. She was older than Tanya — late twenties or early thirties, I guessed — and she was originally from Miami, Florida. More recently she had moved to Switzerland, and at present, at Father Slavko's request, she was serving as a big sister to Tanya. The responsibility of this role, plus her easily discernible innate goodness, soon caused me to revise my initial estimate.

Our visit abruptly ended as Father Svet appeared at the top of the stairs. "Ah, Wayne, good morning! I am ready now, and we have much to do, so come in and let us begin." He greeted my companions, too, and from the exchange it was evident he knew them. I looked at my watch; it was 12:40. I didn't mind; I had thoroughly enjoyed the time with Tanya and Kathleen. We promised to get together later that afternoon in the small grove in front of the church.

Father Svet led the way into a small office across the hall from the apparition room. "This will be a good place to work undisturbed," he said, closing the door quickly.

I had to ask him: "Father Svet, do you know those two?"

"Oh, yes. Kathleen helps us here in whatever way she can, and Tanya — has many problems. Be careful in your friendship with her."

"What do you mean?"

He chose his words carefully. "Tanya needs a great amount of help. She has many personal problems. At times, she is very pleasant and nice to be around, but at other times, she is — difficult. Just be careful that you do not become too involved. She is receiving much help from Father Slavko. But," he smiled, "do not worry about it. Now, let us see what you have done."

For the next three hours we went over the work I had done on the manuscript. He would question me as to why I had changed or added certain parts. Hesitant to say much at first, as I was still in awe of working with this holy man, I finally relaxed and forgot about everything but the work before us.

When we had finished going over what I had completed up to that point, he stood up, clapped his hands on my shoulders, and beamed at me. "This is good!" he exclaimed softly. "We definitely can work together — just as I knew we could."

I was too exhilarated to reply.

We worked it out that I would spend the next nine days in Medjugorje, continuing my editing, after which he would then take me to Konjic, his parish which was about two and a half hours to the north, near Sarajevo. I would stay in the rectory there for a week, never venturing outside during the day, so the Milicia would not know I was there. We would spend that time going through the manuscript line by line. Meanwhile, he would not see me again until the 25th, the fifth anniversary of the apparitions. "We will leave late at night the following day, so as not to be noticed," he added.

As we said our good-byes, I was a little uneasy at the clandestine arrangements; becoming an international incident was the last thing I wanted. But the work came first. Father Svet waved to me and drove out of the rectory parking area in his little white car. As he did, I glanced around furtively, to see if anyone had been watching us. Already, I was beginning to feel like an international spy.

That afternoon, under the trees in front of the church, I found Tanya, Kathleen, and another girl. They were singing to Kathleen's accompaniment on the guitar. Spotting me, Tanya excitedly waved for me to join them, which I did. With Father Svet's warning echoing in my head, I wondered how this vivacious young girl who seemed so happy and at peace here, could possibly have such terrible problems.

Later, I learned that the third girl, who was German and was named Agnes, had also come to Medjugorje with many emotional problems, as well as being physically crippled and able to walk only with the aid of crutches. She, too, was under the care of Father Slavko who had allowed her to be present in the apparition room during an apparition. According to her story, she had been instantly cured of her physical handicap and had left her crutches in the corner of the apparition room, walking out unaided. After returning to Germany, she had gone to her doctor who confirmed that she had no symptoms left and pronounced her completely healthy.

I was seeing much more of Medjugorje now than I had on the first trip. Aside from the spiritual phenomena and miracles and the dramatic conversions there was much more taking place on many levels. And there was also struggle and disappointment — and failure. Not all who came were spiritually transformed. And of course, not everyone coming with physical ailments was healed. In fact, the little village was in many ways not all that different from my own home town of Myrtle Beach. There was good and there was bad here; it was, in a broad sense, a microcosm of the world, the difference being that it had been transformed by the miracle of the appearance of the Blessed Virgin Mary.

Many of the people coming to Medjugorje were like these girls I had just met. They had problems and had come looking for a miraculous solution to those problems. Agnes had found hers, but Tanya was still searching and hoping, as were thousands of others who had made the journey with that one thought in mind. I remembered the comment of Frank Fiamingo, the paraplegic who had been with us on the May trip. I had asked him what he expected to get out of his trip — did he expect to be healed? "I didn't come looking for a physical cure," he had replied. "I came looking for the same thing as you and the others: for my own personal reasons and to renourish my spirituality."

Tanya and Agnes went off to meet someone, but not before Tanya made me promise that we would talk some more the next day. As I started to leave also, Kathleen indicated she wanted to stay a moment longer. "Did Tanya tell you anything about her past?" she asked.

I related the morning's conversation to her, leaving nothing out. "Well," Kathleen went on, "her problem goes beyond the addiction to drugs. She has an alcohol problem as well — and much more. In fact, her first weeks here were confined to bed because she was so sick. Tanya is extremely insecure, which is why Father Slavko has asked me to stay with her and keep an eye on her. I just wanted you to know and to ask you to be very careful with her. Tanya can quickly form powerful attachments."

I assured her that I would deal with Tanya at arm's length and had plenty of work on Father Svet's book, as well as research on my own. I was impressed with Kathleen; far from being spacey, this transplanted American was a deeply caring individual. What had appeared to be a fanatical fasting and penance was a normal response for her — her way of saying yes to God. She was living the message that the Virgin Mary was bringing to Medjugorje, and her obedience was more complete than mine had been. So much for first impressions.

Keeping Tanya at arm's length, however, was easier said than done. The next morning at Mass, she slipped quietly in the pew beside me, asking if it was okay for her to sit with me. I said, of course it was. Later, Kathleen informed me it was the first time she had been to the English Mass in some time. She offered to tell Tanya that I had a great deal of work to do and that she needed to leave me in peace, but I declined. I pointed out that our time together was helping her, as even Kathleen had to admit.

Over the following days, between spurts of editing work on the manuscript, I spent hours talking to Tanya about her problems. Father Svet had been right: at times she was an angel, and at other times it was hard to believe the transformation in the opposite direction. She would do or say things to deliberately provoke me, and would become childishly jealous whenever I would spend time with other people.

This was especially true of the Center for Peace group which had arrived earlier in the week. Sister Margaret was again the spiritual leader, assisted by the ever-optimistic Rose Finnegan. Also, Maureen Thompson's parents John and Maryann, and her younger sister Sheila, were in the group. It was a week of reunion — and relief, for there were hardly any other Americans there, until the group arrived. I especially enjoyed the company of Maureen's parents and sister, leading me to spend a lot of time with them — time previously spent with Tanya.

One evening Sister Margaret, whom I had briefed on the situation, suggested I invite her to join the group's dinner at the Citluk Hotel after the evening Mass, to put her at ease with the Americans. I first checked it with Kathleen, who checked with Father Slavko. At their request I had met one morning with Fr. Slavko, so he would know who this American was who had befriended his young charge. Now, satisfied that my time with Tanya was a help, he gave permission for her to come with me — on the condition that she be home by 10 o'clock.

The dinner turned out to be a wonderful occasion for everyone in attendance. Tanya was as happy as I had seen her, and she literally charmed the whole group. In a sense we were like family to her, and I saw that family life was probably what this troubled girl needed the most.

Keeping my promise to Father Slavko, I took Tanya home on time and returned to Citluk to pick up Sister Margaret, whom I had offered to drive to her guest home just outside of Medjugorje. Heading back towards Citluk, two young girls dancing around in the road suddenly filled the headlights. Recognizing one of them as Tanya, I brought the car to a halt. When she saw me, she was as shocked as I was. "Tanya! What are you doing out here? You know Father Slavko's rule about being in by ten!"

Caught, and not wanting to appear weak in front of her peer, she replied angrily, "I don't care what his rules are! I'm old enough to do what I want!"

I attempted to convince her she was wrong, that in Medjugorje she was under his care, but she was beyond listening. She then informed me that I also could not tell her what to do.

"Come on, get in and I'll drive you home again," I said, trying to ignore this last remark which cut deeply.

"No! We're having fun, and I'm staying here!"

"Okay, do what you want!" I answered abruptly and drove off. How could the same sweet, well-behaved girl who had such a great time with the Center for Peace group a few hours earlier, now be so rebellious and rude — especially to me? There had been many good and sometimes angry conversations between us that had supposedly created a genuine father-daughter bonding. Now, I wasn't sure any of my time with her had been helpful.

That night held another surprise. I returned to Primo's house to find another guest: a photographer from Time magazine's European bureau who had been assigned to cover the fifth-year anniversary of the apparitions, which was tomorrow. Tanya's problems were forgotten for the moment; I was delighted that the apparitions might at last receive international news coverage, especially since more than 100,000 people were expected in the village. We stayed up talking for more than two hours, as I filled him in as thoroughly as I could, even offering to take him around. It was left that I would take him to Vicka's house first thing in the morning for a few special shots.

As we drove there the next morning, he said, "I wanted to tell you this last night, but I didn't want to tell you there at the house: the police are looking for you. They came to see Primo earlier in the day, but he didn't know when you'd be back."

"What?" I slammed on the brakes, almost sliding into the ditch. "Why? What do they want with me?" I was scared. Very scared.

"Take it easy!" my companion smiled. "They know you're a journalist and want to know why you didn't register as one."

"I couldn't. I didn't want them to know that I'm working with this priest — how do they know I'm a journalist?"

The photographer chuckled. "Well, you run around with a typewriter and ask a lot of people a lot of different questions. . . . " He stopped smiling. "Look, you can't fool around with these people. They can pick you up for questioning on any pretext, hold you for a few days and then kick you out of the country. And that's a good scenario!" He shook his head. "You've got to remember: you're not in America!"

Suddenly I realized how stupid I had been, being so obvious about what I was doing. The actions of Father Svet should have been warning enough. . . Now I understood the need for so many precautions, like leaving for Konjic in the dark of night, and of staying out of sight while there. But now it was too late.

"What should I do?" I asked weakly.

The photographer suggested that either I go to the police

voluntarily and try to register, taking my chances — or move out of Primo's house.

"I'll move." No way was I going to the Milicia. "There's a couple of places in Medjugorje where no one would be able to find me." I was pretty sure I could stay at the same home where Sister Margaret was staying, if it was only for a night or two.

What I really wanted to do was to turn the car around right there, get my stuff, and leave Citluk, but the photographer from Time, who knew about Marxist governments from having lived in Poland for a year, shook his head. "Too obvious," he said. "Better to move out at night."

When we reached Vicka's, he assured me that he would rather just wander around on his own for pictures, so I dropped him off and proceeded to the church for Mass. Time had helped me calm down some and begin a rational plan of action. Seeing Sister Margaret near the side of the church, I related what was happening.

"Well," she said matter-of-factly, "you only need a place for one night, since you'll be going to Konjic with Svet tomorrow. Certainly you can stay where I'm staying, and since it's located so far back from the church, no one's going to know you're there," she smiled. "Don't worry about it — just relax, pray, and enjoy the day."

Leave it to Sister Margaret to put the situation in its proper perspective! I decided to follow her advice. Meeting the Thompsons after the Mass, we spent the day climbing the hills and enjoying the festive atmosphere at Antonio's Cafe, a small gathering spot for many of the villagers. Earlier in the week we had discovered that the cafe was owned by the visionary Marija's brother and that Milka, her sister, worked there.

Milka, who had been present on that first day of Mary's apparition and had seen the Blessed Virgin that one time, was now 18 years old. She was a thin, effervescent teen-ager, mature beyond her years and noticeably a favorite among the locals. We immediately became friends. With her knowledge of English limited to a few words and phrases, we still managed to communicate quite well. At times when I had visited her with Tanya, the latter would translate for me. Blessed with an ability to learn quickly, Milka also spoke fluent Italian which she had picked up from the many Italian pilgrims filling the village in the early years.

I was fascinated by Milka's acceptance of having seen the Blessed Virgin only once, while her sister had become one of the six visionaries. When I asked about this in an interview later in the week, she shrugged and replied, "It is better to have seen her once, than not at all."

Did she ever wish that she might have become a visionary like her sister?

"Oh, no!" she laughed. "Then I would have to spend all my time talking to reporters like you!"

I saw something special in Milka. She had accepted her fate, yet there was a discernable sense of wanting to be one of the chosen ones who saw Mary daily; it was well hidden, but it was there. By the time I left, Milka had become one of my favorite people in Medjugorje.

The evening of the fifth anniversary was beautiful, as literally thousands packed the church and the areas surrounding it. Positioned on the lawn in the back of the church, the Thompsons and I were savoring the beauty of the late sky and the cooling breezes while praying the rosary. I had not seen Tanya all day, when suddenly she appeared, contrite and apologizing for her actions of the night before. "Please come with me," she begged, "I can't pray. I need to talk to you."

I excused myself and found a quiet spot in a grove of trees further behind the church where we could talk.

Tanya began crying. She and her friend had met two boys from the village and had stayed out late — very late. Now she was ashamed and didn't know what to do about Father Slavko. "He'll find out, I just know it! And then he will send me home — what am I going to do?"

"You're going to tell him yourself, Tanya, and then accept whatever action he takes."

"No!" As she vigorously shook her head and got up to leave, I patiently pointed out to her all the people who had tried to help her, and all that had been done for her. Now she had a choice: to accept the goodness that was offered to her through Father Slavko's help and living in Medjugorje — or to go on ruining her life. I was surprised how calm I was. It was a blunt, straight, father-lecturing-daughter talk. And it worked. Tanya quietly hugged me and promised that right after the Mass, she would tell Father Slavko and accept whatever fate would befall her.

We returned to the Thompsons and celebrated the Mass. Later, Tanya came running up to us on the lawn, where we had gathered to talk about the day. I knew by her expression that it had gone well with Father Slavko. In a rush of words she described what had happened: "Oh, he was furious with me, but said it was good that I had confessed it to him — I told him you told me to do it — and guess what? He says he'll give you the interview you asked for, if you'll come by in the morning. And he'll let me translate! Oh, I feel so happy!"

Pleased that everything had turned out well for her, I arranged to meet in front of the rectory at nine in the morning. It really had been a wonderful day — and this nine-day period of having "nothing to do" had been wonderfully filled. It had been quite a time of learning, and as I thought about it, I realized that it had been meant to be just that.

But there was still one problem: the *Milicia*. I had almost forgotten about them until the drive back to Primo's house in Citluk. When I arrived, I intended to talk to Primo about it, and if he thought I should go to them and like Tanya, accept whatever befell me, that was what I would do. The photographer from Time had left earlier in the evening to catch a flight out of Mostar, so we were alone. But Primo quickly excused himself for the night, citing the early-morning hour he had to be in the shop. I went to my room, and after a long period trying to decide whether to leave right then or wait until morning, I prayed: "Please, Lord, give me some direction. . . ."

18

In The Apparition Room

Up by five the next morning, I packed my gear and left quietly without waking anyone. This seemed to be the best solution to the problem of the Milicia: just leave and get lost in the crowds at Medjugorje. Later in the day I would return unannounced, pay Primo for the room, and tell him I was going home.

Even at this hour Citluk was a busy little town, much to my surprise — and chagrin, for I had to drive past Milicia headquarters. I sighed with relief as I went by apparently unnoticed, and proceeded to a little cafe outside of Medjugorje for breakfast.

Enjoying a good meal of fried eggs, sausage, and delicious fresh-baked bread, I thought again of how quickly the previous nine days had passed. Here it was already June 26th — my birthday! In the rush and excitement I had completely forgotten it. Now, on this special day, I would interview Father Slavko, savor the delight of an unscheduled day in Medjugorje, and then at midnight leave with Father Svet for Konjic. What a birthday!

At nine o'clock I was in front of the rectory, expecting Tanya momentarily, when suddenly the rectory door opened and Father Svet appeared. "Wayne, my friend, please, come with me." Speaking quietly and gravely, he

179

took me by the arm and led me to a deserted spot behind the church. "We will be alone here."

I had never seen him so serious, and as if reading my thoughts, he added, "Do not be alarmed, but our plans have changed. For reasons I cannot go into, it is not advisable for you to come to Konjic with me at this time." He paused and placing a hand on my shoulder reassuringly, continued: "We must make new arrangements. I will bring the updated manuscript to you tomorrow, and Sister Margaret will take it to the United States, where you will be given a copy. We will work separately, and the Center for Peace will be our courier."

"But Father, I'm not afraid —"

He cut me off with a firm grip on my arm. "Please believe me: it is better this way. I will see you tomorrow, and we will talk some more. Now I must leave."

Well, I thought, fighting off disappointment as we walked to his car, this changes things. As he drove off, I realized I would need a place to stay, after all; hopefully there would be room at the house where Sister Margaret was staying. One good thing: I was free to return home now — and I longed to. I would stay the weekend and head for Dubrovnik early Monday morning, in time to catch the 7:10 a.m. plane home.

As I stood in the parking area next to the rectory, suddenly I was grabbed from behind and hugged. "Happy birthday, John Wayne! Happy birthday!" Tanya danced around me, overjoyed at the prospect of translating for me and Father Slavko. "I've got a very special present for you," she exclaimed, "but you'll have to wait until after the interview."

"Well, I've a got a very special present for you, too, even though it's my birthday," I teased. Tanya had been depressed about my leaving for Konjic that evening. "There's been a change of plans: I'm not going to Konjic,

which means I'll be here with you for three more days."
With that, she gave me another hug and squealed for
joy. She had been on near-perfect behavior since the late-
night incident, and I was genuinely touched by her
exuberance.

But now it was time for the interview. As we entered
Father Slavko's office, it dawned on me that this was "the
room." This is where the apparitions with the Blessed
Virgin Mary took place each evening. Previously, they had
been occurring in the church, specifically in the small
sacristy off to the right side of the altar, until the Bishop
of Mostar had ordered them out of the church. Bishop
Pavao Zanic, a strong believer in the first few months
of the apparitions, was now their number one opponent.
Not a Franciscan himself, he had declared them a hoax,
perpetuated and encouraged by the local Franciscan priests
stationed at St. James Church. For the past two and a half
years the apparitions had taken place in this small, cramped
bedroom-office.

Thrilled to be in this special place, I was even happier
to have an opportunity to interview the intense, thin-faced
theologian/psychologist with gray hair and black-rimmed
glasses. Ironically, he had originally been sent to
Medjugorje by Bishop Zanic, to disprove the apparitions
and reveal them as the fraud that the bishop was now
convinced they were. If anyone could do this, the bishop
thought, it would be Slavko Barbaric. Surely this learned
scholar, conversant in four languages and one of
Yugoslavia's foremost teachers of theology, would soon
put an end to all of this nonsense.

I began by asking Father Slavko about his first days
with the young visionaries. No sooner had he met and
questioned them, than he became convinced that they
were without guile. And if that were so, then the apparitions
were indeed occurring, just as they described. Moreover,

he felt a special burden for the spiritual life of these young people, now with so many pressures on them; in fact, he felt a burden for all the young people of the parish. For inspired by their life-long friends to whom the apparition was appearing and whose lives they could see changing, a number of the young people of Medjugorje were now re-examining their own relationship with God and His church. They were forming prayer groups — and turning to Father Slavko for spiritual direction.

Ignoring the wrath of the Bishop, he began serving the community fervently, working long hours and assisting in every way he could. The counseling group for troubled youths was one result of his dedication. What was his most difficult responsibility? Having to be in charge of the apparition room each evening. Having to be the one to decide who would or would not go into the room.

When asked why these children, he quoted the answer that Mary had given the visionaries, when they had asked her the same question: "I do not always choose the best people."

"That may sound harsh," he added, "but the fact that Our Lady purposely chooses ordinary people gives unquestionable credibility to such phenomena." I knew what he meant: it was difficult to imagine anyone suspecting such simple children of perpetuating — or being directed in — a hoax of such magnitude for five years. Surely in all that time the relentless probing of teams of scientific, medical, and canonical investigators would have uncovered it. Father Slavko added that this was the reason for his giving journalists, clergy, and scientific teams first consideration in deciding who should be present during the apparitions.

Another important point he covered: by appearing to young, uneducated children, the Madonna left room for pure, blind faith. When asked what she expected of the people (in Medjugorje and later throughout the world), she replied, "Let them believe as if they too, see."

What of the faith of the visionaries prior to the apparition? Like many children their age throughout the world, they were aware of the importance of faith, but it had to compete with all the preoccupations and concerns of teenage life. They attended church most Sundays, but it was no big deal if they missed Mass. Prayers like the rosary were said only on special feast days.

And now? Now they were consumed with their roles as recipients of Mary's visits and daily training in spirituality. Was it difficult for them to keep the faith? The constant yearning of pilgrims to see, touch, and talk to them left hardly any time for privacy. Yet each was now filled with a quiet inner peace and acceptance of their roles. And over the past five years, a spiritual maturity had been worked into them that made them far from ordinary any longer.

I nodded; I had been impressed with the poise and grace with which they responded to the endless demands put upon them. And I recalled something Father Pervan had said about them: "Prior to the appearance of Our Lady, they were ordinary children, no different than others in the village. Now, they have been picked up and placed on a new pathway, a new way of life." That new pathway was best summed up, said Father Slavko, in Marija's response to a reporter who asked her if seeing the Blessed Virgin Mary each evening was the highlight of her day: "The highlight of my day is receiving Jesus through the Holy Eucharist in the Mass."

Listening to Father Slavko was a treat. I was learning far more about the visionaries now than I had in all of the books I had read. Which was hardly surprising, considering his credentials and the fact that he was their spiritual director. We went on talking for nearly an hour.

Tanya was superb as a translator, working like a robot, eyes straight ahead and speaking clearly and deliberately each word of translation. Father Slavko was also pleased with her work and let her know it.

Finally, even though I was reluctant to do so, I sensed it was time to bring the interview to an end. Thanking Father Slavko for his time, I turned to go out the door. But Tanya, excitedly motioning for me to wait, whispered something to the priest. "Oh, yes, I almost forgot," he said smiling — and speaking perfect English. "Come to the rectory this evening at five o'clock, if you wish to be here for the appearance of the Blessed Mother. It will be a necessary part of your writing about the apparitions."

I was numb. As a journalist working on a book, I knew I met his qualifications, but it wasn't that. Tanya had obviously told him it was my birthday, and this was her special present for me. It was, without doubt, the most wonderful birthday present I had ever received.

I stood there for a moment, too awed to do much more than utter a quiet thank you over and over, as tears welled in my eyes. I walked outside in a daze, as Tanya jumped up and down in delight at having surprised me. I looked up at the sky and just kept murmuring, "Lord Jesus, thank you."

That afternoon, an hour and a half before the appointed time, I was standing at the foot of the steps leading up to the rectory door, though it would be another half-hour before the crowd began to gather. By 4:30, it was swelling, as people pressed in from all sides, straining to get as close to the base of the stairway as possible. Many were praying fervently, hoping to catch the eye of Father Slavko.

For occasionally, if there was room, he would select a pilgrim or two at random.

Although I had received a personal invitation, negative thoughts kept racing through my head: what if he forgot? Maybe in the crush of the crowd he wouldn't see me. That was why I had taken no chances, positioning myself next to the stairs before anyone else arrived. In fact, I had been hanging around the area for more than two hours.

Standing next to me now was an Italian woman who suddenly began wailing, pleading, and wringing her hands, while the crowd surged forward. I looked up; Father Slavko had appeared in the doorway. He quickly motioned for me and several priests to come up and hurry through the door. We fought our way up the stairs and finally inside.

The Italian woman, never ceasing her pleas, plowed in right behind me, until stopped by Father Slavko, who planted himself firmly in front of her and began a rapid, heated discussion in Italian with her. After much arm-waving and gesticulating by both of them, he began to gently usher her out of the doorway. But the woman would not be denied; sobbing hysterically now and screaming, she clamped her arm around the rectory door so that it could not be shut. I was stunned. This poor woman seemed to have such a great need to be inside. Maybe it was greater than mine. Should I give her my place? It took several people to aid the beleaguered priest in prying the woman's arm loose from the door. Finally, it was shut and locked.

It took a moment for me to realize that I was in the hallway and would soon be witnessing the apparition. But I couldn't get the picture out of my mind of that woman's arm stuck in the door. Father Slavko brought me back to reality as he quietly explained, "Every evening it is the same. Everyone thinks they must get into the room and that their need is greater than anyone else's." He turned his hands up resignedly and shook his head. "I cannot let everyone in; it is an impossible situation!" It was not hard to understand why, of all his responsibilities, he considered this the most difficult.

He opened the door to his office, and we entered. I quickly positioned myself at the far right front of the room to have a good photo angle for a close side shot of the visionaries' faces. Next to me was a video crew of three from some television station. In the next 20 minutes the heat became stifling as the room filled to capacity with priests, nuns, and laity. No one seemed to mind.

I knelt, trying to ignore the sweat dripping from my forehead and joined in the murmur of prayer as one of the priests started the rosary. Outside the window, a muffled rumble could be heard, as they, too, started to pray. Looking around the room, I was struck by the simplicity of this small space that so many desired to occupy. A lone undershirt hung on a hook on the back of the door. A couch positioned against one wall was covered with religious items sent into the room by the pilgrims outside, to be personally blessed by the Virgin Mary. Over the couch was a set of bookshelves with a crucifix just above the top shelf, marking the spot where the Madonna was reported to appear to the visionaries.

I looked around at the faces of the others in the room and saw that all of them, even the priests and nuns, were aware that they were about to participate in an experience of a lifetime. In a few moments we would be visited by a messenger from heaven, the Blessed Virgin Mary. The visionaries had described her as a slender young woman of about 20, wearing a silver-grey gown and a white veil. Her complexion was fair, her hair jet black, and she had a voice, they said, more beautiful than any music they had ever heard.

Suddenly, Marija Pavlović and Jacov Colo, the only two visionaries who would be there this evening, entered the room. We immediately stopped praying as Marija knelt in the doorway, and Jacov, tall and thin and with the typical self-consciousness of a fifteen-year-old, went over to the corner and hunched down, with his hands on his knees. Kneeling somewhat between them, Father Slavko asked Marija to begin the rosary. Quietly she began. I could not take my eyes off her — and was startled when suddenly she looked at me and smiled. I had seen this young woman, now 21, numerous times on videos. She had always appeared to be shy and somewhat frightened by the whole thing. Now, she had a radiant inner beauty about her.

When she finished the first decade of the rosary, Father Slavko nodded to Jacov to commence the second. He pronounced the words clearly and slowly, and I was surprised at how well he did it — until I remembered that he had been taught by the Madonna since the age of ten.

In a few moments the two visionaries got up and stood together in front of the couch and began praying. All at once, they stopped and fell to their knees. My heart leaped as I found myself kneeling next to Marija, less than a foot away! And then it struck me that the Blessed Virgin Mary was present. . . .

Marija wore a look of deep reverence. Her mouth was moving, but no words were coming out, at least not that I could hear. Jacov's lips were also moving. I looked where they were looking. I could see nothing but the cross on the wall, yet a warm, peaceful feeling came over me. I forgot all about taking pictures and could do nothing but thank God for this grace of being here.

My reverence was interrupted slightly when two of the men from the television crew got up and came over to

Jacov, one on each side, picking him up by his elbows; his body seemed frozen in the position of kneeling as they hoisted him in the air, and the camera rolled. His eyes also never left the spot where he was staring when the apparition began, and after about 10 seconds, they lowered him back to his original spot. He went right on, oblivious to what was happening.

Much too soon for me, Marija and Jacov were crossing themselves and getting up. The apparition was over; the Madonna was gone. Marija slipped out and went into the back of the rectory to write down the message that had been given to her. I was filled with sadness, wanting it to go on forever, but I was also filled with gratitude for having been present. I didn't want to leave the room — and saw that the others felt the same way.

But it was time to go, time to re-enter the world. As I stepped out the front door, I was startled by the sea of upturned faces. The moment Marija and Jacov had entered the room, I had forgotten the crowd outside. Now, they were looking at me and the others, searching our faces for some clue of what we had just witnessed. As much as I wanted to share it with them — with everyone — I wished I could just be alone somewhere, to assimilate it all.

There was no way I would ever be able to thank my young Australian friend enough for this special birthday gift — or Father Slavko for agreeing to let me be present for the apparition. But somehow, deep inside, I knew the one to especially thank was the Blessed Virgin Mary. . . .

*"I love you all. . . even when you
are far away from me
and my Son. . . ."*

19

Moments of Doubt

There was no chance to escape the sea of people at
the foot of the stairs. They were surging forward now,
to be as near as possible to Marija and Jacov, and maybe
even touch them, as they came out to go to Mass. As I
worked my way through them, all I wanted was to get
to a quiet place somewhere — anywhere.

But I got sidetracked; the moment I was free of the
crowd, the Thompsons, Tanya, and several other people
whom I had met, descended on me. What was it like?
What did she say? Did you see anything?

The last thing I wanted to do at this time was talk to
anyone, even my friends. But how could I deny them?
"It was — I felt — it was the most wonderful feeling of
peace and complete love I have ever known," I stammered.
Tanya just glowed and hugged me. Finally, I said, "Look,
I'm sorry; I've just got to be alone for a few minutes —
I hope you understand." They assured me they did.

I quickly retreated to the grove of trees well behind
the church and found a patch of grass that gave a full
view of the cross on Mt. Krizevac. It was perfect. Settling
down, I stared at the cross. Just what *had* it felt like to
be present when the Blessed Virgin appeared to Marija
and Jacov? For one thing, it had been impossible to take

189

pictures, or to mentally record details in an objective way — both of which I had hoped to do for my book. Instead I had experienced a personal feeling of great love and a tremendous sense of peace. Physically I felt a warmth come over me, but that was it — no spectacular flashes of light or sounds. In a sense, it was another message, as powerful as the first I had received from the Blessed Virgin. But this time, there were no words; just the same inner sense that God had singled me out for a very special grace. I wondered if the others in the room had had similar feelings.

The most intriguing thing about the whole experience was a sudden, unexplained discernment that my presence there, in that room, was really no different than if I had been in the crowd outside of the rectory; or, simply there in Medjugorje. The special blessing or grace it gave was also given to all present, no matter where they were. I smiled as I thought about it; once again, a lesson in the simplicity of faith.

Hurrying back to the church, I arrived in time for the last of the Mass and the prayers that followed. Sister Margaret spotted me and assured me that everything was set for my staying in the home where she was billeted — but only for one night. For the remainder of my visit I would have to stay somewhere else.

The next morning I dressed quickly and skipping breakfast, went over to the church, as the Center for Peace group would be leaving for Dubrovnik after early Mass. I wanted to be there when Father Svet arrived from Konjic to deliver his manuscript to Sister Margaret, so that I could determine what our working arrangements would be for the remainder of my stay. I was still hoping that there might be an outside chance we could go to Konjic as originally planned.

The Mass ended a little after 8:00. Among the first-timers coming out into the sunlight I noted the same wrenching reluctance to leave that I had experienced a month before. But I was not a part of that, not this time, not yet. I looked at my watch; where was Father Svet? Peering over the heads of the others I could see no little white VW behind the rectory. Oh, well, by now I had gotten used to the way he regarded time; surely he would be along at any moment.

At 8:30, the Center for Peace group began boarding their bus. Still no Father Svet. "Look," I said to Sister Margaret, "you go ahead. If he comes, I'll jump in my car and catch you at your hotel in Dubrovnik and get the manuscript to you. Then I'm going to come back here and hopefully spend a week working with him."

She smiled and said that would be fine, and they departed.

I waited. Half an hour passed, then an hour, then an hour and a half — and I began to panic. Remembering his last solemn words to me, that we would not be going to Konjic because it 'was not advisable at this time', only exacerbated the situation — *anything* might have happened!

By noon I was so desperate, I went into the church in search of Kathleen. She knew Father Slavko's assistant, Milona, and hopefully she could have her call Konjic to see what had happened. She was there, in the front of the church in a pew against the side wall. I slipped into the one in front of her and whispered, "Kathleen, you've got to help me! Please come and see if you can get Milona to put in a call to Konjic, and see what's happened to Father Svet. He was supposed to meet me here at 8:00 this morning, and —"

She looked at me steadily and smiled. "Calm down, Wayne. Why are you so upset? You know how he is — it'll be all right. Don't worry about it."

I stared at her. "What do you mean, 'Don't worry about it'? This is serious!" I added, forgetting to whisper. "I've got to get in touch with him!"

She did not lose her composure. "Wayne: you're in Medjugorje, and you're dealing with Father Svet. Trust God; it'll work out."

"Obviously you don't understand how important this is!" I snapped at her, getting up and leaving the church.

Not knowing what else to do, I spent the next three hours wandering around the church and rectory area, still hoping that Father Svet would show up. I did a lot of mindless walking that afternoon — and very little praying. What had happened? What was I doing here, anyway? Why was I in this dusty little town, four thousand miles from the family that I loved — and missed terribly? How could I be surrounded by thousands of people milling around — and still be lonely and homesick? All at once I was no longer a part of Medjugorje. I didn't know any of these people . . . .

I went over and sat on the low wall that bordered the terrace on the east side of the church. Now I knew, as never before, the meaning of Moses' haunting phrase: *a stranger in a strange land.*

I was shaken. What had happened to my faith? To the vision of my call? To the mission which had brought me here? Less than 24 hours ago, I had been in the apparition room in the presence of the Madonna. The peace from that experience had definitely left me. All I could see now was the dust, and the crowds of pushy pilgrims, the broken window in the church's side door, and the litter everywhere. *This is reality,* said a hard voice within me. *It's about time you faced it.*

It was true; I had been kidding myself for months, spinning a romantic fairy tale. How could I have been so foolish? I shook my head and decided to go back to my room and pack. My ticket had me leaving next Tuesday morning, but all I had to do was go to the Pan Am office in Dubrovnik and get them to change the date.

I felt a gentle hand on my shoulder. It was Father Pervan. "Wayne," he said smiling and holding out an envelope for me, "this is from Father Svet."

"From Father Svet? How? When?"

"He was not able to come today, so he sent this with someone else."

"Thank you — thank you very much!" I said, as he nodded and left.

I tore open the envelope. Inside was a beautiful black-beaded rosary and a note:

> *Wayne, my brother, I could not come for reasons that I cannot go into. I have made arrangements to get the manuscript to you in America, so do not worry about it. You are free now, because I cannot get back to Medjugorje until late next week.*
>
> *We will communicate. Meanwhile, stay and enjoy Medjugorje until you must leave, then go home and enjoy your wife and children.*
>
> *God go with you and your family —*
>
> *Svet*

Suddenly I felt like a ton of weight had been lifted off me. Right there in the middle of that noisy, bustling crowd, I became a part of the Medjugorje experience again. My heart filled with joy — and then I felt ashamed. How could I have ever lost it? How could I have doubted and let fear overshadow not just the purpose of this trip, but all of Medjugorje, my call, everything! How could it have been taken so easily from me?

At that moment I learned a lesson that would last me a lifetime: *never* trust feelings over the facts of faith. Feelings lied; they could deceive you into doubting — everything. Even your faith. Satan used feelings to separate you from God.

The antidote? Prayer. That was the one thing I should have been doing, as I wandered about in a daze. It was the one thing I hadn't done. Instead, in my mind I had played out one dire fantasy after another — rather than battling my way back into God's reality through prayer.

From now on, I would endeavor to "pray without ceasing," as we had been asked to by the Blessed Virgin in many of her messages. And that did not mean endless lip service; that meant to *live it,* constantly. By living in Him. Let your life be a prayer. You cannot be separated from Him, if you are never apart from Him. *He* is reality, not the world's doubts and fears and worries. I had chosen the wrong reality . . . .

That lesson alone was worth the trip, I thought getting to my feet and heading for the church. I looked up, and there was Kathleen, walking towards the rectory. I went up to her and hugged her and just shook my head and said, "Thank you."

"For what?" she asked, puzzled.

"Never mind," I smiled, "just thank you."

There was no way, I thought, going up the steps, I could have put it into words. Kathleen had that unshakeable inner peace I craved, the kind that you did not lose in times of crisis. What she had said to me in church — calm down, don't worry, everything will work out — I had dismissed as foolishness, more of her spacey ways. But it was absolutely true. And now I had the whole weekend to just sit back and enjoy Medjugorje . . . .

Saturday morning found me on the pathway to the top of Mt. Krizevac and its wonderful cross — which was easily my favorite place in Medjugorje and by far the best place to pray. Pausing for a few moments before each of the 14 Stations of the Cross, I thanked God again for the grace of being allowed to be part of all this. I also asked forgiveness for the doubt I had briefly succumbed to on the previous afternoon.

The top was deserted with the exception of a lone woman who appeared to be deep in meditation. After making myself comfortable on a flat rock, I was startled by a cheerful "Good morning!" I returned her greeting, and we began exchanging the usual information. Her name was Francesca Lovatelli, from Italy; she had been to Medjugorje many times. In telling her what had brought me there, I happened to mention my need of a place to stay for the next few nights. Then, by one of those "coincidences" that happen so frequently in this holy place, it turned out she was staying with a family that had a room available for the time I would need one. God had resolved my room problem.

That left only my ticket; it was for Tuesday, but I would go down to Dubrovnik early Monday just to make sure everything was okay. There was still the pall of the police looking for me hanging over my head, and I didn't want to take any chances. In the interval, I once again drank it all in — this time at a relaxed pace, savoring each moment, each meal, each meeting. Tanya spent the better part of Sunday with me and that evening, we bid a tearful, but warm good-bye. I assured her that I would be back later in the year to complete work for my book, and would write and let her know when.

Monday morning, I got up about 3:30, as seemed to be my custom in Medjugorje. I'd packed the car the night before and said my good-byes to Francesca and the family I was staying with, so the day was free. I was glad of that; the drive to Dubrovnik was spectacular, and I wanted to take my time.

But now the thought came to me that the daily flight to New York did not leave until 7:00 a.m. If I got down there fast enough and turned my car in, I just might be able to get on the plane home today, instead of tomorrow. With the faces of Terri and the kids much in my mind, I set out before dawn for Dubrovnik — a good deal more quickly than I had planned.

Before I reached the coast, it had begun to rain — softly, at first, drop by drop, then a steady sifting mist. I didn't care; nothing could dampen my spirits. I was going home!

I got to the airport a little after 6:00, parked the car, and hurried in to find the ticket counter. Except — there was no Pan Am counter. Nor would anyone else change my ticket; I was informed that I had to go back into Dubrovnik, to the Pan Am office near the old city. It was about 12 miles — no chance to get there and get back in time. With a sigh, I set off anyway; maybe with luck the plane would be late. . . . I did not notice that the rain had thickened, and the pavement had become quite slick.

It would have been better if I had never thought of going home a day early, because now it was all I could think of. And I could not bear the thought of having to wait another whole day before seeing them. I glanced up and saw a car stopped in the middle of the road directly in front of me.

I hit the brakes — too hard; the rear end broke loose, and suddenly I was fishtailing out of control, straight for that car. "Oh God, please, no!" I moaned. The only thing going through my mind was: I'm either going to die here in Yugoslavia, or I'm going to smash up this car, and the police are going to find out that the authorities in Citluk are looking for me.

Desperately I yanked the wheel, and managed to send the car into a full spin — once, twice, three times. . . .

"Lord Jesus, please, please!" I cried out. Finally, with a jolt the left rear tire hit the curb, and the car stopped.

The motor died, and there was silence. The only noise I heard was the rhythmic *click-swish* of the windshield wipers. Peering through them I could see no sign of the car that had been stopped in my path. Looking around, I realized that I had come to rest about 30 yards up from a bus stop where people were waiting — and staring at me. Did anyone come to see if I was all right? No, they just stared at me. I was back in the real world again.

I started to shake. I got out and walked around the car. Amazingly, there was not a scratch on it. But behind it on the street were my tire marks, all over the road like black spaghetti — and very close to a drop-off where there was no guard rail. "Thank you, God," I murmured, convinced that there must have been angels at each fender of the car.

Getting back in, I tried the ignition, and it started right up. Carefully I made my way to the old walled city and inquired for the location of the Pan Am office. It was too late for today, but I re-confirmed my seat for the following morning. Then I found a hotel and spent the rest of the day waiting for tomorrow to come.

As the big Pan Am jet lifted off the Dubrovnik runway Tuesday morning, I sighed with relief. Left behind were the worries over the police; I would soon be forgotten by them. And Tanya — I prayed that she would find the spiritual strength to recover fully and go on to lead a productive life. One thing for sure: this time leaving Medjugorje, I knew I would return.

20

Spreading the Message

*Your life will be devoted to the spreading of the message. .
. .* It had been eight months since I had first heard those
words from the Blessed Virgin Mary in my heart, yet they
had never been far from my mind. They came back to
me now as I winged homeward, trying to sort out the
details of this last trip. I had gone over, assuming I would
be helping Father Svet with his new book. Very little had
actually been accomplished on that project, and it was
clear to me now that that had not been God's purpose
in bringing me over. Instead, it had been a time of learning
and maturing; a great deal had been accomplished in terms
of preparation for what lay ahead.

There *would* have to be another trip, of course; deep
down, I had known that, even back in that barren stretch
when I was doubting everything and telling myself the
opposite. I would return, probably before the end of the
year. But in the meantime Terri was going to have to
come and experience first-hand what was taking over more
and more of my life — because it was to be *our* life, *our*
mission. What I was being asked to do would take full
cooperation from her, if it was to succeed. The time for
her to go would probably be sometime in August, before
the kids went back to school. . . .

Of course, she didn't quite see it that way, when I raised the subject soon after arriving home. "You've got to go," I told her at the end of recounting the details of my last trip. "There's too much for me to accomplish without your total support and complete understanding of what's happening in Medjugorje."

"Look, I've read the books," she replied, "and Father Svet's manuscript, too. I'm convinced. I believe it's authentic and coming from God. There's no need for me to go."

I shook my head. "There's just no way you can experience the full impact of the place through someone else." I let it go at that, sensing how resistant she was.

But neither did I abandon it. Not an evening went by that we didn't talk about Medjugorje, and a week later I brought it up again. "It *is* exciting to be so personally involved," she admitted.

"Then you'll go?"

"I didn't say that. Why don't you go for both of us in November?" To my surprise she had agreed without argument when I had told her of the need I felt to return to start work on my own book.

"Terri, I've already been twice; I want you to go. In August."

"I'm not going in August; that's crazy!"

"No it isn't," I persevered. "The kids will be out of school, and I can look after them. If necessary, we can always get someone to come in and help with them."

The line of her jaw became set, and she declared: "I have no desire to go, and that's final!"

I backed off. I knew what the problem was: the kids. She had never been away from them before. But Kennedy was six now and Rebecca two; they could survive without their mother for a week. I didn't press the point, not then.

I did press it a week later. Once again I emphasized

how important it was for her to know firsthand what I was being asked to promote. And once again she stated adamantly that she was not going to leave her children to run off to a Communist land to experience something she already believed to be authentic.

"Terri, the real reason," I said with deliberate calm, "is that those kids are more important to you than — God!" Well, that did it, I thought; now she'll never go. And she probably won't speak to me for a long time, either.

But I was wrong; even as she glared at me, I could tell she'd heard it. "We've got to learn to put God first," I said softly, "even before our kids."

She sighed. "All right, all right! I'll go. But *not* in August."

I was ecstatic. "When, then?"

"I don't know — we'll just leave it open."

The next day in the office, I called the Center for Peace in Boston and found out that their first trip after August was leaving on September 9. I asked them to hold a place for Terri and mailed a deposit immediately. When she came into the office, I told her what I'd done.

She just looked at me and then said, "Well, I guess that's that."

Spread the message . . . Even though I still wasn't quite sure how I was going to do that, one thing I had learned in the last eight months: if God called you to do something, then He would show you the way and help you. All you really had to do was listen carefully, and then do exactly what He told you to do.

Having written the series of columns and some preliminary work on my own book, I had done what I could (for now) with the written word. But what of the spoken word? At the end of the impromptu testimony at the Sertoma Club, a friend had invited me to speak to the Sunday School class of his Methodist church; other Sunday School invitations followed. Word was getting around that I had had a powerful personal experience over in Medjugorje — one which confirmed what God was doing over there. Moreover, the way I related it heightened the God-consciousness of everyone who heard it, regardless of their denomination. Nevertheless, it was still a shock to me when someone would come up afterwards, and unable to control their emotions, would tell me how the talk had touched them deeply. I was not conscious of saying anything special: I had merely related, as straight-forwardly as possible, my own inner feelings.

As I began to receive invitations from churches and civic groups farther and farther away, I remembered the prophetic words of Father Scotti: *This is only the beginning.* Surprisingly, most of the speaking invitations were coming from Protestants like myself. Medjugorje was not just a Catholic phenomenon; it was for everyone — a beautiful message of return to Jesus. And it was contagious: the fact that God was actually reaching down from heaven and interjecting Himself into the daily lives of 20th-century men and women was making people think twice. If it was happening there, in that little village in the middle of nowhere, then. . . why not here?

As the ninth of September drew near, I kept hoping that Terri would begin to get excited about going. In the meantime, I was very excited about something that would take place in Boston just before her return. The Center for Peace was bringing Father Tomislav Pervan, the pastor of St. James, over to America for a two-month speaking tour, and they were starting with a weekend retreat in Boston — for those friends of Medjugorje for whom spreading the message had become their mission. I was delighted to be invited.

Finally the day of Terri's departure arrived. I tried not to be too cheerful, since that was the farthest from how she felt, but neither could I entirely suppress it; I knew what was in store for her. I also knew that the Center for Peace people would look after her. Most of all, I knew she was in God's hands. He would make this pilgrimage uniquely meaningful for her.

From the airport I went to the office, where I found my secretary Denease in a state of frustration. The eighth and final column in the Medjugorje series had run just before I had left on my second trip, and requests for reprints had continued to build. "You know," Denease fumed, "it used to be they just wanted the earlier columns they'd missed. Now they want all eight to send to friends!"

I started to laugh — which was clearly not the right thing to do.

"Do you know it takes *nine pages* to copy the whole set?" she went on, with a look that stopped my laughter. "Do you know how long that takes? Do you know how long our copier is going to last? And half of them forget to include a self-addressed, stamped envelope!"

"Calm down, calm down," I said, trying not to laugh again, "we'll do something about it, I promise. How many requests are actually coming in?"

She subsided somewhat, now that I was taking her seriously. "We're getting between 15 to 20 a day now."

"That many?"

She nodded. "All told, I would guess we've sent out about a thousand."

"You're kidding!"

I had no idea it was that many. I went into my office and shut the door — and wondered what could be done to make distribution of the columns easier. It occurred to me, then, we still owned the press. We could print anything on it we wanted to. . . so, why not print the columns in the form of a tabloid? It was cheap, easy to handle, ship, or mail; and I could even include a few pictures from my trips to Medjugorje. Initially, we'd print about 3,000 copies, as it would also serve as a good pass-out, when I gave talks to the local civic clubs and churches.

I spent the morning editing and updating the columns and lining up the layout. Then I called in Denease and informed her that I'd solved the problems of distribution of the articles. She was happy — until I handed her the corrected copies to type-set. "This'll take me two or three days," she groaned. I just smiled; Denease always said something would take a couple of days — and then she would go and knock it out in four or five hours. Which is what she did this time.

Meanwhile, I wrote the lead-in, telling briefly how I had gotten involved and how I had heard in my heart a distinct message which began *You are my son* . . . . For so long I had hesitated to put that down in cold print. I didn't mind telling friends, and now eagerly shared it with other pilgrims. But to lay it out there for strangers to read and evaluate was another thing. Well, the time for "journalistic objectivity" had long since passed. If this was going to be my life's work, I would have to tell it *exactly* as it was.

When the typesetting was ready, I spread the pieces out on the layout table and started putting the tabloid together. It was printed a couple of days later. Denease was thrilled; the new tabloid, which was eight pages, fit perfectly into a business envelope, and needed only one stamp, instead of two.

On an impulse I bundled up 500 to take to the retreat. Sister Margaret had been asking for copies of the columns for the Center for Peace, and there might be some others there who would want them. We were all to meet at Kennedy Airport, so that we would be there when Father

Pervan arrived, and then we would all drive together to Ephrata House, a retreat center about an hour's ride from Boston.

The look of astonishment on Father Pervan's face when he saw us made it all worthwhile. There weren't very many of us, really, but those that were there had played key roles. There were Stan and Marge Karminsky, a Pennsylvania couple whose home-made videotape on their trip to Medjugorje had been copied thousands of times and distributed all over the world; there was Terry Colafrancesco, a young businessman who had started a Medjugorje information center called "Caritas," in Birmingham, Alabama; and Sister Margaret and several others from the Center for Peace whom I had previously met. In all, there were about 40 people from all over the country who were involved in making Medjugorje's message from the apparitions known.

On our way to Ephrata House, someone in our van asked how I had become involved with Medjugorje, and I told them. I finished just as we arrived and was surprised to see that several people had tears in their eyes. There was more sharing the next morning, after John Hill had told us about the Center for Peace and Father Pervan's forthcoming trip. There were more tears as well, for God was drawing us close together. How good it was to be with others who felt similarly called, and who had had their own times of testing.

During the dinner break that evening someone had arranged a book table, although most of the titles displayed there were well familiar to all of us. I asked if I might put my columns out, and they said, of course. Within half an hour, they were gone. During the course of the break I met Peter Crary, an attorney from Fargo, North Dakota, who like John Hill had never been to Medjugorje but was nonetheless totally convinced of its validity and importance. He was impressed that a Lutheran Protestant had become so involved in the apparitions of the Virgin Mary. "When you get home," he said, reaching in his wallet and pulling out a hundred-dollar bill, "send me as many copies of your columns as this will buy."

"Whoa, Peter, wait a minute! I'm not selling these things; I'm giving them away. Just tell me how many you want, and I'll send them to you."

He shook his head. "You don't understand. I have a lot of Lutheran friends out there, and so far nothing I've been able to say or do concerning Medjugorje has reached them. But I have a strong feeling that this will. Now how many can I have?"

I rough-estimated the cost of printing and shipping at about $25 a thousand and promised to send him four thousand as soon as I reprinted.

Hearing of the arrangement, a lady from Michigan said that she wanted four thousand also, and Terry Colafrancesco ordered two thousand for Caritas. I was stunned. With no effort on my part, suddenly I had orders for ten thousand copies!

But there was no time to dwell on it, for Terri was coming home from her pilgrimage. It was too much to expect that she would step off the airplane as I had, yet I could not help hoping .

My hopes were put on hold. Terri had had a memorable introduction to Medjugorje, but it had not turned her life upside-down, as mine had. She was glad she'd gone, and she allowed as how she might go again — but not right away. Then she said something to me that made all of my efforts to get her to go worthwhile: "Once I got there, I forgot you, the kids, and even my address; for the first time in my life, the single-minded purpose of loving God above all else became a reality. . . ."

When she had recovered from jet-lag and come into

the office, Denease had shown her a copy of the columns in tabloid form. The two of them then came into my office, Terri leading the way.

"You printed 3,000 of these?" she exclaimed with a teasing smile. "What are you going to do with them?"

"You don't like it?"

"Well, it's a good-looking job, but you could have run 500. You've got enough to hold you at least two years, and they'll probably line every bird-cage and litter box in the area!"

She was laughing now, and Denease behind her was laughing, too. "I had no idea you were going to print that many!"

"Well," I said, "before the two of you get too big a laugh out of this, let me inform you that I have orders right now for 10,000 copies!"

They stopped laughing.

"Where did you get orders for 10,000?" Terri asked, and I told them.

For a moment they just stood there, speechless. Then Terri, admitting that was pretty good, added, "But there's no way you can do them for $25 a thousand."

I sighed; on that she was undoubtedly right. Yet that was the figure I had promised them at, so we decided we would stick with that price and see how they would do.

We printed the ten thousand and included a little addendum to the effect that if you wanted extra copies they were $25 a thousand, $15 for 500, and so on, and sent them out. Before long we began to get requests for tens and fifties and hundreds. . . and then Peter Crary called. "Could you send me another 5,000 copies of those articles? I've got the money coming to you."

"Peter, are you insane? What are you going to do with them?"

"I've got people asking for them all over the place out here! I'm almost out of the ones I've got."

I couldn't believe it. Shortly after that, Terry Colafrancesco called and ordered ten thousand more. The price was still $25 a thousand, and when Terri found out I had printed the second run without raising it, she was concerned. "We're going to lose our shirts at that price!" she exclaimed, and she was right; we lost thousands. But I didn't care, and neither did Terri, really. As she put it, it was like a payback for the all of the good things that had happened in the last eleven months. We had sold our newspapers and the printing business was paying the bills. We certainly had little to complain about.

But we knew we couldn't go on like this indefinitely; if the orders continued to come in at a steady rate, we would have to up the price. Finally, after the third printing we had no choice. I raised the price to where, if the volume got high enough and stayed there, we could break even. "Well," said Terri, "if we're going to distribute the columns as a non-profit venture, we might as well run it as one." And so, Weible Columns, Inc. applied for status as a non-profit enterprise.

And then a funny thing began to happen: people started sending in more than they should have. Some people were ordering a thousand copies and sending us $100, with a request that we use the extra where it was most needed. I received a letter from a man who ran a tree nursery in Spokane who sent a check for $500 and ordered only 7,000 copies; he wanted the extra money to be a donation to pay for copies for those who could not afford them. Stunned, I wrote him back and tried to express my gratitude for his donation.

The next week I got a phone call from him: "You sent me 7,000 copies of these things!"

"Yes, I know."

"But I only ordered 700!"

"Wait a minute," I said, getting his letter out of the file. "No, sir, I'm sorry, but you did order 7,000."

"I did? My goodness, what am I going to do with 7,000?"

"Well," I laughed, "I've come to the point where I don't believe anything happens by accident any more. God obviously intended for you to have ten times as many as you thought you needed. Don't worry, He'll show you how to make use of them." And He did.

Then I got a letter from a lady in California who ordered 500 copies and sent $1,000. I wrote her back: "I just want to make sure you know what you're doing. If this is a gift, I thank you profusely, but I wanted to be sure." It was a gift.

The next thing I knew, all the money we had lost had been made up.

Meanwhile the orders kept pouring in, and now with them we were also receiving personal letters. Apparently the Holy Spirit was using the columns as an instrument to touch hearts and even change lives. I was deeply affected by the ones which began, "It was the 'You are my son' part that got me. After that, I *had* to read the columns — and what a difference they've made!" I would just shake my head; to think that I had ever hesitated to mention her message, out of fear of being thought a fool.

People wrote in saying that the columns were the perfect way to inform others of Medjugorje — easier to read and assimilate than a book, and yet comprehensive enough to tell the story. By the time I was getting ready to go back to Medjugorje in November, we had already shipped an incredible 40,000!

Terri was saying that we might reach 150,000, but secretly I was more optimistic. I dared to dream for a million.

*"You have forgotten, that through prayer,
you can stop wars, and you can alter
the laws of nature. . . ."*

21

Rita's Story

Wonderful things happened at Ephrata House. It was
a blessing that Father Pervan would be able to tour the
United States, bringing the events of Medjugorje to all
corners of this country. It would also help him to
understand these enigmatic Americans who were now
streaming into his little village by the thousands. The
retreat also marked the first time that those of us working
to make Medjugorje's message known had gathered
together to share our stories and ideas, and it launched
the columns as a tool for spreading the message. But the
most memorable event was the powerful witness of Rita
Klaus, a school teacher from Evans City, Pennsylvania,
a small town near Pittsburgh. Rita's story was the last item
on the agenda — and that was where it belonged, for
nothing else could have followed it.

As she began to relate the events that culminated in her
presence at the retreat, we sat there, spellbound and overwhelmed. Truly Ann Debeats, the energetic young woman
who ran the Center for Peace for John Hill and was serving
as the leader of the retreat, had saved the best wine for last:

> I'm very new to Medjugorje; in fact, I hadn't heard
> about it until February of this year. I read about it

in the *National Catholic Register* and was very interested. Shortly after that, I ordered a book called *Is the Virgin Mary Appearing at Medjugorje?* by Rene Laurentin. I read it, and I believed immediately. I began to pray more and to fast, and asked my children to pray the rosary. But I guess I'm getting ahead of my story.

Three months ago, I had Multiple Sclerosis. I had had it for more than 25 years. I was first diagnosed as having it when I was 20 years old, and it was difficult to accept. Of course I went through all the channels of denying I had it; I just would not accept it. As it began to progress, I rationalized it was something else. It was ruining my life; I was depressed and very angry inside — and very hurt. Yet I wanted to do what God wanted me to do.

About five years ago, a friend asked me to come to a healing service, but I really wasn't into the Charismatic Movement, so I tried to get out of going. But my friend wouldn't take no for an answer, and my husband pointed out that I had tried everything else, so what could it hurt to go?

The service began with the praying of a rosary, so that wasn't so bad. I was sitting in a pew towards the back of the church, and when the procession of priests started, I felt someone grab me from behind. At first I was totally embarrassed, because I had already made up my mind that I wasn't going to volunteer to go to the front for special prayers or anything. Then something strange happened; I felt this wonderful peace come over me. It was as if all the unhappiness of the years of suffering through this disease suddenly disappeared.

Returning home that evening, I vowed to improve my spiritual life. Up to this point, I was very bitter towards the Catholic Church. Though I had continued to attend Mass, I was simply going through the motions. Now, I wanted to make up for that. I told my pastor what had happened and asked him to pray that I might continue to be at peace.

By the end of that year the paralysis was in both legs and my arms. This, of course, upset me because of my work as a teacher, and because of my husband and children, and the hardship it put on them. But I had a good parish. Neighbors drove me to school, my husband scrubbed floors, and the kids helped out where they could.

Meanwhile, my legs became severely deformed, and the bones began to bow. My right knee became completely displaced because of the spasticity of the leg; the knee-cap came off and slid over into the interior of the leg. Also, there was now no feeling left at all.

At this stage I was forced to go to a rehabilitation hospital. It was time to face up to the fact that I was handicapped — and to begin life in a wheelchair. My husband could accept the braces and the crutches, but he couldn't stand the wheelchair. Yet it was something we both would have to face and live with. We loved the outdoors and liked to go camping. This would really slow that down for us.

But there were some good things happening. Many people pitched in to help, and the state came in and installed thousands of dollars worth of equipment in the school where I was teaching and in my home.

As I said earlier, I had sent off for the book about the apparitions at Medjugorje. I was really impressed and told my husband about it, but he's not Catholic — he's Lutheran, so it didn't have much effect on him. Anyway, we tried to improve our prayer life,

and I personally set aside an extra hour each day
for meditation.

Then, one night in June this year, as I lay in bed
finishing my rosary, I heard a voice say, Why don't
you ask? I don't know why, because I had never asked
before to be healed. I had come to accept my
handicap. But it just came to me as I lay there. So
I asked with all my heart for her to ask her Son
to heal me of whatever I needed to be healed. At
that moment I felt a bubbly feeling go through me,
and I don't remember anything else as I fell asleep.

When I awoke the next morning, I didn't think
about the night before. I had a Scripture class I
attended at a nearby college, and I prepared to go
to that class. My husband helped me into our van
which was equipped with hand controls for me, and
he placed my wheelchair in the van as he always
did. When I got to the college, there was always
someone there to help me and get me to class.

I didn't notice anything unusual right away.
Suddenly, as I sat there studying with the rest of the
class, I began to experience a feeling of warmth in
my feet and legs and an intense itching. But there
was no way this could be happening, as I had no
feeling in my feet and hadn't for several years. Then
I looked down at my feet and not only were they
itching, but my toes were wiggling! I was totally
dumbfounded!

I didn't remember another thing in the class; in
fact, I don't even remember leaving the class and
getting into my van. All I wanted to do at that time
was get home and tell my family what was happening
to me.

As I arrived at my house, I remembered that there
was no one home. I had complained earlier that I

had no strawberries and would they please go to the strawberry farm and pick some for me if they had time that morning. Evidently, they had gone and not returned in time to get me into the house. They did have the foresight to leave my crutches at the bottom of the three steps leading into our house. Occasionally, if I needed to get into the house, I could do it with the crutches. But it took a great deal of difficulty to do it.

Well, I sat there in the car for about 15 minutes, waiting. I was filled with disappointment because I wanted so much to tell them what was happening. Then, I had to go to the bathroom. My handicap also included bladder and bowel dysfunction, and I had been in class all morning. . . . so I had to get in and get in right away!

I stretched out of the car and got the crutches Ray had left for me within easy reach. I could not, however, lift my leg with the heavy braces on them. I stood there for a few minutes and then thought that if I could feel my feet — maybe I could also lift my leg. I tried it, and it went up the steps with no difficulty. My heart was pounding!

Once in the house, I went to my bedroom on the first floor and leaning against the bed to unlock my braces, I looked down at my legs. I thought they looked kind of funny; then I looked again and it hit me that my right leg was completely straight! I had had two surgeries on it to attempt to straighten it, but neither had been successful. In fact, they had finally released the kneecap (surgically) to let it go with the rest of my knee, stating that was all they could do with it. A severe valgus deformity had resulted from the years of spasticity and muscle imbalance.

As I looked now, it was straight. The kneecap was where it was supposed to be. My legs were perfectly straight!

At that point, I completely flipped out and began screaming that my legs were straight. I kept saying, "Thank you Blessed Mother! Thank you Jesus!" But it still had not sunk in that I was healed. Shaking, I took off the braces and stood up on my legs, unassisted, for the first time in years. I looked down again; they were like anyone else's legs! Finally it struck me that something very wonderful had happened.

I walked down the hallway. . . *walked down the hallway,* with my crutches under my arm. When I got to the base of the stairs, I thought: well, if I'm really healed, I can run up those stairs. So I dropped my crutches and did it — and then ran back down and up again. And I just kept shouting "Thank you!" over and over. I went a little hysterical, weeping and laughing at the same time. . . . I was in shock. I felt like St. Paul when he was knocked off his horse.

Finally, when I had sobered up a little, I decided to tell someone so I tried to call my pastor. But I kept dialing my own number! When I got through to him I said, "Father Bergman, I'm healed! I'm healed! I don't have MS anymore!" And he answered, "Who is this?" I said, "This is Rita — I'm fine, you don't understand, I'm healed!" Then, after a moment of silence he said, "Rita, I want you to sit down, take some aspirin and call your doctor — promise me you'll do that!"

I didn't know what else to say, so I just hung up on him and called a good friend who also taught at St. Gregory's. She recognized my voice, but by this time, I could hardly talk, and she thought something terrible had happened. She flew to the house, and that's something because we live way out in the country. I remember I was standing in the middle of the living room floor, jumping up and down when she arrived; soon we were both jumping up and down as she realized what was happening.

My friend calmed me down some and said we needed to find my family so that we could tell them, so we left for the strawberry farm. Since we had to go by the rectory of the church, we decided to stop and *show* my pastor that I was healed. He was in the study, and when he saw me standing in front of him, it hit him what had happened. All Father Bergman could do was stare at me, and he kept saying, "Sit down, Rita, you haven't used those muscles for a long time!' I told him I was fine and that I felt like I was 17 again!

We left there and headed for the farm, but when we arrived, my family had left, so we were off again for the house. When we got there, my friend ran in to get Ray who came out, white as a sheet. He thought something must have happened, because my car was still there and the braces and crutches were in the house, and that an ambulance must have come and taken me to the hospital.

I jumped out of the car and ran to him. My oldest daughter just stood there in tears and completely dumbfounded and choked up. She's twelve and my other two daughters are ten and seven. They had never known me any way other than handicapped.

It was. . . an indescribable scene. My oldest was crying, the middle one just stood there with her mouth open, and my little one said, "Oh, goody! Now we don't have to do housework anymore!" She followed that with, "You look silly, Mom!"

After awhile, we all calmed down and decided we better call my doctor. Would you believe, he was out playing golf! The next day, I went back to my Scripture class, but I didn't know what to do about them. If I told them, the class would be totally disrupted so I decided to go in the wheelchair. That was the hardest thing ever — to have to sit there in that chair knowing I was well. Later, when I returned home we were finally able to contact my doctor.

We told him what had happened, and he kept saying, "That can't be! That can't happen; it's impossible!" He asked my husband if I was walking, and he said, "No, she's running!" He asked us to come to the hospital right away.

When we got there, everyone on the staff was waiting. I had just been there a couple of weeks before that. They were stunned. My doctor thought it was a joke, saying I must be Rita's twin sister. He then conducted a lot of neurological tests and found everything to be perfect. After exhaustive tests, all he could do was hug me and cry and ask me what did I do? I told him all I did was ask. How many times? Once, I answered him, but many people have been praying for me for years. He then asked, did I use up all the prayers, or were there still some for him? It was wonderful.

Since this has happened to me, many things in my life have changed. I witness now to other MS patients, and to groups. And I pray a lot to God and His Holy Mother. I just ask you to pray that whatever I do, I do it well. Thank you, and God bless you.

We sat there too stunned to react — then there was thunderous applause. Rita's story was the final cap on a spiritual weekend that had already been incredibly full.

But there was more than just her story that attracted me to Rita. I felt a strong kinship to her. My sister, Lola, had Multiple Sclerosis. I had introduced her to what was happening at Medjugorje and then let her make her own decision as to its authenticity. She had been hesitant at first, as she, too, was Lutheran. But after reading much of the material and reviewing the video tapes, and hearing my own story, she was convinced.

Now I couldn't wait to tell Lola about Rita and her healing — and Rita about Lola. As soon as I could get through the crowd that had immediately surrounded Rita, we sat down and began talking. "I think if Lola could have a picture of you to go with the story," I told her, "that would give her great faith and hope." Rita obliged by letting me take her picture and then had a picture made with me. Even as I thanked her, I somehow knew also that this would not be the last I would see of Rita Klaus.

22

Finish What You Started....

My schedule was fast filling with talks in and around
the Myrtle Beach area, and the columns continued to
be in demand. Jim and Rosie Stoffel had become
wonderful friends and were a tremendous help in my
spiritual education. Several times I was able to assist Jim
in showing the videotape from the Center for Peace, and
Rosie was a special inspiration. She had been battling
throat cancer for several years, yet always seemed so
energetic and upbeat. The Stoffels had been to a number
of special healing masses, but as was often the case, the
real healing was spiritual — for both of them. And because
of this, they were able to continue as normal a life as
possible.

But all was not a bed of roses. I was beginning to discover
how difficult writing a book could be. After endless hours
of organizing material and outlining the project, the time
had arrived to sit down and actually begin putting thoughts
on paper.

I really wanted to write this book. Many had already
been written, but nearly all had been authored by
Catholic priests and dealt mainly with the early days and
attempts to explain what it all meant from a theological
standpoint. As yet, no one had written about what

happens to the individual who goes, sees, feels and is converted to full commitment to God. That was what I wanted to do.

But as I spent day after day staring at a blank page in my typewriter, I started to be assailed by doubts. They seemed to come in waves — how was a Lutheran Protestant, now deeply and emotionally involved, supposed to write objectively about a supernatural religious phenomenon steeped in Catholic history and tradition? Why had the national media persistently ignored such a significant story? Most important, who was going to actually believe that I had personally received a message from the Blessed Virgin Mary?

All at once the whole thing seemed too improbable for anyone to take seriously. I tried to recapture the fervor I had once felt, but the built-up euphoria of the whole experience had diminished to hesitancy and loss of confidence. Days set aside to begin writing turned into weeks of inactivity, as increasingly I justified not having time to write because of all the speaking invitations that were coming in.

I was not denying anything of what had happened to me; the feelings of conversion and renewal were still there. But as the volume of the columns going out increased and began to spread into many states, I began to believe that they might actually be the "book" I had felt such a strong urging to write.

By the end of October my paralysis at the typewriter had gotten to the point of desperation. Then, one morning as I sat in my office trying to motivate myself, I picked up the Bible which I kept in my office. I looked at it for a moment and then prayed, "Lord, please show me what to do," — and opened it at random. My eyes fell on II Corinthians 8:10:

I want to suggest that you first finish what you started
to do a year ago, for you are not only the first to propose
this idea, but the first to begin doing something about
it . . . .

I sat there for what seemed an eternity, literally trembling and awed by the simplicity and directness by which God speaks to us. The fervor and confidence were back, and they overshadowed all doubts. "Thank you," I murmured, and began to make preparations to return to Medjugorje in November and begin work in earnest on the book.

By the time I boarded the plane in New York, I was reasonably certain what needed to be done. First, I would interview as many of the visionaries as possible, and for this I was going to need Father Svet's help. I had contacted him in the hope that he might introduce me to them and possibly act as translator. In any event, I would continue to help him on his own writing.

Once again I rented a car in Dubrovnik, and this time I had no trouble finding the way to Medjugorje. Through Rose Finnegan of the Center for Peace, I had written to Grgo Vasilj, requesting to stay again with his family. This was the family with whom I had stayed on the previous trip, and had been accepted as a friend.

Quiet and pensive, Grgo was a hard-working father of six. A deeply spiritual man, he had built a prayer room for his family, which included his father and mother, and every morning at 6:30 a.m. they would gather there for prayer before breakfast. On my previous visit I had considered it a great privilege when he had invited me to join them.

A construction foreman by trade, Grgo had been inspired to build the prayer room because of his daughter Jelena. Quiet, and with strikingly beautiful eyes, Jelena had received a special gift from heaven in December, 1982.

In school one afternoon, she had heard the Virgin Mary's voice — a phenomenon known as inner-locution. The same gift was given to her playmate, Marijana Vasilj (no relation), both girls being only ten years old at the time. As with the visionaries, it had been occurring regularly ever since.

Jelena and Marijana did not see the Blessed Virgin as the visionaries did; they saw her "with the heart." Yet their inner-locutions were so similar to the messages that the others were receiving that Jelena, the more outgoing of the two, was frequently referred to as "the seventh visionary."

According to her, the Blessed Virgin was giving them teachings concerning the spiritual life. In May, 1983, she told Jelena to advise a priest that the Madonna desired a young people's prayer group to be established in the parish. She would lead them and give rules of sanctification: members would have to renounce everything, putting themselves totally at God's disposition. Some 56 boys and girls came forward to follow the call.

There was a special fascination for me concerning Jelena's gift: it was so similar to what I had experienced — and continued to experience from time to time. I felt it was no accident that I had been privileged to stay at Grgo Vasilj's home, and to share prayers with his daughter.

Extremely shy, Jelena would hardly even look at me at first. But gradually, as she grew comfortable with my being around, she was even a bit mischievous and loved to tease her sisters. After a couple of days she began to answer my questions. When I asked her about the messages that she was receiving for herself, she replied that they were mostly instruction on the ways of holiness. One of the first had been for her to start her day with a prayer to the Holy Spirit, and as stated, she had been asked to start a prayer group which she had done.

Holiness did not come easily to her (did it come easily to anyone?), and often her father would have to rouse her, if she was going to be in the prayer room in time for their morning devotions. He would also have to fuss at her occasionally when groups of pilgrims would come to the house, and she would refuse to talk to them. Jelena, now fourteen, and a typical teen-ager in many respects, was similar to the other visionaries, in that she was neither good or bad. Yet she was chosen by the Madonna — even though she preferred early-morning sleep to prayers, liked television and had a fondness for M&M candy (which I would try to remember each trip).

On this trip there was also a deep disappointment and hurt cutting into the joy of having returned again to Medjugorje: Tanya was gone. I discovered that she had gone to Italy two months earlier — and was back on drugs. It was a bitter lesson: no matter how many prayers were said or how many people offered aid, unless the recipient chose to accept the help, it would not work. Acceptance came from faith and a free-will choice. I was reminded of Jesus in His home town of Nazareth, unable to perform major miracles because of the lack of faith of those with whom He had grown up.

Yet I was not ready to give up on Tanya. My prayers for her would only increase. I knew that inside this young Australian a war was raging between evil and good; and I was determined to offer all prayer possible in hopes of good winning. Tanya represented to me the ongoing struggle we all had in remaining in the grace of God. We could accept that grace and live under its protection, or we could reject it; the choice was ours.

I recalled the time Tanya had accompanied me, along with Kathleen, for an interview with Jelena. Having done such a wonderful job with Father Slavko, I had asked her if she would help me with Jelena. They had not met prior to our meeting that last weekend I was in Medjugorje; in fact, Tanya had not even heard of Jelena's inner-locutions.

About half-way into the interview, after Jelena had related how the Madonna had begun "talking" to her, Tanya suddenly turned to me and exclaimed, "This is a lot of bull-___!"

"Tanya, don't say that! What is the matter with you?"

"Listen, I've spent lots of time around the visionaries, and I know they're not lying, but this — well, I don't believe her!"

I glanced at Jelena who was not sure what was being said but sensed something was wrong, and then at Kathleen who merely shrugged and offered no help. Finally, after regaining my composure I told Tanya to tell Jelena that the interview was finished. "And now," I added in a firm voice, "I want you to tell her that you don't believe her."

Tanya smiled. "You think I'm afraid to tell her?" She turned on Jelena and began gesticulating and speaking emphatically in Croatian.

I could not believe the change that came over Jelena. Her shy, quiet demeanor was replaced by a look of serenity and a half-smile. She appeared to be not the least upset or intimidated by Tanya's verbal assault.

I asked Tanya what Jelena had answered.

"She said the two of us would have to get together and talk about it, that's all."

Frustrated, I got up to leave. But as we thanked Jelena, she said something else to Tanya and took her by the hand.

"Oh, no!" wailed Tanya, "She wants to talk to me *now!*"

"Good," I said, "we'll wait for you outside."

Forty-five minutes later, Tanya and Jelena emerged from the house, smiling. Once again, the angelic side of Tanya was evident.

"I believe her now," she said quietly.

"Why?"

"She's so honest, and so — open. And after hearing of some of the things the Blessed Mother said to her, I realized it's the same things the visionaries tell me."

As happy as I was that such an embarrassing situation had turned into a valuable lesson for this struggling teenager, I had been even more intrigued with the change that had come over Jelena.

While Tanya's subsequent regression was a painful disappointment, still it was good to be in my second home again, to climb Podbrdo for meditation and to slip into St. James for Mass. And this time, there seemed to be more Americans present; there were *two* groups from the States — Sister Margaret Sims was leading one from the Center for Peace, and Terry Colafrancesco headed a group from Caritas. Word was getting around.

Something else was different: people were beginning to recognize me from the columns. Many told me that they were there *because* of the columns. That overwhelmed me.

Terry asked me to speak to his group, and I agreed, thrilled to be able to give a talk right there in Medjugorje. We went to the grove of cedars between the church and Mt. Krizevac. There, in that lovely oasis of serenity, amidst gravestones going back several hundred years and with the great cross providing a silent backdrop, I talked to them of Medjugorje: what had brought me, what I'd seen, and what God was still showing me — and would show them, as well.

One evening when after Mass, some of the Center for Peace people who had heard that I had given a talk to the Caritas group, asked me to speak to their group also, and they hastily arranged for us to meet in the basement of the rectory at 9:00 the following morning. They told me that there would be 20 or 30, but word traveled quickly. There were more like 50 or 60 when I got there. Again I inwardly prayed for grace and for the Holy Spirit, not Wayne Weible, to be heard.

When it was over, Sister Margaret came up and gave me a long hug and said, "That was beautiful! Just keep it up!"

I went to Mass, inwardly thanking God repeatedly, and was profoundly moved by the service. After the Eucharist, I was there on my kneeler, eyes tightly closed, in prayer deeper than usual. All at once, I began to see many faces. They were clear and vivid, and seemed to be floating in a brown-gray mist. Then the individual faces began to fade and were replaced by masses and masses of people.

Suddenly, above them was a dazzling white light, brighter than any I had ever seen, yet I could look right into it. As I watched, there, in the middle of it, Jesus appeared in a white robe. Slowly He opened His arms and extended them down to all the people below.

The vision was extremely clear, and it lasted for a long time. I was so caught up in it, that when it finally faded, and I opened my eyes, I was surprised to find that the service had ended some time before, and I was nearly alone in the church.

I got up shaking and marveling at what I'd seen — nothing like that had ever happened to me before. Quietly I went out of the church and met Shannon Brennan, a young woman with the Center for Peace group. She had been sitting next to me during Mass.

"I'm sorry, Shannon, I couldn't —"

She stopped me. "You don't have to explain anything; it was obvious that something special was happening to you."

I told her of the vision; I had to tell someone. We began walking toward the little community where the visionaries lived and were soon joined by a friend of hers. They had not yet been on the "Hill of Apparitions," as Podbrdo was popularly known, and urged me to go with them. After the beautiful vision, all I wanted to do was pray; the Hill seemed to be the best place, so I agreed.

As we reached the base of the Hill, Shannon noticed a crowd of Americans outside of Marija's house, which was just up the road. "Oh, let's go see Marija before we climb the Hill," she exclaimed.

I agreed immediately. Marija was probably the most influential of the visionaries, but more important, I wanted to see her sister Milka. I had interviewed them both, but had spent more time with Milka. Marija stood half-way up the flight of steps to her front door, semi-surrounded by a crowd of American pilgrims whose questions she was quietly answering through an interpreter. At one point her eyes briefly met mine, and I thought for a moment that she half-smiled. Ridiculous, I told myself; with all the interviews she gave daily, she couldn't possibly remember one that had taken place five months ago.

After another fifteen minutes or so the American group departed. Shannon and her friend left also, telling me to meet them on the Hill when I had finished speaking to Marija. I was about to go up to her, when a couple of Italian men who had been lingering on the fringe now moved in and monopolized her time. Patiently she answered their queries, speaking Italian fluently, and when at last they left, she turned to me.

"Marija," I began, "my name is —"

"Wayne!" she exclaimed, coming over and greeting me with a kiss on each cheek. "How are you? It is good to see you again!" English was not easy for her, but her spontaneous warmth needed no interpretation.

"You remember me?" My jaw fell open.

"Yes, of course I remember you from interview with

me and with Milka. Milka has, how you say, great respect for you."

I was stunned. "Is she here?"

"No, Milka is in Germany, to take care of sister-in-law who has new baby."

"Well," I smiled, "I will come back and see you later. Father Svetozar will come with me," and I turned to leave.

"No, no," she laughed, "you come up now!" And taking me by the hand she led me up the steps and into the kitchen. For the next twenty minutes or so we talked about what was going on in Medjugorje, and what her life was like. ("Very busy. Very little time like this. But it is good.") I was surprised at how much she seemed to understand — and astonished at how well she was able to communicate, despite the broken English. We were actually having a conversation — not an interview, just a nice chat. But afraid of saying something really stupid, and not wanting to push my luck, I got up and said, "I will come back with Father Svet."

"You come any time," she said, seeing me to the door, "you come back."

I nodded and waved and went down the steps. And then, when she had gone inside, I could contain my jubilation no longer and ran up Apparition Hill, anxious to tell Shannon about my conversation with Marija. For there was something very special in that meeting: she was not Marija, the visionary, but Marija, my friend. It was the beginning of what would become my closest relationship with any of the visionaries.

That was a Cloud Nine day from beginning to end. In the afternoon, Svet drove down from his parish to give his weekly talk at the church, and when he was finished, we hugged one another in greeting. "I have good news!" he said, as we walked to the fringe of the yard bordering the church. "I have arranged for you to come to Konjic and stay in the monastery for four days!"

"That's great!" I said, happy to at last have an opportunity to spend more than a few hours with him. "When?"

"I must go back tonight, but you come tomorrow. And we will talk about your book, not mine — although I do have some thoughts I would like to write with your assistance."

The drive up the Neretva River to Konjic was spectacular. Once again, I did not have a road map, but Svet assured me that it was simply a matter of following the road to Sarajevo which ran straight through Konjic. About two hours later, I arrived.

Expecting a village not much larger than Medjugorje, I was surprised to find that Konjic was a bustling town. I found Father Svet's church, a magnificent structure with the monastery next to it. He was there to greet me and took me to the room where I would be staying. I winced; Konjic was considerably higher than Medjugorje, which meant that it would be much colder. And in true monastic tradition there was no heater. But Svet, as if reading my mind, smiled and gave me the small heater in his own room.

That evening we had supper in the refectory with the other priests. It was a festive occasion and a wonderful experience to be with Franciscans other than at Medjugorje and learn about their lifestyle. Afterwards, we went to Svet's room to start work. "I need your help with some notes that I have made. They are not for my book; they are just some thoughts that possibly I may use at a later time — or you can use them for your book."

So we began — Svet reading and adding as we went along, and me typing and advising. At times we would stop and debate a point. I would suggest a small change, and he would state his preference for leaving it as it was.

After awhile he slapped my knee and smiled. "This is good!"

"What do you mean?"

"That we can sit here and debate these insignificant points, and now, you can even choose to disagree with me." He smiled when he saw it finally register: Father Svetozar Kraljevic, my spiritual hero, was no longer high up on a pedestal to be held in awe; while he was still an overpowering figure, he was now also a close, personal friend and a brother in Christ.

We put in three hours that evening and spent the whole next day similarly occupied. We took a break about midway through the day to stroll over to the open market across from the church. Everything from food to coffee grinders was for sale, and Svet purchased a little grinder. "This is for Terri," he said, giving it to me.

"If you knew how little time my wife spends in the kitchen," I laughed. "But she'll love it, because it's from you." Terri had met Svet on her September trip and had immediately felt the same way about him that I did. She would be thrilled that he thought of her, but that was typical of him. No matter how many new "brothers and sisters" from the pilgrimages to Medjugorje he acquired, he always had a special word, or a few moments to listen, for each of them.

That afternoon, Father Svet was scheduled to say Mass at 5:00. As he went to prepare for it, I took a seat in the shadows at the back of the church, about 20 minutes early. The church was freezing, and I could not stop shivering, even though I was well dressed for the cold. One by one, the townspeople came in, until there were about fifteen in all. I took small solace in the fact that they appeared to be every bit as chilled as I was. To take my mind off the cold, I slipped to my knees and started to pray.

Abruptly, I stopped shivering; in fact, it was like I was in some sort of a vacuum. And then, I felt a message within me — exactly as I had several times before. It was not an audible voice, nor was there an accompanying vision. Yet, it *was* a voice, and a strong one. All it said was: *Bring Milka to the United States.*

I was startled. At that moment, Milka was as far from my mind as China. I hesitated, then asked, half aloud, "Why?"

There was no reply — just a strong sense that I was to do as requested.

I filed it away in my mind with a mental note to talk to Svet about it. There was now within me a calm acceptance of being the recipient of these inner messages. After my previous experiences and the time spent with Jelena, I was beginning to comprehend that anyone could be thus used as an instrument of the Holy Spirit.

The opportunity to talk to Father Svet came the next morning, as he drove me to the site of a proposed new church for the parish. All of the income from his writing went towards its future construction, and he was sure it would be a reality soon. Svet was in civilian dress for the trip. Out of the brown robe of the Franciscan Order, he seemed somehow less imposing. But the grace was still in his bearing and the holiness in his eyes.

He did not seem surprised, when I told him of the message concerning Milka. "Well," he said thoughtfully, "when we see Marija tomorrow, tell her about it and see what she thinks." He had agreed to return to Medjugorje with me, to act as my interpreter.

On our way back to the monastery, we were just getting to the center of Konjic, when we heard a din of honking horns. At a little crook in the road where several streets converged, it seemed as if everyone in town had arrived there simultaneously — and no one was giving an inch.

It never occurred to me that there could be a traffic jam in such a small town in the mountains of Yugoslavia, but here we were, stuck in the middle of one.

Father Svet tilted his head, then shrugged and got out of the car. He went to the center of the mess and started directing traffic, beckoning this car to back up a little and that one to come forward. I could not tell if anyone recognized him, but all were obviously relieved that somebody was finally doing something. The honking stopped. In less than five minutes the intersection was clear, and everyone was on their way.

"Sometimes," he said smiling as he returned to the driver's seat, "you have to take action yourself and make change."

I laughed at him and shook my head. I had just witnessed my Franciscan friend giving a living demonstration of the famous prayer of his patron saint, which went something like: *Lord, grant me the courage to change what can be changed; the patience to accept what cannot be changed — and the wisdom to know the difference. . . .*

Early that afternoon, while Svet ran an errand in town before we left, I sat on my bed after packing and thought about all that had happened to me since that fateful evening when the Mother of Jesus had spoken to me. Everything was becoming crystal clear. I could see Medjugorje and all of its significance and ramifications as I had never seen it before. And my own role in the scheme of things was also clear. Now I understood why I had been called back for the third time in less than six months. It was a learning period. Svet's role was his influence and guidance. Quietly I began praying the rosary, using the one he had given me.

There was a soft knock at the sill of the door which I had left open. I looked up and Father Svet was standing there, staring at me with a beautiful smile. "This is the way I am going to always remember your visit here — you, in this room, praying your rosary."

I couldn't say anything, as my eyes filled.

"Well, if you are packed, we shall leave," he said, bringing us back to the business at hand. I took my bag and followed him down to where the cars were parked. He led the way back to Medjugorje, and I had no trouble keeping up. As we reached the outskirts of Mostar, he signaled me to stop and got out and came to my car. "We will have some coffee now."

"You sure you want to stop here? It's only about 40 more minutes." He assured me he did.

Over cups of the thick, strong espresso that I had grown fond of, he said, "Wayne, I have made a decision; we are not going to work on my new book for awhile. I am going to devote my time with you to help you with your book."

I started to object, but he held up his hand, and I sensed that he had given this much thought and prayer on the way down. "You must write this book now and let nothing interfere with it. Take your time and make sure it is accurate, but you must do it."

I just nodded.

23

The Learning Continues

Father Svet pulled into the yard behind St. James' rectory, while I parked as near as I could, conscious that it was once again my last day in Medjugorje. As I got out of the car, he said, "We will have lunch in the rectory first, before we go to Marija's house."

We were joined by a Father Nicholas, a quiet young priest who had only been at Medjugorje a few months. He was anxious to tell Father Svet about something that had just happened, and as he began relating it to him in Croatian, Svet held up his hand and turned to me: "Perhaps you should get your notebook and take notes; this sounds like something for your book. I will translate for you." I did as he suggested and started writing furiously, as Father Nicholas related the story of Mira (not her real name), a woman in her early thirties from a small village in Northern Yugoslavia.

Mira had been raised in a devout Catholic family, but having fallen in love with a young man who was actively involved with the Communist Party, she drifted away from the Church. Her priest warned her that she was headed in a direction that could only bring hurt to her and her family, but she did not listen, and they were married. With her new husband's affiliation with the Party, it was no longer appropriate for Mira to continue going to Mass.

As the priest had predicted, she grew estranged from her family, even when her first child was born — a boy who was crippled with a form of Muscular Dystrophy. In the ensuing five years this tragedy plus the increasing pressures of life took a fearful toll on Mira. She suffered from acute anxiety, for which she took medication in ever larger doses, until she developed epilepsy. The frequency and severity of her seizures progressed to the point where she was hospitalized in Zagreb in the fall of 1986, suffering from as many as thirty attacks a day.

For 17 days the doctors tried every conceivable treatment but were unable to help her. Her condition steadily worsened, and perhaps as a result of the radical medication she was receiving, she went blind. Finally they told her husband that there was nothing more they could do for her. He might as well take her home, for she was going to die.

A pall hung over their house for the next two weeks, as Mira lay in her bed and the two of them waited for the inevitable. But somewhere during that time an extraordinary thing happened: Mira began to hear a voice. *You must turn to God and pray,* it seemed to be saying.

Concluding that she was delirious from her illness and medication, her husband tried to soothe her. But she persisted and now began to insist that the voice said she must go outside. Here her husband drew the line. The doctors had said she was to stay in bed, and fearing that any activity might hasten the end, her husband kept watch to make sure that she did.

But eventually he had to leave the house, and as soon as he did, Mira managed to get out of bed. Slowly she made her way to the front door. No sooner had she opened it and was standing outside than she had a vision. The

Blessed Virgin Mary appeared to her and said: *You can be healed.*

Mira dropped to her knees. "Blessed Mother," she cried, "please, heal my son; he's only five."

Your son is not responsible for his affliction, but his suffering will be the salvation and conversion of many people. Do not ask for him; ask for yourself. Go to Medjugorje, and you will be healed.

That was all. Mira's blindness returned, and she crawled back into the house and to the bedroom. When her husband came home, she tried to tell him what had happened, but he did not believe her; indeed, he was saddened that her delirium seemed to be taking a turn for the worse. She begged him to take her to Medjugorje, but that, he said, was out of the question.

Mary appeared to her again in her bedroom. "Blessed Mother," Mira cried, "my husband will not take me to Medjugorje!"

Do you know anyone in this village who can pray for you?

"No," the woman answered, "they've all turned from God."

Nor do I. Go to Medjugorje, and with that she disappeared. Mira became driven. All she could talk about was going to Medjugorje. When her husband in despair decided that the only recourse was to take her back to the hospital in Zagreb, she became hysterical. Finally, to quiet her, he agreed to take her to Medjugorje. On November 8th, they took the train to Mostar, and on the 9th they arrived in Medjugorje (the same day that I had, I realized).

Her husband took her directly to the church, and as they entered he noted that she was calmer than she had been in months; strangely, she had had only a few epileptic seizures during the travel.

The church was empty, and he guided her to a pew down in front on the right side. (Hearing that, I remembered seeing her there when I came in that Sunday afternoon.) All afternoon Mira prayed, and suddenly about an hour later she had an urge to look up. She did — and was astounded that she could physically see the statue of the Virgin Mary in front of her. Her sight had returned!

Her husband stared at her, dumbstruck. She got up and went outside, where she found a visiting priest who was hearing confessions. She made a long and emotional confession, and then told him what had just happened. He encouraged her to go back in and continue to pray, and the next day she should find one of the local priests and tell him what had happened.

But the following day when she went looking for one of the Medjugorje priests, they were all away on errands. Finally on Tuesday morning, she told Father Pervan and Father Nicholas her story. Her sight was perfect, and she had not had even a mild seizure for more than 24 hours! She was confident that she was completely healed.

She went home converted — and so did her husband.

It was a stunning story, and I was especially struck by the aspect of her child suffering for the redemption of others. How many had wondered why there was so much suffering in the world. . . . Here was one instance that was tied directly to the suffering Christ, who died a horrible death so that we could be forgiven and redeemed for God. The young Franciscan had given us the story right out of St. James' journal, exactly as it had been recorded. It was like hearing a new parable.

We thanked Fr. Nicholas and left for Marija's, and because the sun was shining we took the path through the fields rather than drive. It would take twenty minutes longer, but after Mira's story, the extra time would be welcomed for private thoughts.

Marija was waiting for us at the top of the steps to her front door and again gave me a warm greeting. It was

interesting to see her with Father Svet. She had a deep
respect for him but also a fondness which was apparent
as she absently removed a bit of lint from the sleeve of
his cassock as they talked. I watched her as they chatted
in Croatian, catching up on the news, and thought to myself
again how beautiful she was. But not in the conventional
sense; there was a spiritual beauty which emanated from
her — the same sort of beauty which was evident in the
countenance of Mother Teresa.

"Well," said Father Svet, switching to English, "now we
need to get to work. Why don't you tell Marija your story.
She can understand English a little, but I will repeat it
in Croatian."

For the next twenty minutes I told her of the events
in my life during the past year. Throughout, I tried to
communicate that I was not looking for anything special
— and yet all the while I could not help wishing that
I could say: Marija, please, would you ask the Blessed
Mother if I'm doing what she has asked of me? Like so
many other pilgrims, I had this deep-seated desire for a
special sign or possibly a few moments of seeing her as
the visionaries saw her. Deep-down, I knew this was selfish
and focusing on the wrong things, but nevertheless it was
there.

Somehow, from the intensity of my emotion as I looked
in her eyes while Father Svet was translating, she seemed
to know my heart. "Yes, I understand," she said in English,
nodding with a half smile. We took a break. She got up
and fixed us some coffee, and brought out some rolls
for us. "Milka made these before leaving for Germany,"
she said, looking at me and smiling.

All of a sudden I became aware of something unusual:
there were no bunches of pilgrims lined up in the street,
waiting to see her, no young Italian groupies coming inside to hang out, no presumptuous tour guides barging

in to make demands of her. There were — no distractions of any kind. *Incredible* — as if God had carved out this time and given it to us.

But now came the hard part; I was going to have to tell her about what had happened to me up in Konjic two days ago. What was she going to think? "Marija, I have to talk to you about Milka."

"Milka?" she responded, not waiting for the interpretation. "What about Milka?"

I told her about receiving the message, adding that as I thought about it afterwards, it seemed to be for a prolonged visit — three months, at least. Perhaps it was for her to learn English, I concluded lamely. There were still few Americans coming to Medjugorje at that time, but I could foresee — no, *knew* — the time was coming when the majority of the pilgrims would be from the States.

For a long time Marija looked at me without saying anything. Then she smiled, and with Father Svet interpreting she said, "I cannot speak for Milka. I do not see any problem with her going to the United States . . . but you must ask her yourself."

"How? She's in Germany."

Marija went to a drawer and took out some stationery. "Here, you write her a letter and leave it with me. When she comes home in January I will give it to her. Then you can telephone or write to her." She shrugged. "We will see what happens."

Encouraged, I asked her, "How do *you* feel about it?"

She thought for a moment before replying. "If you think that the message you received is from Our Lady, you should obey what she is asking."

I noted that she refused to commit herself, but this was not the time to pursue it further. I had done what I could; it was in God's hands now. As we left, Marija once again told me in English to come back anytime, adding, "God bless you."

Next, Father Svet took me to Mostar, where he wanted me to meet and interview Ivanka. She wasn't home, but her father was, and we talked to him. Father Svet had warned me that his wife had died shortly before the events in Medjugorje had begun, and I made a note not to ask any questions that might stir painful memories. Asking him about his life, I learned that he had spent much time working in Germany and had done quite well. He had a house in Medjugorje, as well as this one in Mostar.

What was it like, having a daughter who was a visionary? He hesitated, then chose his words carefully. "I feel that we are very graced to have this. That she should be involved in this has had a profound effect on the whole family — on her younger sister, her cousins, everyone. But it has also had some bad effects — too many people coming around, too many questions, too many journalists . . . ." He smiled to let me know that he didn't mean me, but I decided to save the rest of my questions for his daughter.

He offered us some coffee while we waited, and after about five of the little cups Ivanka came in with her younger sister. As soon as she saw Father Svet, she went over and gave him a hug. Then, looking at me and seeing the note pad in my hand, she began a long string of Croatian directed at Svet. I did not need an interpretation to know that this was not exactly a hearty welcome. Father Svet responded in Croatian, and again it was not too hard to tell what he was saying, as he shook his head and frequently said, "No, no."

But instead of calming down, her resentment level increased, and now she was walking around, raising her hands in the air. Sensing that I was the last straw, I was mortified and nudged Father Svet, shaking my head and nodding towards the door. All I wanted to do was leave

— gracefully if possible, but certainly as quickly as possible!

But he ignored me and kept talking to her, calmly yet persistently. She was, however, in no mood to be placated, and finally I could stand it no longer. "Listen," I said under my voice to Father Svet, "I really don't want to create a problem here. If she doesn't want to do this, that's okay; let's just go." I stood up to leave.

"No," he said quietly, pulling me down in my chair, "be patient."

He talked to her some more, every so often gesturing in my direction, and to my surprise she abruptly sat down. "It's okay," Fr. Svet said to me, "everything is fine." Ivanka, still somewhat stiff and formal, nodded and smiled at me, as he spoke.

Svet explained that she was not happy with the recent BBC film in which he had convinced her and Mirjana to agree to interviews, especially with some of the personal questions that had been asked of her. In fact, Ivanka was not happy with the public role the life of a visionary called for. She was also still saddened that she no longer was an active part of the daily visits from the Madonna. I had seen that, on the day of the fifth anniversary as she sat on the lawn with friends. During the time of the apparition, I had noticed that she lowered her head in evident sadness. This, plus many interviews that had not appeared in print or on film as she had given them, was why it had taken some time for Svet to reassure her that my point of view would be sympathetic.

To confirm that, I told her my own story just as I had earlier that afternoon to Marija, concluding that I was here more as a pilgrim than as a journalist. She laughed and held out her hand, which I happily shook.

I asked her some general questions about her life, where she was and where she was going, and I emphasized that

I was not there to write an exposé. "I'm looking for your personality," I told her, "what you as a person felt then — and now — and where your role as a visionary has led you."

She really opened up after that, chatting at will and giving much more than was asked. Later, she brought out a photo album to show me. I noted one snapshot, taken a couple of years earlier, in which her hair was cut off. It had grown back now, and through Father Svet I said, "I like your hair better long. It's as though you haven't really changed, in spite of all that's happened. You're the same, even though you're 21 now."

At that she beamed and began to talk about her forthcoming marriage which at the time was still supposedly a secret — except that her friends knew it, which meant that all of Medjugorje knew it. "Well," I said with a smile, "I'm not going to ask the question that everyone asks (when would they marry?); I'm just going to say I'm very happy for you, and I think this is very good."

It became more of a conversation than an interview, as we continued to talk about Medjugorje. And then I asked, "Where are you going to live after you get married — here in Mostar?"

"No, we want to come back to Medjugorje," she replied, and it seemed to me she was a little anxious about it. Then she added, "I don't know what to do about it." As she spoke, she was looking directly at me; we were having an eye-to-eye conversation, even though Father Svet was interpreting. Again as with Marija, I was no longer a journalist; I was a friend.

Suddenly she asked me, "Do you think I will be able to go back to Medjugorje and live a good, quiet life with my husband?"

I looked at her sadly and shook my head. "No, Ivanka,

I don't think you will. People will never leave you alone. They will want to continue to come to you, and it's probably going to become even worse, because you'll be married."

She wrung her hands. "I don't know what I'm going to do!"

I reached over and put a hand on her arm. "For all of these years you've depended on the Blessed Mother to guide you. She's come to you and given you this and led you this way. She's blessed you in the fact that you're getting married, even though she asked you about the religious life. But when you said that this was what you wanted, she said that was your decision . . . and she has blessed what you're doing!" I paused. "Ivanka, she's going to continue to take care of you!"

The funniest look came over her face, as if to say: yes, you're right! And all of a sudden it hit me: who did I think I was, sitting here, telling this visionary who had spent years having daily visits with Mary, that everything was going to be okay? But I had blurted it out, out of consciousness of her concern. All at once we looked at one another — and laughed, simultaneously struck by the unlikeliness of it.

I turned to Father Svet and said, "I don't know what I was doing, telling her those things."

He just laughed and said, "It is okay; she was meant to hear them."

After that we were true friends, chatting endlessly until Father Svet reminded me that they had not yet had their dinner. So we departed, and as Ivanka gave me a hug, I said, "I'll see you in Medjugorje."

"Yes, that will be good," she added, waving good-bye.

It was harder to say good-bye to Father Svet. We found a quiet restaurant in one of the hotels in Mostar and had a long dinner filled with wonderful conversation.

It was midnight as we finally parted. The one consolation was that I now knew that I would be coming back again — and more than once.

24

On the Road

It had been an exciting trip, but it was good to be home again — at least I thought so, until I walked into my office a couple of days later. There, piled in stacks on my desk was so much mail you would have thought that I had been away for a year. "Denease!" I cried, "What is this?"

"Two weeks' mail," she replied innocently.

"What is happening? How could this be just two weeks? It's all over the place!"

She laughed. "Do you know how many copies of the columns we're sending out a week now? Close to fifty thousand! And those are not requests you're staring at; we've already filled those. All I put on your desk were the personal letters to you from people who've read the columns and wanted to write you about them."

Stunned, I went to the desk and sat down and took the one from the top of the nearest pile. It was from a woman in Illinois:

Dear Mr. Weible:

Last Thursday a friend gave me your columns. I had heard of Medjugorje casually and thought it sounded impossible. Then I read your columns. I no longer think it's impossible; in fact, God is more

real to me now than at any time since my confirmation . . . .

There were at least a hundred more in that vein. It
took me all day to get through them, and by the time
I finished I was speechless. I gathered up a handful to
show Terri. "I know," she said, smiling, "I've been reading
them."

"What am I supposed to do with all of this?"

"Print more columns," she answered cheerily, "and sit
down and begin answering some of them. Maybe you can
do that while you travel."

As it turned out, there would be more of that, too.
I had received my first out-of-state speaking invitation,
for the first few days in March. One of the Center for
Peace pilgrims on my last trip was a New Orleans woman
named Lettie Bindewald. She had heard me speak in
the basement of the rectory, and after Mass that morning
she and some friends had climbed Mt. Krizevac. I had
gone up myself in the afternoon, and I met her group
coming down. Lettie was a little startled to see me, and
took a piece of paper out of her shoulder bag. "I wrote
this on the top," she murmured, "and meant to give
it to you later. Don't read it, till you get to the top
yourself."

I did as she requested. It was a note, telling how touched
she had been by Medjugorje, and that the thing which
had had the greatest effect on her was to hear this
Protestant speak. "I love my Catholic faith," she wrote,
"but I have had this strong urge to spread this message
to the Protestants. Until I heard you talk, I didn't know
how. Now I do."

I was touched by the note and saved it. She later wrote
me, and in my answer I agreed to come and speak sometime
in the future. And then she called. "I didn't think I'd be
calling so soon," she said, "but there's a group of people

here who have read your columns and would be glad to sponsor you."

I accepted, telling her that it would be the first time I had spoken outside of South Carolina; in fact, I had never spoken more than fifty or sixty miles from home.

"Great," she replied, "David and I would love to have you stay with us, but we're happy to get you a motel room, if you'd prefer it."

"No, no, I'll be glad to stay with your family," I said quickly. That surprised me because normally I would have preferred a motel room. But this was different; I wanted to be with people who loved Medjugorje as I did.

I told Terri about the call and that I had accepted the invitation to go there and speak. Of all the cities in North America, there was more Medjugorje interest in New Orleans than anywhere else. I had no explanation for it, but I certainly had plenty of confirmation: that was where we shipped by far the greatest numbers of columns. And this was borne out by Terry Colafrancesco and Peter Crary.

"Oh boy, here we go," she responded in a tone that was hardly enthusiastic. "Now you're talking about leaving the state to speak." She was even less pleased when I told her the dates. "That's the weekend I have to go to Texas for Doris' wedding," she moaned. "I told you that!"

As soon as she said it, I remembered. But I was still optimistic. "Look, why don't you go to Texas, and as soon as your sister's wedding is over, catch a plane for New Orleans? I'd really like it if you could be with me."

She thought about that for a moment, then shook her head. "I don't know about leaving the kids for that long."

I determined to stay positive. "We can get someone to stay with them — Come on, you'll like New Orleans." She reluctantly agreed.

Terri knew what was coming. Ever since I had appeared on the Sally Jessy Raphael show in February, speaking requests had been coming in from all corners of the country. The number of columns shipped had also picked up.

This particular television show was internationally syndicated and was a major break in getting the story of the Medjugorje apparitions out on a national media level. As it happened, the other two journalists on the show with me were both from New Orleans — Jim Bailey and Mary Lou McCall, a television news anchor team for a local station there. After learning of the apparitions, they had convinced their station's manager that a trip to the village to do an in-depth news series would tremendously boost the station's market ratings. Thousands of local residents from the heavily Catholic population in and around New Orleans had made the pilgrimage to Medjugorje, or had heard about it. There was an insatiable thirst for more information about the phenomenon.

Prior to making the trip, the interests of these journalists were strictly professional; like me, they were simply in search of a good story — and maybe a national award to go with it. "We were looking to possibly expose the whole thing as a hoax and maybe win an Emmy," was the way Mary Lou put it, somewhat embarrassed now. This modern-day career woman, attractive and intelligent, was Catholic, but before making the trip to Medjugorje she had not been to Mass in more than two years. Jim Bailey, on the other hand, was a professed agnostic with a family background that was nominally Baptist. The last time he had been in a church was for his own wedding.

They returned from Medjugorje with an outstanding, professionally objective documentary on the apparitions — which did indeed boost their station's ratings far beyond the expectations of all concerned. They also came home with the unwavering conviction that the Blessed

Virgin Mary truly was appearing to the visionaries. Their lives would be changed forever — just as mine had been. Later, they would travel far and wide to bring the message to people of all faiths.

The show — the first to present the story of Medjugorje nationally — thus had the added appeal of three journalists who had initially been unreligious skeptics and who had had their lives transformed. It aired in February, 1987, and quickly became one of the most popular segments in the show's history. Thousands of letters and calls poured in to their studios in St. Louis, requesting more information about the apparitions. It was shown on a delayed basis during the next six weeks to more than 85 cities, including most of Canada and England. This single half-hour show did more to positively educate the public about the appearance of the Blessed Virgin in Medjugorje, than all previous media efforts combined. And now I was going to New Orleans. . . .

I was met at the airport on a Saturday morning in early March by Lettie, David, and their four kids. Judging from his silence on the trip to their home, David did not fully share his wife's enthusiasm for my visit. This big, quiet man had heard me speak in Medjugorje, and he was smiling now, but I sensed that David Bindewald was a man who did not commit himself to anything impulsively. Like the fabled Missourian, his attitude seemed to be: okay, if you're for real, show me.

They had scheduled two talks that day — one in the afternoon and one that evening. Terri had left for Austin on Thursday, and was to arrive in New Orleans at about six, just about the time we would be leaving for the evening talk. No problem, Lettie assured me; they would have a friend meet her and bring her to the meeting.

On the airplane that morning I had tried not to think about the trip — but I wound up thinking about little else. I had prayed, of course, that God, by His Holy Spirit, would give me the words to say and the way to say them. I knew I shouldn't feel anxious, because that was saying I didn't really believe He would come through — but I couldn't help it.

Now, I was here, and it was time to go to the first talk, in a large Catholic church with a very large parking lot — which was almost full by the time we arrived. And there were still 45 minutes until the talk!

As we got out and started to walk up to the front door, people started coming up and waving copies of the columns, saying "Please, Wayne, would you autograph this for me? Could I get your picture with my husband ? I saw you on television. . ." And many just plain thank-you's for writing the articles.

Pretty soon I was surrounded. I didn't quite know what to do, so I began signing copies of the columns, not because I wanted to, but the look on some of the faces convinced me that it was better than saying no to them. I glanced at David Bindewald and imagined him thinking, "Now I see what it's all about; this guy has got his glory going for him here!"

Lord, take this from me, I prayed. When I start to speak, let them see You in this, not me. And I felt His peace descend once again.

As we walked up the aisle to the front, I couldn't help notice that the church was jam-packed. Then, when I heard the pastor whisper to Lettie that they estimated there was about 1,200 people there, my eyes widened, and I started to panic.

But all at once they burst into applause. I was overwhelmed — and grateful. I knew that they were really applauding God's work in Medjugorje; I was just His messenger. And I felt the Blessed Virgin Mary's presence, a feeling of approval that I was fulfilling my commitment to spread the message she was bringing from her Son. I smiled and waved and was now anxious to begin.

The moment I started to speak, I realized that God was answering my prayer and giving me the words. I didn't know what I was going to say next, but it poured out of me, and always it was just exactly right.

We had a question-and-answer period afterwards, and that, too, was as electric as the talk. It seemed that each question was something that must have been on a great many people's minds. And by the grace of God, He seemed to be giving me answers that shed light and brought help.

Finally the pastor held up his hand and said, "This will have to be the last question. Wayne is speaking at another church tonight, and we don't want him to be worn out — or late!" I looked at him, surprised. It seemed like barely half an hour had passed, instead of three times that long.

When I came down off the podium after the closing hymn, the pews emptied as people surged forward, all asking questions at the same time and requesting that I pray for them. I was in a daze. Never had I experienced anything like this! I felt embarrassed and happy at the same time, and somehow detached, as if I were standing away somewhere looking at what was happening . . . .

I attempted to concentrate on one person at a time. A lady began, tears in her eyes, saying how much she appreciated the talk and then went right into a complicated family problem. There were many such one-to-one exchanges, one right after another. After about 30 minutes, Lettie gently but firmly reminded me that we had to go immediately, as we were already running late. And so we practically had to fight our way out of there.

The next church, also Catholic, was smaller, but it was even more packed than the first one. Some 900 people were waiting, we were informed, as we approached the front door. Happily Terri arrived right behind us, and was I glad to see her! But as she saw the people standing in the back and the aisles, she was taken back. "My gosh!" she gasped under her breath, "I don't believe this!"

And then, as we made our way up the aisle, she gripped my arm tightly and whispered teasingly, "What are you going to tell all these people?"

"Terri," I whispered back, "don't say that!" And I began to think: am I going to say the same things I said at the afternoon session?

There was the same sense of anticipation and the strong presence of God, as there had been before. I had just gotten started when the priest came up and said, "I'm sorry to have to interrupt, but we have a problem; there are a dozen cars outside, parked in the no-parking zone. The police have warned us about this in the past, and we don't want them to come and start towing cars away, so we're going to have to move them now. Here are the license plates. . . ."

By the time he finished reading off the twelfth plate, and the twelfth person had made his way out of the pew, the electricity was gone. I tried to pick up where I had left off, but I felt bereft, like I was pushing a huge boulder up a steep hill. Only towards the end did that special Medjugorje feeling return, and I felt buoyant in my heart again. Once more the words came unbidden to my lips, as did tears to many eyes.

When I finished, the same thing happened as before: throngs of people pressed forward to say hello, to shake hands, to confide problems and ask for prayer. This time, I was able to stay a little longer with them.

On the way home Terri said softly to me, "That has got to be the best I have ever heard you speak."

I was startled, for she was not one for easy compliments. "After that interruption about the license plates," I replied, "I felt it was so hard. And it had been so easy before — it did not get easy again, until the very end."

"Well," she said, surprised, "that may have been so for you, but it was not so from where I sat. The whole thing was beautiful, just right. Now don't let that go to your head," she added with a quick smile.

The next day, Sunday, I spoke in the morning and afternoon. At the latter, incredibly, the talk was interrupted by the priest admonishing people about parking; it was another overflow crowd. Then, as a final treat, Lettie had arranged for me to speak at a Lutheran church that night, close by their home. "We did this for you," she said. "It's a brand-new church and a small one, so don't expect more than 40 or 50 people."

"Fine," I smiled, "whoever God wants there will be there."

As we were finishing dinner, she said, "There's one thing I forgot to mention: each time you've spoken, you've talked about the rosary and how much it means to you. Well so far, that's been fine. But tonight, since these people are Lutherans. . . well, maybe you should consider not mentioning the rosary."

"Why?" I asked, surprised. "I've also been emphasizing that the rosary is a prayer to Jesus and —"

"Yes, I know," she hastily added, "but this is a very delicate message. The Catholics are going to understand that, but possibly the Protestants won't."

Terri turned to me. "You know, I think she has a point."

"All right," I smiled, "but I'll just see what comes."

When we got to the church, I was grateful that it was the last session. Not having done this before, I had not realized how totally exhausting several days of speaking could be. Counting a radio interview, this was my sixth lecture in two days, and I honestly wondered whether I could get up for it. But then, it was a Lutheran church. . . and besides, it was not going to be me, I reminded myself.

The church was only half a mile or so away, and we got there in no time. But again there were so many cars parked on the road leading to it, that it took us longer to walk to the church after leaving the car, than it had to drive there. The pastor was excited when he greeted us: "We've got more than 400 people in there!"

"Remember," whispered Terri, as we went in, "no mention of the rosary!"

Hardly had she spoken, than a young Catholic woman named Eugenie, whom I had met in Medjugorje, came up and, looking around, said softly, "Wayne, if you want to tell them about the rosary, I've got a hundred of them here!" and she patted her large purse. I didn't look at Terri.

When I got to the front, there was no microphone; they had not expected anywhere near this large a crowd. No matter, I was confident the Holy Spirit would amplify as necessary. As we started the opening hymn, I realized how glad I was to be able to share this with my Lutheran people.

That night I had such a great burden for the Lutheran Church to come alive that I came on perhaps more strongly than I normally would have, emphasizing the need for more spirituality and that we had to open ourselves to the Holy Spirit. I was really getting into what was going on over in Medjugorje, when all at once about half-way through, I stopped. I was struck by a tremendous urge to tell them of the rosary.

Pulling mine out of my pocket, I held it up and said, "I'm going to tell you something: I pray this rosary every day. Now many of you don't even know what a rosary is, and many of you are going to look at this and say,

'That's Catholic.' " I paused. "Well, let me tell you, I don't look on this as being Catholic. To me this is a prayer to Jesus Christ. And that's how I pray it, as a prayer to Jesus. You go through the whole rosary, and it takes you right through His life, from His birth to the Crucifixion and the Resurrection. And if you do it prayerfully, not by rote, meditating on who He is and all that He has done, it cannot help but draw you closer to Him. You may not feel particularly close to Him when you start, but you'll be there by the time you're finished."

I glanced over at Terri who just rolled her eyes to heaven. "Of all the spiritual things to do with prayer that I have gotten out of Medjugorje," I concluded, "this is the one I cherish the most." I finished by pointing out that there was a young woman in the back who had a hundred rosaries and would be glad to give one to anyone who desired one.

As I finished the talk, they broke out in loud applause. And in the back, as they were announcing coffee and tea and doughnuts in one of the assembly rooms, there was a muffled commotion. People were mobbing Eugenie for rosaries! She told me later that they were gone in two minutes.

Instead of going for refreshments, I slipped outside. It was about the first time I had been alone in three days, and my heart was full, even though my body was exhausted. Then, all at once I was filled with absolute joy. I sensed that Mary was right next to me. Instinctively I knew she was there because of what I had said about the rosary, and that she was pleased. I resolved never to avoid talking about the rosary, if that was what the Holy Spirit was leading me to say.

That trip to New Orleans seemed to open a floodgate of speaking invitations, and I began to travel everywhere — Indianapolis, Pittsburgh, Philadelphia. . . . I enjoyed it immensely, regardless of how tiring it was. Because it was thrilling to see the hand of God working among His people.

And now, despite having to be away from home frequently, Terri approved. "Well," she said when I was complaining about how I was going to keep track of it all, "why don't you set up a trip every other week or so and try that?"

I knew what it was costing her to say that. It was not just the absence of a husband and a father; it meant she would have to run the printing company pretty much alone. She would be left with all the problems and the headaches. . . . I just looked at her and shook my head.

By Easter of '87, my dream of reaching a million copies of the columns had been surpassed — by an additional million! The volume of orders just kept increasing. It now took three printing plants to keep up with them, and one day Terri mused aloud, "You know, maybe the columns really are the book you're supposed to write. I realize you've been through this before, but — "

I vigorously shook my head. "No, Terri, I've got to write the book; maybe now's not the time, but it has to be done."

Meanwhile, traveling and speaking was more important. It was time to take the message on the road.

*"I urge you to offer every sacrifice with love.
I desire that you who are helpless
begin with trust. . . ."*

25

Mary Margaret

There were two other trips in the spring of '87 that were notable. The first was to Nashville, Tennessee, where I had been invited by the Dominican Sisters of Aquinas Junior College. I had made it clear when I journeyed to New Orleans, that there were no fee requirements — only air fare and a place to stay. That would be the standard wherever I traveled to speak about Medjugorje.

I was shocked to find it would cost over $500 to fly to Nashville, as was my contact at Aquinas, Sister Mary Louis, for the announcements had already gone out, and the college's auditorium was booked.

"We only have $250," she said plaintively, "but we really want you to come — I don't know what we can do."

"Don't worry about it, Sister," I answered, "We'll pick up the balance." She met me at the airport, and I found her to be a wonderful, humble nun. That evening I had the privilege to address an assembly of Dominican Sisters. What could a lay Protestant, I thought as I began, possibly have to say that would inspire a group of women who had dedicated their lives to total service to God? Somehow I was able to overcome my initial hesitancy and relate to them the story and beauty of Medjugorje's message. Again, the Holy Spirit was strongly present, and the time spent with these special daughters of God was mutually rewarding. I realized afterwards that they were like any other group; they had needs, fears, doubts and a desire to know of the miracles that confirm God's love for mankind.

The next afternoon I spoke at the college and was scheduled to give another talk that evening. As was becoming standard, the auditorium was packed, surprising only in that it was an afternoon talk. When I finished, a woman pushed her way through the throng of people that crowded around me, and grabbed my arm. "Wayne, you don't know me, but I've just returned from Medjugorje with a group of people from here. . ."

"That's wonderful! I'm glad you were able to go and see — "

"Excuse me," she interrupted hurriedly, "but I'm double-parked, and I've been sent by several members of the group to tell you that we want you to come to dinner this evening, and we can't accept a no; so I'll pick you up here at five, and I promise to have you back in time for your talk tonight — is that okay, Sister?" she asked Sister Mary Louis who was standing next to me and was as dumbfounded as I was.

"Well," she said, looking at me with a shrug and a smile, "it's up to Mr. Weible."

"I guess it's okay," I said weakly, for I did feel an inner urge telling me to accept this unusual invitation, even though I didn't want to leave the campus area. This business of being "wanted" by so many people didn't set well with me, and I would have just as soon gone to my room and enjoyed a couple of hours of quiet time.

"Great!" she exclaimed. "I'll pick you up right outside the auditorium at five sharp."

True to her word, Mollie Gavigan, as she introduced herself, was there at the stroke of five. As we drove to her home, she gave me a little background on the pilgrimage from which seventy people from Nashville had just returned.

"Most of us went because of a couple here, Gino and Jeannie Marchetti," she began. "They have a little two-year-old daughter, Mary Margaret, who has Cystic Fibrosis. Jeannie went, hoping that Mary Margaret might get into the apparition room and be healed."

She went on to tell me that a reporter and a camera-man from one of the local TV stations had accompanied the group to do a special report, concentrating on the Marchetti family and their dream of a miracle cure for their daughter.

The group had found the weather there in early March to be terribly cold and windy, yet they were warmed, as so many had been before them, by the extraordinary hospitality of the villagers with whom they stayed. My good friend, Father Svetozar, had once again come into the picture. They had met him on one of the roads there and recognizing him, had asked him to pray over Mary Margaret for a healing. Father Svet, in his simple and humble way, had told Jeannie that it would be better to pray for happiness for her child, rather than for a healing.

"Jeannie really was disappointed," Mollie added. "She had read and heard so much about Father Svetozar, she just knew that he could bring about this miracle."

On the day before the group was to leave, the Marchetti family had gained entrance to the little bedroom-office in the rectory to be present for an apparition of the Blessed Virgin Mary. When it was over, Gino and Jeannie realized that the real miracle was *their* healing; they could now accept their daughter's condition. While Mary Margaret returned home still suffering from the symptoms of Cystic Fibrosis, the Marchetti family accepted God's will no matter what it entailed.

"That's beautiful, Mollie," I murmured, touched that once again the miracle of Medjugorje was focusing on our acceptance of life as it was. How I wanted everyone to know of this, and to concentrate on that aspect of Medjugorje's apparitions, and not on the phenomena and such holy mysteries as rosary chains changing to a golden color, or the sun spinning, or the cross disappearing from the top of Mt. Krizevac. Medjugorje was simply a gift of God's infinite love for each of us.

But having arrived at Mollie's home and spending a few minutes with Jeannie who was holding Mary Margaret in her arms, I noticed she was having a hard time keeping her emotions in check. Finally losing the battle, she began to cry openly. "Could I just talk to you — alone somewhere?" she asked through her tears.

We immediately went into a back bedroom. Mary Margaret was such a strange contrast to her mother's distress; she sat in Jeannie's lap, calm and happy.

"Listen, I know that God gave us the grace of being able to accept my baby's condition; and I do. But is it wrong for me to keep asking that she be healed of this disease?" Jeannie lowered her eyes to her child and added quietly, "maybe I'm not grateful enough for what God has already given us with our trip there."

What could I possibly say or do for this woman? Who could really know the suffering of a mother for her child, other than another mother? I heard myself saying, "Jeannie, it's not wrong for you to continue to want Mary Margaret healed; what you must do though, is *fully* accept the will of God, and love her and thank God for her regardless of her condition. . . ."

I paused, taken back at the words that had come so easily. It was easy for me — or anyone else who did not have to suffer through such an ordeal — to say these things. Yet it was clear: give Him complete surrender and accept whatever is given in life.

But there was also a strong feeling in my heart that this child would be healed, and I heard myself saying to her mother: "Mary Margaret's going to be well."

I reached into my coat pocket and took out my rosary. This particular rosary was like a part of me. It had been specially made for me by a very wonderful woman who lived a short distance from Myrtle Beach. She had given it to me as a special gift, having made it herself out of "Job's tears," a special seed that was ideal as beads for a rosary. I handed it to Jeannie. "Here, I want you to have this and to pray for Mary Margaret with it."

"Oh, I can't — "

"Yes, you must," I added. "Listen, I'm going to lay my hands on Mary Margaret and pray for her — now."

I couldn't believe I was doing this! Never before had I ever prayed over anyone, but something was telling me to do it. It was as though there was a war going on inside of me, for another voice seemed to be saying: "Are you crazy? Who do you think you are, giving this woman hope that her daughter will actually be healed?" After the prayer, I repeated to Jeannie that Mary Margaret was going to be okay.

We walked out of the room, happy, dazed — and on my part, more than a little frightened. What if Mary Margaret did not improve? What if I had given hope to this desperate mother, only to find out later. . . .

Yet inside, I knew everything was done as it was meant to be done.

We had a wonderful dinner, and the crowd for the talk at the college that evening was even more packed. I left Nashville the next day tired but happy.

A funny thing happened on the way home. The flight from Charlotte to Myrtle Beach was overbooked, and they needed volunteers to give up their tickets for a later flight.

Since it was Friday, and I was in no special hurry, I volunteered — and received in compensation a round-trip ticket good for any destination in the United States. It did not strike me until about half-way home that this free ticket was worth far more than the extra I had paid for my round-trip to Nashville. Once again, God had given far more than had been offered.

Three weeks later, as I was leaving my office on my way to the airport for a trip to Indianapolis, the phone rang. It was Jeannie Marchetti.

"Jeannie," I said, "much as I would love to talk, if I don't leave for the airport this second, I'm going to miss my flight. Look, I'll call you from Indianapolis, and—"

"Wayne! Mary Margaret is well!" she cried, her voice quavering with emotion. "She's well!"

My insides were churning, as I heard myself say to her, "Of course she is! I told you she would be okay."

"How did you know?" Jeannie was laughing and crying for joy at the same time. "I mean, after Father Svetozar prayed over her and then to get inside of the apparition room, and now — "

"Jeannie, the healing began at Medjugorje. You didn't understand Father Svet at the time, but when he said to pray for happiness, he was telling you to accept God's will, regardless of the outcome. I don't know how I knew, but the Spirit of God works in ways we simply can't comprehend. All I know is that I felt I was supposed to pray over her, and — I knew she'd be fine. I'll call you; I've got to go."

I hated to cut Jeannie short, but that plane was not going to wait — although I was so tremendously happy inside, I felt that I could get to Indianapolis without it. How wonderful to be used as an instrument of the gift of healing — and how frightening, as well!

I was met at the airport by Mary Ann Barothy, a public relations professional who had set up my tour of

Indianapolis. She informed me that we were going to drive to Terre Haute, to visit the convent at St. Mary of the Woods College, for a short talk. Once again, I would be addressing a group of nuns.

As I finished the talk, I thought of the gift of my rosary to Jeannie Marchetti. Still filled with wonder at Mary Margaret's improved condition, I told them her story and how I had felt compelled to pray over her. "You see," I concluded, "God takes a small gift like my rosary which meant so much to me, and in exchange, He gives this child and her parents the gift of happiness. Mary Margaret is going to be okay."

As we were saying our good-byes to the Mother Superior and some sisters outside of the room in which I had spoken, an elderly nun walked up to me, her hands extended. In them was a beautiful ruby-beaded rosary. "Take this," she said, her eyes filling with a beautiful light shining through tears. "I've had this rosary for more than 25 years; now I want you to take it — and give it to someone who needs a healing."

We were stunned. Almost automatically, I reached in my coat pocket and pulled out a small, wooden-beaded rosary fashioned out of plain cord. Terri had placed it in my pocket as I was preparing for my trip, telling me that she had brought it back from her trip in Medjugorje. "You might find someone who needs it," she had added casually.

"Here, Sister," I said, handing the rosary to her. "I'll give you this one in exchange; the Blessed Virgin Mary blessed it in the apparition room at Medjugorje."

It was as though time suddenly stood still — and we were all enveloped in a feeling of holiness that was beyond words. It was a feeling that lasted throughout the five-day tour of the Indianapolis area, and one that solidified my call: God did indeed want His message of love, renewed through the apparitions at Medjugorje, taken on the road.

"Pray in such a way that your prayer,
your surrender to God, may become
like a road sign. . . ."

26

Complete Surrender

I smiled as I prepared to go back to Medjugorje for the fourth time in a little over a year. The village had a way of doing that; once you'd been there, you had a yearning for more. Nowhere on earth was there another place with such a sense of peace.

But this time my desire to return was more than spiritual; I wanted to get some rest. The previous six months of non-stop travel, talks, and interviews had taken a toll. I was flat worn out and seriously in need of having all batteries recharged.

One thing would be different this time: I would be going with Global Group Tours, the organization that arranged the trips for the University of Steubenville. Before Medjugorje, I had never heard of the small Franciscan campus in the obscure coal town on the Ohio River. Now I knew it to be a spiritual powerhouse, where students literally put God first, and where continual revival seemed to be in progress. Student prayer groups met at all hours of the day and night, and a religious vocation was regarded as a viable career alternative. But most important to me was the fact that the university had committed itself to spreading the Medjugorje message, including group pilgrimages to the village.

The head of Global Tours was a man named Dale Krieger whom I had met first by phone, and later in person at New Orleans. Lean and lanky, Dale was an easy-going Southerner who looked and acted like nothing ever really fazed him — despite the uncertainty and unpredictability of the travel business. As I came to know him better, I realized that this remarkable calm was rooted in an unshakeable faith that no matter what happened, God was in charge.

Dale had been brought to the crux of his faith by the tragic death of his 18-year-old daughter after an automobile accident. As he waited in the hospital, praying for her, he came to grips with his own belief. Up to that time, he had not given much more than lip service to his Catholic faith. During the subsequent period of recovery following her loss, he rediscovered his love of Jesus — which would later lead to active involvement in taking pilgrims to Medjugorje.

From the start we had hit it off, and it seemed right that I make my next trip with his group. My plan was to fly over with them in the latter part of July, then stay an extra week, before returning home with another of his groups. I would still be on my own for the duration of the stay — or so I thought.

When we got to Dubrovnik, I again went to the car-rental booths — and discovered that in eight months the prices had more than doubled! Apparently the rental agencies, realizing that Medjugorje-bound pilgrims who desired independence would not balk at exorbitant prices, were charging all that the traffic would bear. And that was only a harbinger of changes to come.

When Global's bus (with me on board) crossed the bridge into Medjugorje, I hardly recognized the place. Lining the road now were tourist offices and cafes, and souvenir booths hawking everything from plastic Madonna statues to pizzas; many items for sale had nothing whatever to do with Medjugorje. Stunned, I asked Dale what had happened.

He explained that the majority of the merchants were itinerant Gypsies who had no particular interest in Medjugorje — but a great deal of interest in the money of the pilgrims it attracted. These Gypsies had steadily moved in and established stands until they were only about fifty yards from the church itself. The priests had strenuously objected and were trying to have them removed, but so far the Government had not exactly been supportive.

As our bus waited in line in what had become an ongoing traffic snarl, I happened to look out the window as a Gypsy woman got out of a Mercedes (!), from the back seat of which she extracted a doll and a blanket. As I stared in disbelief, she wrapped the doll in the blanket so its details could not be seen. And then, looking around, she assumed a sad-eyed expression and stuck out her hand. It was soon filled with dollars by the first group of pilgrims to pass by.

Feeling sick, I told Dale what I had just witnessed. He shrugged and said that the priests were warning the pilgrims not to give money to the beggars, but beyond that there was little they could do. People felt that they were doing what the Blessed Virgin Mary's messages were asking of them, so they continued to give to the bogus poor.

I shook my head. What was happening to this village that I loved and regarded as my spiritual home? It was being turned into a commercial circus by a pack of thieves who had to drive long distances to get there. I wondered if the new pilgrims would be able to find the holiness that had led to the conversion of millions in the past six years.

There were more disquieting surprises in store. After settling in at the home of Grgo Vasilj, where I would be staying, I headed for St. James. The church had always been an oasis of tranquility for me, regardless of what might be going on outside. As usual, there were clusters of people in the grove in front of the church. All at once, one pointed towards me, and they came from all sides, asking questions and snapping pictures.

I was flabbergasted — and embarrassed. Terri had warned me that with three million copies of the columns out there, my days of public privacy might be over, but I was totally unprepared for this.

I was finally able to disengage myself and make my way up the steps to the church. Others started towards me, but I pretended not to see them and hurried into St. James, which fortunately was between services and relatively empty. Going to the pew in front of the statue of the Blessed Virgin Mary on the right side, I knelt down and bowed my head and thanked God for bringing me back. In less than a minute, I felt a tap on my shoulder. I turned and looked up into the face of a middle-aged woman with a bag on her shoulder from a tour agency I'd never heard of. She was beaming down at me, while her husband stood behind her.

"Excuse me," she began, "you *are* Wayne Weible, aren't you? The Protestant who wrote the articles on Medjugorje?"

I nodded, forcing a weak smile.

"I'm sorry to bother you, but I had to thank you: you've changed our lives! You're the reason we're here! A friend gave me your columns, and that did it. For the first time in my life, my faith means something to me. We just had to come."

I nodded and thanked her, and turned back to my prayers, looking beseechingly at the beautiful statue of Mary. "Blessed Mary," I blurted out under my breath, "I don't want all of this attention!" I had come here to rest, to get away. What had happened to the peace here? I looked at the statue's face, almost wanting to ask for a smile, a gesture. . . .

The response was not at all what I expected. Suddenly I once again felt the Blessed Virgin speak to me: *Why are you looking for me in signs? I am everywhere you are. Go out to the people and do what you said you would do.*

I got up and walked out of the church, feeling about two inches tall. Being a messenger for God, I realized, was a 24-hour-a-day, 365-day-a-year calling. It was not just when an audience was applauding or the TV lights were on. It was whenever and wherever the message was needed, in season or out, whether it was convenient or inconvenient. People's lives were changing, and every possible encouragement was needed to make those changes stick. Meekly I vowed to learn tolerance and patience and to be an interested listener, no matter how tired I was or how inane the questions.

Outside the church, people again crowded up, and this time I went out of my way to visit with them. There were groups from California, Alabama, Phoenix. . . and in each it seemed important to people to let me know the role that the columns had played in their decision to come. I was glad now — glad for them, and glad for my call.

Someone asked, "If we can arrange a time with our tour leader, will you speak to our group?"

"Well, yes, but I just got here, so you'll have to get back to me ."

"Is there any time you would prefer?"

"Other than the English Mass in the morning and the Croatian Mass in the evening, any time is fine."

"Where would you like to speak?"

I remembered the Caritas group whom I had spoken to on my last trip had preferred the grove behind the church. "Do you know that little cemetery in the cedar grove on the path to Mt. Krizevac? We'll do it there at four o'clock."

The ancient cemetery with the breeze sighing through the tops of the evergreens had an incredible sense of peace and the presence of God. That afternoon, as I talked to them, I just poured out my whole heart.

After that, word got around quickly that I was in Medjugorje. I was asked to speak six more times that first week, and finally, when there were more requests than I could fill, someone urged me to see Father Philip Pavic, the American priest of Croatian heritage who was now stationed at Medjugorje, about speaking in St. James.

Father Philip, a large, grey-bearded theologian with warm, brown eyes that offset his imposing size, had been immersed in studies at Notre Dame in Paris after spending twelve years in the Holy Land, when the Blessed Mother had called him to Medjugorje. He was in charge of matters concerning English-speaking pilgrims. When I got over my embarrassment and explained my predicament, he arranged for me to speak in St. James on Thursday afternoon. Father Svet usually came down from Konjic to speak on Thursdays, but this week he would be coming on Friday instead, so it would work out perfectly.

I was thrilled — and scared. Not in my wildest dreams could I have imagined receiving such a privilege.

In the meantime, there were previous speaking obligations to fulfill. One was for the Center for Peace group, headed again by Sister Margaret and assisted by Bernie and Ellen Hanley. I was delighted to discover that Rita Klaus and her family had come as guests of the Center. Just a little over a year after her miraculous over-night healing of Multiple Sclerosis, Rita was finally able to come to the little Village of Apparitions.

Bernie had asked the two of us to give talks to their group at a special luncheon. Rita spoke first and ended in tears; in fact, the entire group was in tears. As I began, I found it to be the most difficult speaking assignment I had yet faced. I was simply overwhelmed by Rita's words, as well as by the role that the Center for Peace had played in my own involvement. Then, in the middle of the talk, *I* broke down in tears. That had never happened before, and I was embarrassed — until I realized that everyone else was crying, too. It was an emotion-filled luncheon, but one that accented the goodness of God, as these were tears of happiness.

Afterwards, Rita agreed to sit down with me and give me some additional background material for my book. She came from "a *very* Catholic family," as she put it, and had felt a calling from God at the tender age of eight years. At 16, she had entered a convent in Omaha, Nebraska, and had served five years as a novice, before taking her vows. During all this time she was afflicted with a progressive illness which was finally diagnosed as Multiple Sclerosis.

"The worst part," she continued, "was that the Mother Superior didn't believe me. I looked healthy, but I suffered days of dizziness and sometimes couldn't even walk up the stairs. She thought I just wanted special attention."

Rita eventually had to leave the convent and was deeply distressed. She didn't understand why this was happening to her, when she wanted so badly to serve God as a nun. Other problems began to surface. She could not find employment because of her condition. Finally, her doctor told her not to tell potential employers that she had MS. He felt that she would have at least five or six years of stability, and that her best bet would be to go to the East or West Coast to live. "I had done some teaching in the convent, so I decided to go to Pennsylvania, attend school, and get my degree. I found a job that would allow me to teach in the daytime and go to school at night."

Eventually Rita met her husband Ray, and after a long courtship they were married. Life seemed to be progressing well, but she was bitter towards the Church. She still went to Mass, but it was more out of habit than desire. Later, when the disease finally overcame all of her efforts to combat it, she became depressed and withdrawn. "I tried everything but prayer. Our marriage settled down, and Ray was great. We had three children, but still, I had this terrible bitterness that life had dealt me such a bad deal."

I nodded — and wondered how many wounded souls that described.

"As you know, the turning point came in 1981, when a friend invited me to go to a healing service with her. Ray said I'd tried everything else, so why not this?" She shook her head at how casual it had all been.

"So, I went. And once I got there, I wished I hadn't come. I just knew that people were staring at me, and I wanted the floor to open up and swallow me. Then, as the priests were coming up the aisle, one of them grabbed me from behind and began praying over me. He prayed and prayed. I was mortified and kept thinking what is going on here? But a great sense of peace came over me — and I began praying with him. It was the first time in a long, long time that I had felt this way. I knew it was a spiritual healing. I no longer cared about the disease: whatever God wanted, I would accept, and I would be happy."

I sat there mesmerized by Rita's complete surrender to God's will. This again, was the key to the message coming out of Medjugorje. Rita's surrender had developed into a glorious witness of God's all-giving love in her physical healing. But what was far more evident was the beauty of her spiritual healing. She and her whole family now belonged totally to God.

"And of course, you know the rest: on that night of June 18, 1986, I asked God to heal me of whatever I needed to be healed, and the next day, I was no longer a victim of MS."

I stared at her, my eyes widening. Then I shut off the tape recorder and got up and took a few steps away.

"What's the matter?" she asked, startled.

I just waved my hand, unable to speak. That *date!* That was the date on the back of the photograph!

I told her about the photo of Jesus that Maureen Thompson and I had found on top of Mt. Krizevac, how it had been perfectly dry when everything else was soaked with dew; how it had that date, June 18, 1986, written on the back of it — and nothing else. And how we had found it on May 7, more than six weeks earlier.

Rita and I sat there for a long time without speaking. There was no doubt in either of our hearts that it was somehow connected with her healing. But, I realized, the mystery of the date was not important — not compared to the total surrender of her will to God's will. Surrender — that was the real key to our new lives as Medjugorje messengers.

As always, my time in Medjugorje was fruitful. On that trip which had been intended for rest, I wound up giving fifteen talks, including one of the most important I would ever give — in St. James Church on a hot Thursday afternoon.

About an hour before I was due to speak, I sat down on the ground outside the church and rested my back against its cool stone exterior. My mind was anything but cool, as I gazed at the Gypsy booths lining the road to the church. Their owners were busily hawking their wares, imparting a feeling within me that was anything but conducive to preparation for a talk on the ongoing miracle of Medjugorje.

And then, as I tried to concentrate and pray, asking the Holy Spirit to give me the words I would need, a beggar woman came up to me, with three dirt-smudged little children trailing behind her. She held out her hand, and when I didn't seem to notice her, she tapped her extended palm demandingly with the finger of her other hand.

Well, I knew that the priests discouraged us from giving to the Gypsy beggars, but — what if this one were an angel in disguise?

I reached into my pocket and pulled out everything that was there — about four thousand dinari (equivalent to seven dollars).

She took it and shook her head. "No, no," she said, "*dollar,*" and she held out her hand again.

"That's all I have," I answered, amazed that she would ask for more.

"No!" she retorted. "You give me dollar."

I looked at her, not believing what I was hearing, and she turned her hand over to show me what she meant. In it was a roll of dollar bills that must have been three inches thick. Pointing to them, she demanded, "You give me dollar!"

I just shook my head and waved her away. But seeing the gold cross which hung around my neck, she now reached for it and said, "You give me this!"

Now I was getting mad. I got to my feet to shoo her away, but the young children began grabbing my hand and rubbing their little bellies and crying. It was obvious they had been coached by their mother — if, indeed, she was their mother. I quickly left and went around in back of the church to get away from her, now thoroughly depressed. She may have been something in disguise, but it was no angel.

I now began to pray in earnest, and eventually I was at peace again. I was even grateful for this squalid incident, and especially its timing, for it showed me so clearly that despite all the carnal commercialism of the hustling "real" world that was encroaching on Medjugorje, the beautiful core of spirituality — the unique touch of Jesus — was intact. That was the deep ocean current; the rest was merely surface distraction.

I slipped into the church through the rear entrance, and after a brief introduction by Father Philip Pavic, I went to the podium. And froze. I was used to being a member of the congregation, when the church was so full one could barely move. I was not used to seeing it that way from the opposite perspective. This holy place.
. . what could I possibly —

Not *me*, I reminded myself. *God* had brought me here. He had opened the door and filled the church. Now, by His Spirit, He would provide the words He would have them hear. All I had to do was open my mouth and speak them.

I gave one of the most complete talks on Medjugorje I had ever given. It was well received, and afterwards Father Philip gave me a tape of it for Terri. I thanked him, never realizing that, like the columns, there would eventually be countless thousands of copies, distributed around the world.

I wasn't the only one to get a copy of the tape that day. In the audience was Mary O'Sullivan, from Ireland. She, too, had asked Father Philip for a copy — which she took back to Ireland, where she had it produced and on the market in a matter of days, using the proceeds to bring priests to Medjugorje. By the time I made my first trip to Ireland, more than 15,000 copies had been sold.

So far this trip had been anything but restful. But I didn't mind — it had become a time of complete surrender.

27

Controversy from Within

On Sunday, we were in for a special treat. It was the parish's annual Confirmation Sunday, and as was traditional, the Bishop of Mostar would be coming to Medjugorje to administer the first Eucharist to the class of young confirmands. It was a gala occasion, one of the most festive days of the year for the village.

There was an added sense of excitement because of the bishop's presence. Since the early days of the apparitions, Pavao Zanic, Bishop of Mostar, had waged a steady campaign to discredit them. His stance had created confusion, uncertainty and outright rejection of the authenticity of the phenomena by many Catholic priests and religious, and this, in turn, had affected the acceptance by clergy and lay people of other faiths.

The bishop's opposition was hard to understand in the face of so much good fruit coming from Medjugorje. For me and literally millions of others, the apparitions were a joyous and hope-filled confirmation of the message of Jesus. How could the leading local authority of the Catholic Church oppose them? Not only did he not believe in them, but he had become their most bitter and zealous opponent.

The irony was, in the beginning Bishop Zanic had been a strong advocate of the apparitions. Such was his interest that he visited the parish five times in those first weeks — much to the chagrin of Father Jozo, pastor of St. James, who at the time had his hands full. The last thing he needed was the bishop's visits adding to the confusion. Still, he had invited Bishop Zanic to celebrate the Mass on July 25 which was the Feast of St. James, the church's patron saint.

In the bishop's homily during this Mass, he proclaimed his belief for all the world to hear:

Six simple children like these would have told all in half an hour, if anybody had been manipulating them. I assure you that none of the priests have done any such thing. . . . Furthermore, I am convinced the children are not lying. . . .

One thing is certain: something has stirred in people's hearts. Confession, prayer, reconciliation between enemies — that is a most positive step forward. All the rest we must leave to Our Lady, to Jesus, and the Church, which one day will most certainly give its opinion on the matter.

These were strong words indeed from a man who would later deem the apparitions to be a hoax, perpetuated by the Franciscans. Father Jozo had warned the bishop not to commit himself too soon, for, as he later reflected, he sensed the bishop was a man who made his mind up quickly and then refused to change it.

Bishop Zanic was not a Franciscan, and therein, perhaps, lay the root of his opposition. In September, 1980, the year before the apparitions began, as the newly-named Bishop of Mostar, he immediately began shifting the parishes in his diocese from Franciscan to secular authority (ie., under no particular order). The Franciscan priests, many of whom had served these parishes for years, were outraged, as were the vast majority of their parishioners. At their specific request, many of the

Franciscan priests continued to minister to the needs of the people.

When the bishop learned that the Franciscans were ignoring his orders, he retaliated by making an example of two popular young priests, initiating action to have them expelled from their order and from the priesthood. This created a furor between his office and the local Franciscans.

Here, the story took a strange twist. Shortly after the apparitions began, the visionaries were persuaded to bring the matter of the two young priests before the Blessed Virgin Mary. Even more surprising was the fact that she commented on the problem. According to the visionaries, the Madonna stated that the Bishop had been "misled and misinformed," and should "reconsider" his banning of the two young Franciscan priests who were innocent of any wrongdoing.

That did it. When Bishop Zanic learned of this alleged message, he exclaimed, "The Blessed Mother of God would never speak to a bishop that way!" From that moment on, he became a resolute foe of the apparitions.

In January, 1982, the bishop set up a commission to study the apparitions objectively and thoroughly, so that the Church could make a final ruling on their authenticity after they ceased. The commission was composed of four men who announced they would be going to Medjugorje to investigate and interview everyone concerned. It was known beforehand that three of them were opposed to the apparitions. As it turned out, they did little; only one member, Franciscan priest Ivan Dugandzic, visited Medjugorje regularly.

Two years later, a new commission was established to replace the original, since the first had done nothing except irritate the Vatican with their lackadaisical approach to the investigation. The new commission was expanded to fourteen and included members of the medical profession. The mixture, however, was no more balanced than before: at least ten members were known opponents of Medjugorje. The bishop appointed himself as commission president and chairman, and went on record as declaring: "I *am* the Commission," adding that he would "crush the apparitions."

The commission did not disappoint him. In April of '86, he traveled to Rome, to present its preliminary findings, rumored to be negative. But there, the Bishop of Mostar received a shock. On his return home, it was reported that he confided to some pilgrims that Cardinal Joseph Ratzinger, head of the Congregation for the Doctrine of the Faith, had chastised him. Allegedly the Cardinal told him he disapproved of his methods of investigation and asked him not to make a judgment on the apparitions at that time.

Shortly thereafter, in an unprecedented move, the Vatican dissolved Bishop Zanic's commission and established a new commission, comprised of all the bishops of Yugoslavia (BCY) and headed by its cardinal. They, and they alone, were given the authority to set up a new study of the apparitions, after which they would make an official recommendation to the Pope. In the meantime, as the new BCY commission set about gathering its evidence (which could take several years), the Bishop of Mostar was expressly instructed not to involve himself further in the matter of the apparitions, about which he was to maintain silence.

While the Church's official stance would be some time in coming, unofficially, it was supportive. By all reports, the fruit of Medjugorje's apparitions had been uniformly good; people's lives *were* being changed. Medjugorje information centers were springing up all over the world by pilgrims who had come and seen, and were now trying to do what the Madonna was asking, by spreading the message. One unique aspect of the Medjugorje experience was the broad spectrum of people affected; doctors, attorneys, engineers — rich and poor, men and women from all walks and social structures. All seemed affected in a like manner.

In the light of so much positive evidence, the Pope's own reaction was hardly surprising. In a public audience the year before, a dozen Italian bishops had asked him if they should permit their parishioners to go to Medjugorje. His response was widely reported: "Why do you even ask the question? If they are converting, praying, fasting, going to confession and doing penance, let them go to Medjugorje!"

But the more pilgrims who came to do just that, the more it irked Bishop Zanic. Against the Vatican's orders, he continued to make inflammatory denunciations, and any journalist who wanted a debunking interview by a church authority knew where he could get one. Officially, the bishop continued to thwart what he now considered to be a Franciscan conspiracy in any way that he could.

Yet recently there had been hope for improvement in the relations between the diocesan office and the parish. For the past few months the bishop had made no unusually derogatory statements, and several priests from Medjugorje had been to visit him on small matters without friction. In fact, he had been more than just civil; he had been downright genial. So, maybe there *was* hope. Maybe the peace of Medjugorje was descending to cover even this volatile situation. Everyone I talked to was hoping that this Sunday would mark the first step on the path of reconciliation. Surely, the bishop would have kind words for these young confirmands on such a happy occasion.

On Sunday, as soon as the English Mass was over, I found Bernie Hanley, and we hurried out to get a glimpse of the infamous Bishop Zanic, who would be trailing the procession of confirmands and priests to the large outdoor campsite where Mass would be held for this celebration. The sky was clear, the sun brilliant, and the young people were all dressed in white with blue sashes, and all smiling. The priests were smiling, too — in fact, everyone was. Except Bishop Zanic. Short and stout, and regaled in mitre and crozier and the full ceremonial vestments of his office, he decidedly was not smiling.

At Father Pervan's signal, the procession began, led by an upraised cross which was followed by the children, the priests, and the bishop — and Bernie and me at a discreet distance. At the campground an outside altar was waiting, along with the entire village, dressed and scrubbed at its Sunday best. They were joined by numerous relatives from nearby villages and towns. Watching respectfully from the perimeter of the grounds were many of the pilgrims then in Medjugorje. All told, the congregation numbered more than a thousand.

Bernie was holding his camera up in the air above his head, trying to get pictures, while I prayed, Lord, please, open this Bishop's heart and his mind. Fill him with the Holy Spirit. Let him understand how beautiful this is. Let him see how many people are here, and how many have come out to share in this occasion. Let him be touched by what You are doing in Medjugorje.

The Mass began with beautiful Croatian singing, some of the most inspiring I had heard; its power led me to believe that my prayer only echoed those in the hearts of many who were present. The Gospel reading went smoothly, and then Bishop Zanic stepped forward to give the homily. He spoke rapidly and emphatically, and while I did not understand the words, it was not hard to understand their meaning. He was shaking his finger, and his rising tone was growing increasingly intense.

I had no trouble reading the crowd's response: all smiles had vanished, replaced by expressions of stony endurance. Something was wrong, terribly wrong. I glanced over at the Franciscan priests, men whom I had grown to know and admire. They were staring down at the ground, while Father Pervan looked straight ahead, unblinking, his expression revealing nothing.

I looked over at Bernie who was still busy taking pictures. "Bernie, something's not right here," I murmured. "This is more like a funeral than a confirmation service."

"I don't know what's going on," he whispered back, "but it's awfully quiet."

When the bishop paused in his diatribe, three men burst into applause. I glanced at the nearest one who was beating his hands together — until he realized that only two of the other thousand were doing likewise and quickly stopped.

By the time the bishop concluded his remarks, any lingering joy for the occasion was gone. Everyone just wanted it over. And when it was, instead of the cheerful visiting one might have expected, the people silently dispersed and went their separate ways.

But not all of them; a few, deeply hurt and angry that their children's first communion had been ruined, went up to the bishop and started to tell him exactly what they thought of him, until Father Pervan quickly intervened and sent them home.

Later, we ran into a Croatian tour guide we knew, who confirmed our suspicions. The bishop had proclaimed his opposition to Medjugorje's apparitions more strongly than he had ever stated it before. And the people? "They were angry," the tour guide related. "Some even told him to his face that he was a liar and that he was not welcome in their village."

I returned to Grgo Vaslij's home to find his family and friends enjoying a banquet in the courtyard of the house, celebrating the confirmation of Grgo's 13-year-old son Andrija. Through Marija, his oldest daughter who could speak English, I asked Grgo what he thought of the bishop's homily. With a grim smile, he and all of the others at the table who had heard the translation of my question turned their thumbs down.

Later, from a transcript of Bishop Zanic's remarks, I learned the reason why. At one point he accused the Franciscans in Medjugorje of perpetrating a deceitful lie: "He who preaches such untruths about God, Jesus, and Our Lady, to the faithful, deserves the lowest rung in hell!"

A dismayed Father Philip Pavic recalled, "People just kept silent. They could hardly believe what they were hearing. . . that the bishop, in mitre, crozier and full vestments from the altar, was imploring the Divine Right and consigning us to hell for an invention of a falsehood about Jesus, Mary, and God Himself."

The bishop interpreted the silence of the congregation as a sign of approval — "a sign that the people who live there are tired of it (the apparitions) and don't believe the story anymore."

Such an assessment was hardly borne out by the daily lives of the villagers. To me, the real tragedy was that after six years the Bishop stubbornly remained blind to all the good that had been done in the parish — not to mention around the world — as a result of the apparitions. Before them, none of the five hamlets had been able to get along with one another; now peace and harmony reigned in the mountain valley. Before, Mass attendance had been sparse; now it was so full that they had to institute an early, before-work service to accommodate those who wanted to attend daily. And how did he explain the deepening devotion of the young people? At a time when elsewhere they were turning away from their parents' religion in droves, here they were leading the way back.

I recalled what he himself had said in the beginning: that such simple children could not possibly sustain a hoax under intensive interrogation for even half an hour. Well, how did he explain their story having held up for six years under unimaginably rigorous scrutiny and investigation?

As I walked slowly to church that evening, along the now-familiar pathway through the fields, I remembered the verse that to me best defined Mary's appearance in the little village: "Jesus said, I praise You, Father, Lord of heaven and earth, because You have hidden these things from the wise and the learned, and have revealed them to the merest of children. . . ." (Matthew 11:25).

28

The Mission Goes Abroad

Terri frowned as we pulled out of the airport parking area. "You look as tired as when you left; in fact," she added with a wry smile, "you look even more tired! I thought this trip was going to be an opportunity for you to get some rest."

I took a deep breath, then said, "I thought so, too. But I worked harder these last two weeks than any previous trip there. We need to sit down and have a serious talk about this mission I've been given."

She threw me a smile, seeming to ignore my last comment. "I'm anxious to hear about what happened: did you have any time with Father Svet?"

"I mean really talk, Terri. About everything."

She nodded again, no longer smiling. "Okay, we'll do it this evening, after the children are in bed."

As that time approached, I was not looking forward to it. While Terri had been as openly supportive as anyone could ask, it was the things she *wasn't* saying that were getting to me. Whenever I told her of a planned speaking trip or a return to Medjugorje, I could sense her disappointment. After eleven years together, she didn't have to say anything; I knew exactly how she felt. And lately, as the tempo increased and the speaking engagements grew more frequent and further away, her subconscious resentment was beginning to leak out in little side comments.

Of course, I was not always as considerate as I should have been. I would forget that each person came to God at their own pace, at the pace they were comfortable with, and in my desire to "help her along," I had become a little too critical at times.

Well, it wasn't going to get better; in fact, it was going to get a whole lot worse. That was what we had to talk about.

I didn't plan how I was going to say it; once I started, it just poured out. I began by telling her that the most important thing that happened on this trip was that I had received a much sharper vision of my call, and what my mission would be. Or rather, what it was going to cost — all of us. Because it was going to pick up. "I'm going to be doing more and more traveling around this country — and out of this country. I'm going to be going back to Medjugorje more often. And at the same time I've got to get the book done."

I stood up, too excited to stay seated. "I've never felt such a sense of urgency — about all of it. I've got to get out there and do absolutely as much as I can, and as fast as possible!" I looked down at my wife. "So — there's going to have to be a tremendous sacrifice from all of us — me, you, and the kids."

"Well," she said calmly, "I can accept that. But you have to understand something: you're human. You can only do so much. Mary doesn't want you to go out there and burn yourself out. If you do, you're not going to be of any use to her or us or anyone!"

I could see her point — but I knew what had to be done. So, I hesitated before replying and then said in as reasonable a tone as I could manage, "I'm not worried about burning out. Spiritually or mentally I don't think I ever could. All I'm saying is, this is the way it's going to be for awhile. And listen, it's not going to be fun for me, either. I love my son and daughter — and their mother — and my other children. And I'm not going to be able to see you or them as often as I would like. . . . and they're already saying, 'Dad's crazy, running off doing all these silly things!' "

That had become a real sore point. My four older children were definitely products of our times; they did not go to church and happily embraced the new philosophy of, "If it feels good, do it!" I had pleaded with them to try to understand that their father had received a message straight from heaven, and of course I wanted them to benefit from it. But whenever I raised the possibility of their going to church, I was usually met with that here-he-goes-again look.

Lisa, my oldest, and the only one to have graduated from college, would at least listen and discuss it with me. But Angela couldn't understand what had happened to me. Several times she had called Terri to express her concern over her father, that I was actually a little touched in the head. My two sons, Michael and Steve, simply looked at me as having become a religious fanatic. Finally, Terri sat me down one evening and said, "Look: talking's not going to do any good with them; you just live it and pray for them to understand. That's what you've been given from Mary, the knowledge that you can turn to prayer for your needs. And that's what you talk about in your lectures: *live the message.* Try doing it with your kids!"

So now, with this new frustration, I should have known she would again come up with a sensible solution. She paused a few moments, then said, "Look, we'll make a simple deal, okay? I'll put up with all this, if you'll just do two things for me: first, get off my case about becoming spiritual — let me be the judge of what I need to do or not do to find spirituality; second, when you're home, remember that you're a husband and a father. Put us on the front burner, okay? Then we'll let everything else take care of itself. I'll hold the fort at home, and you go out there and be the 'holy man' Mary wants you to be."

She was smiling mischievously, her eyes were dancing as she said it; knowing how much I disliked that expression, she deliberately used it whenever she wanted to really get my attention. She had definitely gotten my attention.

I laughed. "Okay, okay! Just don't call me that!" Silently I thanked God for the grace of such a wise and understanding partner, and truly she would be a full partner in this mission. I thought of the scriptural account of Jesus sending His disciples out, two by two; that was how I viewed *our* mission.

In the coming months there would be plenty for both of us to do. By early fall, to my utter dumbfoundment the number of column-tabloids shipped passed the four-million mark — and they were now going out at an incredible 70,000 *a week!* I was traveling everywhere — trips were being planned for Ireland, Trinidad, even Alaska, as well as practically all of the States. If there was ever any place that I had one day hoped to see, it looked like that wish was going to come true in the next couple of years.

And there was more radio and television — my appearance on the Sally Jessy Raphael show seemed to open the gates for interview invitations. The one that blessed me the most was being Mother Angelica's guest on her national television program in Birmingham, Alabama. I was already impressed by her from all I had read and learned from those who knew her. Here was this cloistered nun who had felt called to get the Gospel of Jesus out by starting a television station, which she did.

It was incredible because she had no money, and no direction from her order to do this. She just decided she was going to do it. This charismatic nun would see pieces of equipment in studios during interviews and say, "That's just what I need!" And she would keep talking to people, until finally she started gathering all these little pieces together. The next thing she knew, she was on the air.

There were many bumps along that road, but God was with them, and those sisters knew how to pray. Today, via satellite on her Eternal Word Television Network (EWTN), she had one of the widest audiences of any Christian talk show. That much I knew, and I also knew one of her producers, Jack Sacco, whom I had met in Medjugorje on the June '86 trip.

It was Jack who escorted me through the studios and took the time to tell me about Mother Angelica and her association with Medjugorje. After thoroughly researching the apparitions to ensure they were in line with church doctrine, she had been quick to make them known.

When I actually met my hostess that evening, half an hour before air-time, she was everything I had expected, and more. Mother Angelica was as open and friendly as anyone I had ever met, and in no time I felt as if we had been friends for years. She was also quite sharp and had a remarkable memory. As we talked, she mentioned several things from the columns, from which it was obvious she had read them carefully.

She couldn't get over the fact that a Lutheran would be doing something like this. I told her that what was happening over there was for everyone. "But let me tell you how something you said once was a great help to this Lutheran," I added. "I was listening to one of your tapes while driving to a talk one evening, when I heard you say: 'Never apologize for the Blessed Virgin Mary!'"

She laughed. "I've said that more than once."

"Well, it was like a knife going into me. Because I realized that up until then, in my talks to Protestants I had been down-playing her role. I would say to them that I didn't care if they believed it was Mary appearing, or some angel, but that something was definitely going on there. When I heard you say that, it struck me that out of ignorance, I was actually denying her, when I knew that it was she who was appearing there and who had called me."

Mother Angelica took my hand and beamed. "Wayne, we're going to have a beautiful program."

And we did. The studio was jam-packed with people wanting to see this Lutheran who had written about the Blessed Mother. A talk-show guest, I had found, could generally tell how an interview show was going by how quickly or slowly time seemed to pass. With her I was startled when we reached the end of the hour; it had seemed more like fifteen minutes. And it had been fun! As we had started the program, Mother Angelica, talking about the fact that literally anyone could be called to be a messenger, added, "In fact, God can pick up any dodo off the street and use him."

The studio audience started to giggle, and she paused and looked at them. Then she turned to me and hastily added, "Oh, I don't mean you!" The audience roared with laughter, and we joined them.

Afterwards, I felt like I could ask her for some personal counsel, and the following afternoon in her quarters I told her what was on my mind. I was awed and somewhat intimidated by the physical healings that had taken place in the course of this wonderful mission I had been given. I knew that she had experienced many gifts of the Holy Spirit, and I wanted advice. Everywhere I traveled, people would ask me to pray for them, and I would be happy to do so. Sometimes, the prayer request would be for physical healing, and — there had been healings. . . .

Quietly and with great serenity she explained. "The spiritual gifts of the Holy Spirit are just that: gifts. They're given to be used when they're needed, when we're called upon to use them. We don't hang out a sign that says, 'Healing Done Here' or 'Prophecy Spoken Here.' When you feel the leading from God, use the gift, then step back and wait until next time. That way, you know the gift comes from Him, and that it isn't you doing it."

She paused and looked me in the eye. "But the greatest gift you have is that you are Mary's messenger."

I felt a profound sense of thanksgiving and humility hearing her say that. And a real sense of relief. I would never forget her advice.

Everything seemed to accelerate after that: in late September Milka Pavlovic, after finally receiving her visa, came for a three-month visit. The only trouble was that due to a mix-up in her picking up her ticket in Dubrovnik, her departure had been delayed a week. Which meant that when she finally did arrive, I barely had time to meet her plane in New York and take her home, before having to leave the next day for a nine-day speaking tour in Ireland. I was more than a little worried about that, for Milka knew hardly any English. But fortunately she and Terri hit it off, and by the time I got home, she was really enjoying herself and felt very much at home with the family.

Meanwhile, I had fallen in love with Ireland. Thanks in no small measure to the advance-work of Mary O'Sullivan, there was considerable curiosity about this American Protestant who talked about the Blessed Mother appearing in Yugoslavia. The phenomenon was not exactly new to them; they had had their own visitation by the Blessed Mother — at the town of Knock. A strange and wonderful thing happened, as my plane prepared to land at Shannon. Having been so rushed to pick up Milka, I'd had little time to really think about my trip to Ireland. I was beginning to get excited as I peered out of the window at the beautiful, green countryside. Then, once again I heard that now-familiar gentle message from the Madonna: *Go to Knock.* The funny thing was, although I had read about the apparition at Knock (there had been only one appearance), I didn't know that Knock was located in Ireland!

So, when I was met by Sean Conroy, a jovial and dedicated Irishman whom I had first met in Medjugorje, I asked him, "Sean, is the Knock Shrine far from here?"

He looked at me, his head tilted. "Why do you ask?"

"Well, I'd really like to go there, if it's at all possible."

"Funny you should bring that up: we were planning to take you there, but then your schedule got so filled up that we dropped it out. But it's not that far from where you'll be staying tonight." He thought for a moment. "Tell you what: we'll drop off your bags at the home of the family you'll be staying with, grab a sandwich, and we'll drive you on up there right now!"

So we did. Knock was about sixty miles away, and on the way Sean filled me in about the pilgrimages people made to Knock.

Knock was one of the more fascinating of Mary's previous apparitions. It had occurred in 1879, during a fierce rain storm on August 21. More than 20 people saw the apparition which appeared on the side wall of the small church, and many viewed it for over two full hours. The Blessed Virgin Mary was life-size, and she was joined by two other figures whom the villagers identified as St. Joseph, and St. John, the Evangelist. The entire scene was bathed in a brilliant white light, and was untouched by the driving rain.

The other figures were not as big or as high as the Virgin Mary, who seemed to be about two feet off the ground. She stood erect, her hands elevated to shoulder height. She wore a large cloak of a white color, hanging in full folds and somewhat loosely gathered around her waist. She also wore a rather large crown on her head.

St. Joseph, who was described as having gray hair and beard, was bent slightly toward the Blessed Virgin, and St. John was to the right of her. He appeared to be a young man dressed in Mass vestments and holding a book in his left hand, while the other hand was raised in blessing.

But it was the scene in front of the figures which intrigued me the most. There appeared to be an altar on which was a young lamb. One of the villagers described the lamb as being covered in golden stars or small glittering lights. This was clearly a symbol of Christ, the Paschal Lamb.

It was this part of the apparition that struck me as strong evidence confirming Mary's role as intercessor; here she was, gazing in adoration at the Sacrificial Lamb, Jesus — seemingly *pointing us toward Him.*

"The Pope made a special visit here in 1979," Sean concluded, "and it's become a very popular place of pilgrimage."

When we got there, I felt like I belonged. It was Sunday afternoon, and the large open plaza near the original site of the apparition was absolutely jammed with people. They were just beginning a procession as we arrived.

"What's happening?" I asked Sean, as I gazed at the front of the line which was about six or seven people across and stretched out for at least a hundred yards.

"They're doing the Stations of the Cross."

There were people in wheelchairs, and old people being helped along by children. . . . I was so moved, I couldn't speak. We got out and went into the basilica, where the procession had originated. Slipping into a pew and praying, I felt a warm, gentle blessing and anointing for the whole Ireland trip. I sensed that it came directly from Mary, and that this was the reason she had asked me to come here.

Beginning that evening and everywhere we went, the churches and the halls were packed beyond belief. Nowhere had I met people more hungry, more open to the possibility that God, out of His great love for man, was taking extraordinary measures to call mankind back to Himself.

There were priests and laymen alike, and that night one priest, a big, ruddy-faced fellow, wore a troubled expression during my entire talk. When it was over, he came up, and there were tears streaming down his face. He just hugged me and murmured, "Thank you," over and over. And then he asked me to pray for him.

Several nights later, we were in a theater and sitting next to me in the front row before we began, was another priest. He looked at me and said, "You're the man who's come to talk about Medjugorje?"

"Yes, Father."

"Well," he said chuckling, "I'll tell you right now: I'm very skeptical. But I've got an open mind, and I've come to listen, so lad, you'd better be at your best!" He may have been smiling, but I could tell he meant it.

Towards the end of my talk, I took out my rosary and held it up and told the audience how important it was to me. It was a prayer to Jesus, I said, and it didn't belong to the Catholic Church alone; it was for all of us, everyone who loved Jesus.

When I stopped a few minutes later, there was a standing ovation. And the priest who had spoken to me beforehand came up on the stage and said, "God bless you, lad, God bless you!" He hugged me and added, "Just want you to know: I can believe that!"

"Well," I managed, "that's good, because if just one person is helped by my talks, it's worth it."

"I want you to do me one favor though," he paused, looking at me.

By that time I was so happy that a priest had been touched, I said, "Ask it, Father, anything you want."

He hesitated. "Well, would you — exchange rosaries with me?"

I was shocked. Mine had been made for me by a young lady in nearby Surfside Beach back home. From the moment she had given it to me, I had never been without it, and I did not want to part with it now. But . . . . "Sure, Father," I said, "here."

He took it and gave me his. Old and faded, the wooden beads were almost worn out from passing through his fingers. "I've had this for twenty years," he said slowly. "I got it at Fatima."

He looked at it fondly, and suddenly I realized that it was as hard for him to give up his, as it was for me. In fact, it was much harder for him — it must have been like saying farewell to a dear friend. Should I stop him? No, somehow God was in this; we each seemed to sense that, and we made the transfer. At that moment I was inundated with people and didn't see the priest again.

The next morning, the two ladies who were to take me to my next meeting came to pick me up. I didn't know what it was about Irish women, but they all seemed to drive as if they were in a road race. It was one thing to go 65 on the inter-states back home; it was another to do it on a narrow, winding two-lane road bordered by high hedges and ancient stone fences — and on the left side of the road! While they were chatting merrily away, I was sufficiently scared to start doing some serious praying. I got my rosary out — my new-old rosary — and

was stunned. The thin metal chain joining the beads had
changed color!

I had heard rumors of this phenomenon in Medjugorje,
of pilgrims' rosaries turning to gold, and in the beginning
had discounted them as over-enthusiasm or wishful
thinking. But after being shown a number of them, I had
begun to wonder: since you've called me to this, how come
you haven't given *me* a golden rosary? And now she had.
I didn't know if the links were pure gold or not, and it
didn't matter; last night they were silver, and now they
were gold — or at least a burnished golden color. And
to think that I had almost refused this gift!

That whole trip was a gift. It was hard work; we were
flat out the whole way, with me occasionally speaking three
times a day. But throughout I felt the presence of the
Holy Spirit, providing fresh inspiration and anointing. And
just when I began to wonder if I could go on, there would
be a brief but sweet respite.

We wound up the tour in Dublin Friday night, at the
city's 3,000-seat National Stadium. On our way there, Sean
asked me how I was doing.

"I'm dead beat," I replied honestly, "all I want to do
is get home and sleep for a week." And then I laughed.
"But I imagine the Holy Spirit will do whatever needs
to be done; He always has."

Sean nodded. "Aye, He has, to be sure. Have you noticed
it hasn't rained during all the time you've been here?"

Now that he mentioned it, I recalled that the sun had
indeed been bright and shining every day of my trip. "Is
that so unusual?"

"Why do you think we call it the Emerald Isle? Rain
is almost an everyday occurrence here."

When we got there, every seat was filled. And once again
the Holy Spirit did not disappoint. Three hours later, as
we came back outside and got in the car to drive to the

airport, the heavens opened up, and the rain sheeted down, so hard that we were slowed to a crawl.

On the plane home, I was too tired to sleep. Well, I had better get used to it; other than the occasional respite that was going to be my life from now on. My schedule for the coming year included several other international trips, plus two more visits to Medjugorje, and countless speaking engagements in the States. And that was only the first six months!

But I would never forget Ireland — mainly because of a beautiful vision I experienced following one of the talks. We were once again in a church packed beyond capacity. After Mass and the talk, we were kneeling and praying for the brokenness of Northern Ireland. I was deeply touched by the priest's plea for the healing salve of the Holy Spirit to come upon the people of that area. As I knelt with my eyes closed, I remembered a passage from a beautiful book I had been given called, *The Poem of the Man-God*, by Maria Valtorta, who was alleged to be a visionary and stigmatist. In the passage, Jesus was trying to explain His love to His disciples, when John, His young, fervent follower, came up to Him and placing his arms around His waist and laying his head on Jesus' chest declared, "Master, I love You."

So taken by the remembrance of this scene, I silently prayed in earnest, "Oh, Jesus, let me put my arms around Your waist, and let me put my head on Your chest and simply say, I love You!"

Suddenly, I saw and felt Jesus lay His head on my chest. It was so real, I gasped, and nearly fell over.

Now, flying home, I closed my eyes and felt His presence once again. . . .

*"I beg you to give Our Lord your past and
all the evil that has accumulated
in your hearts. . . ."*

29

Milka

I arrived home from Ireland to find our temporary addition to the family happy and well settled in. True to form, Milka Pavlovic had adapted well in the week and a half that I had been in Ireland. She and Terri had developed a good relationship, and the kids treated her as if she had been living there for years. Terri had enrolled her in a special education class to learn English; she had already picked up enough of the basics to be comfortable with us.

From the moment I had met Milka, I knew there was something special about her. This Croatian teen-ager who had been blessed to have seen the Madonna on the first day of the apparitions — and seemingly cursed to have been excluded as one of the six thereafter — was fiercely independent and fully capable of taking care of herself.

Yet I had detected in her a wistfulness and a longing to be an integral part of the grace that had come to their little village. And I had the feeling, after receiving the startling message from the Blessed Virgin Mary to bring Milka to the United States, that she would play a significant future role in the apparitions. Meanwhile, arranging for her to come to America was my immediate assignment, and after making a few phone calls to our embassy in Belgrade, I knew it was not going to be easy.

As soon as I had arrived home in July, I contacted the office of South Carolina's senior Senator, Strom Thurmond, hoping to receive a little political support. He obliged — quickly; in less than three weeks I received a succinct telegram from Milka: HAVE VISA. SEND TICKET. I later learned that this tough 18-year-old had taken a plane to Belgrade alone, gone to the American Embassy and in ten minutes had obtained a visa.

Terri and the kids were elated. I called Father Svet's cousin, Jozo Kraljevic, who lived in Mostar (twenty miles from Medjugorje) and asked him to help arrange Milka's departure. Jozo had taught English for years in the schools of Mostar, and was well acquainted with the visionaries and their families. He had frequently served as an interpreter for various media crews investigating the apparitions. Next I called Dale Krieger, and through his travel agency, Global Group Tours, Milka's ticket was arranged.

All she had to do was travel to Dubrovnik on Friday, pick up the ticket, and board the plane on Sunday. I would be giving talks in Pennsylvania that weekend and planned to fly to New York on Sunday morning to meet her and escort her home to Myrtle Beach. There was just one small problem, one which seemed to afflict more than a few Croatians: a general indifference to time. Milka failed to pick up the ticket on Friday, going to the agent's office on Saturday instead. A different clerk was on duty, and not being familiar with the arrangements she refused to give Milka the ticket.

Unaware of this, I went to Kennedy Airport to meet her Yugoslavian Air Lines flight — which she was not on. With the help of a sympathetic JAL agent, I discovered that while she was indeed listed on the passenger manifest, she had never boarded the plane.

There was nothing to do but go home and start over. Again through the assistance of Jozo Kraljevic, I was able to re-schedule her for a flight arriving on Friday — the day before my trip to Ireland. There would be just time to take her home, introduce her to the family, and leave. Not the ideal way to begin her first visit to America, but — all problems were forgotten as she cleared customs and greeted me with a weary smile. We arrived home a little before midnight, thanking God for her safe arrival.

Her three-month stay passed incredibly swiftly, filled with far more things to do and places to go than one would have thought possible. Yet even as busy as she was, Milka occasionally felt strong twinges of homesickness. And she was far from over-impressed with big, beautiful, bountiful America. Immediately she reacted to the pace and stress of our daily life; to her it was far too filled with meaningless activities that prevented the family closeness she was used to in her little village. "Too much, too much!" she would say in her broken English, and her favorite expression soon became: "Go slow, take it easy!"

We did everything *but* go slow and take it easy. Milka went to English class twice a week, where she became good friends with a Japanese girl; though neither of them could speak English, they communicated beautifully and were soon inseparable. When not in class they were out together exploring Myrtle Beach. We even squeezed in a trip down to Disney World.

But by far the highlight of her visit was her witnessing about the events in Medjugorje. I had determined not to exploit Milka in any way during her visit with us, and it was only at Terri's insistence that I reluctantly agreed to take her on a couple of my speaking engagements.

And I found that Milka was perfectly capable of giving her testimony of what had happened on that first day, and what effect it had had on her life.

As word got out that she was staying with us, requests came pouring in. I discussed the matter at length with Milka, emphasizing that she did not have to do this; as far as I was concerned, her primary goal was to learn English and to become familiar with Americans, two things that might help her play a supporting role back in the little village.

Not only did Milka agree to give her testimony, but she took to it with a fervor. Using a local Croatian as an interpreter, she gave the details of that first day when she was privileged to see Mary, and she willingly answered questions afterwards. To the audiences, it was as good as having one of the visionaries present; in fact, I looked on Milka as a visionary. The only differences were the daily rendezvous and personal messages with the mother of Jesus that the others experienced.

As a special favor to Peter Crary, I had agreed to a five-day tour in Fargo, North Dakota, where Peter had established a Medjugorje center and with volunteer help had already distributed in excess of two million copies of the columns. When I called to ask him if it was all right to bring Milka, he was ecstatic. "Are you kidding me?" he exclaimed. "She'll be a wonderful addition!"

Peter even made arrangements for Slavko Zovko, a Franciscan priest stationed in Milwaukee, who had been born and raised in Medjugorje, to serve as interpreter throughout our stay. Father Slavko, who had served with Father Svet in New York City, had traveled with Tomislav Pervan, pastor at St. James in Medjugorje, when he had come to the States for a two-month visit. Like so many of the Franciscan priests I had met, he was a simple but holy man, fully dedicated to his calling — with a way about him that quickly put you at ease.

We met up with him in the airport at Minneapolis which gave us time to reacquaint ourselves and for him to meet and learn a little of Milka's background. We began talking about the apparitions and the variety of phenomena that were occurring at Medjugorje. One of the most intriguing to me were the mysterious pictures taken there, on which people would find images reportedly of the Blessed Virgin. Like his Franciscan brothers at Medjugorje, Father Slavko cautioned me not to put too much stock in them.

"I usually don't," I assured him. "People send me all sorts of photographs, purportedly of the Madonna's face in clouds, in tree trunks, in shadows in their gardens. And several, connected with Medjugorje, have been proven to be fakes." I paused, then removed one from my coat pocket, where I had been carrying it when I traveled, ever since Jim Stoffel's daughter Karen had given it to me. "But this one has really touched my heart."

I had showed it to Milka before, but on the day she had seen the apparition she had been too far away to note the details of the face. Now I passed it to Father Slavko. "The story behind this one is unique," I went on. "When I first saw it, I was overwhelmed by its beauty and felt that, regardless of its origin, it would be my image of Mary at Medjugorje. In fact, I plan to use it on the cover of my book."

He looked at it and nodded. "It *is* a beautiful picture," he said, looking up at me, "but one must focus on the message, which can easily be verified by Scripture. Your picture, I'm afraid, cannot," and he returned it with a smile.

Undaunted, I went on to tell him the story: according to Karen, a nun from the Vatican, on pilgrimage to Medjugorje, had been invited into the apparition room. During the time of the visitation, she had taken a picture

of the crucifix on the wall above where the young
visionaries appeared to be looking. When the photograph
was developed, a close-up of a young woman's face
appeared on the film. Karen had received a copy of this
photo just before leaving for Medjugorje herself, and after
Ivan's talk with her group she had an opportunity to ask
him if it looked like the Madonna.

Ivan, like the other visionaries, was normally turned
off by such requests concerning pictures. He glanced at
it and started to turn away — then turned back. "Yes,"
he said slowly, studying the photograph, "it does look like
her." Then he smiled. "Only she is even more beautiful!"

While I agreed with Father Slovko about not trusting
any photographs, nonetheless, this one would always be
my image of Mary.

We were met at the Fargo airport by Peter and his mother
who informed us of a special welcoming party at Peter's
home. "The people coming tonight," he explained, "are
the volunteers who have worked so hard to get your
columns out and make this a successful speaking tour.
They're thrilled to finally get to meet you. I know you
are going to be surrounded by them asking questions and
all, but if you would, please try to give them a little extra
time."

"Don't worry," I assured him, "I'll be glad to."

As we left the airport, Peter's mother took Milka and
Father Slavko to her home where they would be staying,
to drop their bags off before joining us. Peter, meanwhile,
had some other friends that he wanted me to meet, and
so they would probably get to his home before we would.
As we went up the steps to his front door, he again
mentioned how happy all the volunteers would be to see
me. We walked in — and were surprised that no one was
in the foyer or the living room. Going back into the den,
we discovered that practically everyone who had been

invited was crowded in there — and in the center was Milka Pavlovic holding court!

"Gee Peter," I said with mock sarcasm, "I don't know if I can take all of this attention!" We both laughed. Milka was the highlight of the evening and was especially effective with the young people present. She touched many hearts that evening just by her presence. The volunteers saw her as a real part of Medjugorje that they could see and touch and hear.

And it was like that everywhere we went — Father Slavko was simply icing on the cake. At my request, in addition to interpreting, he agreed to tell of his life in the little village. And thus my own testimony was brought dramatically to life by the witness of *two* of the local villagers. I was surprised to realize that although Peter had packed something into just about every moment of our time, it was by far the easiest tour I had made up to this point.

One afternoon, we were scheduled to speak at a convent, and as always, I was a little nervous about speaking to a group of nuns. This afternoon would be even more difficult, for these were cloistered nuns; I would be speaking to them without actually seeing them.

The fact that these women had made such a total dedication of their lives to God stayed with me throughout my talk — evoking such deep feelings that I was completely wrung out when I finished. Then, through Father Slavko, Milka gave her witness with confidence and innocent charm. I marveled at how accomplished she had become in such a short time, adding a little more detail with each speaking engagement.

Afterwards, the Mother Superior asked us if we would spend a little more time with them, and of course we agreed. We sat on one side of a large, open window, with the sisters on the other side. I was surprised when one of them asked about pictures of the Blessed Virgin that had reportedly appeared on pilgrims' film after they had returned home. I looked at Father Slavko and said quietly, "Do you think it would be all right if I showed my picture to them?"

He grimaced and then said, "Well, yes, why not? What harm can it do?"

I pulled the picture from my pocket and briefly explained the story behind it, then handed it to the Mother Superior. The sisters were awed as they passed it among themselves, finally returning it to me. I tried to slip it in my inside coat pocket as I answered a question, but for some reason it refused to fit. A few moments later, I tried again with the same results. Rather than create a distraction, I placed the picture on the window sill, thinking I would wait until the informal interview was over.

We spoke with the sisters for nearly an hour, and then, as we prepared to say our good-byes, I once again tried to slip the picture into my coat pocket; it still wouldn't fit. Abruptly, I heard that now-familiar inner-voice: *Give them the picture. . .*

Give them the picture? This picture which meant so much to me? I couldn't believe it! But — I obeyed. "Here, Mother, why don't you keep this picture, as a remembrance of our visit?"

The sisters were overjoyed. They could hardly believe I was giving it to them — and neither could Father Slavko.

"But you loved that picture so much," he murmured in amazement, as we walked to the car. "How could you give it to them?"

"I honestly don't know, Father, but I felt I was being asked to do it, so I did. My wife's going to shoot me," I added as an afterthought; Terri felt the same way about the picture as I did, and had been reluctant to let me take it on the trip.

That evening, we stopped for dinner at the home of the couple who had arranged the speaking engagement for that night. As we sat down at the table, the wife slipped me an envelope and said, "I wanted to give you these — it's a very special little miracle from Medjugorje." I opened the envelope and inside were two copies of the exact picture I had given to the sisters! "You can keep one and give one to Milka," our hostess was saying. "It's just what I always imagined Mary looked like. The story behind it is —"

"Never mind," I smiled at her, "I know the story."

I just sat there, staring at the pictures. Once again, a gift given from the heart had been returned with interest. And what a gift!

The tour ended in Minneapolis at St. Mary's Basilica, with an audience of more than a thousand. Following the presentation, there was a reception, and everyone was invited to come and meet us. The crowd was far more exuberant than usual, and I could see the pressure building in my young Croatian charge. Since Milka's first presentation in the States, she had expressed a deep dislike of the adulation that normally followed such talks, and here in Minneapolis it was worse than ever. Then came the topper: a heavy-set woman rushed up to her and tried to kiss her hand. Milka immediately pulled it away and asked the lady not to do that. The woman, unfazed, then shoved a twenty-dollar bill into her hands.

That did it. Milka dropped the money and ran out of the reception hall.

"Milka — wait!" I yelled after her, but she didn't stop. Surrounded by people, I had difficulty extricating myself, but at last I broke free and ran out, to find her waiting in the car.

"Let's go, let's go!" she demanded. "It is enough! These are crazy people!"

"Milka, I'm sorry! That lady —"

"Is not just one lady, is many people; they want picture, autograph — *I am not movie star!*"

"It's okay, we're leaving," I said, trying to calm her down. "Let me find the people who brought us, and we'll leave."

About fifteen minutes after we left, Milka had calmed down, and we decided to stop for pizza, one of her favorite foods. The incident at the reception was soon forgotten, and later she was able to look back on it and laugh.

Milka's visit to America ended with an early trip to New York City, so that we could give a talk at the Croatian church, before flying to Yugoslavia. We stayed at the home of Fino Guaradino, a successful businessman who had traveled to Medjugorje in June, 1986, and found conversion. Fino was anxious to show Milka New York, and was a gracious host. He and another good friend whom I had met in Medjugorje, Penny Abbruzese, had organized a center and were deeply involved in distributing information and witnessing.

It was the perfect ending to a glorious and educational stay for Milka. I felt that my mission had been accomplished, as she was now able to speak very good English, and I prayed that this experience of her being a witness for Medjugorje would prompt her to continue to speak out. She was especially effective with young people, and there was an urgent need to reach the youth of Medjugorje at this time. For the steady progress of Medjugorje as a place of holiness had been mirrored by Satan's progress. New restaurants had added bars, and these were fast becoming a gathering place for the younger generation of Medjugorje. Added to this was the impact of sudden affluence on families who had always been poor and who had no experience dealing with the problems it brought.

I will never forget an earlier conversation with Grgo Vasilje, concerning television. Many of the villagers were

now purchasing them, and Grgo had been able to re-
sist the pleas of his children to get one. Jelena enjoyed
watching it with friends, and when I asked him about
letting her go to friends' homes to watch it, he stated,
"That is still better than getting one here; then we would
be watching it all of the time, and prayer would decrease."

However, when I had returned in October, Grgo had
purchased a television set. The pressure from his children
had been relentless, and he had finally given in. Now,
he thought it wiser for them to be at home where he
could at least control the time they spent watching it, and
of course what they watched. The young people of
Medjugorje needed examples to follow, and Milka was a
natural leader.

Due to a mix-up, we failed to get off the airplane in
Zagreb as we were supposed to, and wound up arriving
in Medjugorje at one o'clock in the morning. Milka
immediately woke up her older sister; it had been a long
separation, and the one person this independent teen-
ager was closest to and depended on most was Marija.
As she tried to describe the past three months in five
minutes, Marija was as excited as she was. Asking a steady
stream of questions, she insisted on preparing us
something to eat.

Suddenly the fatigue of the long trip hit both of us.
Milka ate a little and then declared she was going to bed.
I was also tired and ready to turn in, but Marija, up now
and wide awake, wanted to talk. She began telling me
something about the President, but I couldn't quite
understand.

"Your President, he call me — here, at my house!" she
exclaimed.

I wasn't sure I was hearing right. "You mean — President
Reagan of the United States?"

"Yes! He call but — he cannot talk," she said, searching

for the right words. "I talk to his office, his secretary."

I was astounded. "Why did he call?"

"I sent him a letter about Medjugorje, about Our Lady's coming and asking for peace. He is meeting with Gorbachev for treaty, and I wanted him to know about Our Lady."

I pressed Marija for more details, but aware of her limitations with the English language, she urged me to get the details from Kathleen in the morning. When I did, Kathleen beamed as she related how President Reagan had been affected by the simple and direct letter which she had put into English for Marija, telling of the Blessed Virgin's call to peace at Medjugorje.

"Alfred Kingnon, the U.S. Ambassador to the European Communities was visiting here with his wife on a personal, three-day retreat before returning to the States for the signing of the missile treaty by Reagan and Gorbachev," Kathleen explained. "He was fully struck by the apparitions, even more so when he met Marija. Later, she had invited him for lunch, and it was then the idea came that maybe he would carry a personal message from her to the President, since he knew him personally."

Kathleen smiled at the recollection. "It all just fell into place. I sat down with her to help with the English, and that was it. The best part was that when he gave it to the President and told him about it, the latter was deeply touched. That was why he tried to reach Marija by telephone. But you know how this system works," she chuckled. "He was cut off twice. Then, on December 8th, his secretary reached Marija and told her how much he had appreciated her letter."

"That's incredible!" I murmured. How simply and directly God worked here! A young Croatian girl who claimed to see the Madonna daily, was able to touch the heart of the most powerful political figure in the world.

"The best part," Kathleen went on, as Marija sat close by confirming the details, "is that as the President was entering the room to sign the treaty — which just happened to be December 8th, the Feast of the Immaculate Conception — he turned to the ambassador and told him that he had been deeply affected by the message of Medjugorje and wanted "Those two girls to know it."

This news helped offset the sadness of saying good-bye to Milka who had become like a member of our family. She had cried when she said good-bye to Terri — and she was not one for tears. But another bit of news made it easier. The commission investigating the apparitions had asked Marija, Jacov, Ivan, and Mirjana, to come to Split for their first in-depth interviews. Marija arrived back in the little village Sunday, the day before I was due to leave. I was in the bell tower visiting with Father Pavic who lived there, when Marija came up and knocked on his door. She was a little surprised to see me there, but was absolutely beaming with happiness.

"Oh, Father," she exclaimed, "it was wonderful! This commission is very good and asked us good questions. I am very happy and pleased with them!" She said she would tell him more later, but it was nearly time for the apparition, and she had to go.

Later that evening at her home, Marija mentioned several more times how happy she was and how good it was to have a commission that appeared to be taking the investigation seriously. She said that the previous two commissions had never asked relevant questions and that the majority of their members never even bothered to come to Medjugorje, or be in attendance for an apparition.

Then it was time for me to leave. I was departing from the village at midnight as my flight left early in the morning out of Dubrovnik. I hugged Marija and thanked her for everything and then took a few extra moments to thank her mother and father. I turned to say good-bye to Milka, who was staying in the background. Very formally, she stuck out her hand and said thank you — and then with a smile told me: "Go slow, take it easy."

I hugged her and went quickly out to the taxi, not wanting this tough little teen-ager to see my tears.

30

The Final Harvest

The spring of 1988 found me busier than ever. But whenever I was home, I made a determined effort to be the husband and father that Terri had asked me to be. By the grace of God, I was able to do that; in spite of the stress of my schedule, we seemed closer as a family than ever.

In fact, during school break in April, I surprised them by announcing that the whole family was going to Medjugorje, so Kennedy and Rebecca could know firsthand why their dad was traveling so much. And as an added surprise, I planned the trip through Ireland. We would journey there and then join one of the Irish groups on pilgrimage to Medjugorje.

Terri was ecstatic. The one place she had always wanted to visit was Ireland. We had talked about going once we had sold the newspapers, but that was before our involvement in Medjugorje. Now she was going to go — and with her kids.

We stopped over one night in Ireland and then left the next day for Medjugorje, celebrating Easter there. After six days, we returned for four more days in Ireland, and one day in London. All of this was possible because of frequent flyer miles I had accumulated through my numerous lecture trips in the last year.

Medjugorje was pretty much the same as I had left it on my last trip in December when I had taken Milka home. The only unfortunate part was that Marija was not at home during our visit. I had wanted Terri to meet her and spend time with her, but Marija and fifteen members of the prayer group — including Kathleen — had been called by the Blessed Virgin to a small town in Italy, for five months of contemplative prayer life. They would not return to Medjugorje until the middle of August. Nonetheless, it was a wonderful time of family sharing. We would never forget being there together as family, or our time in Ireland. And now Kennedy and Rebecca understood.

Everything was going remarkably well, with one exception: the book that I was supposed to be writing was not getting written. During the past two years of research I had amassed a small ton of notes and cassette tapes which I had piled into a huge stack. Yet in all that time I had actually completed exactly 34 pages of working manuscript. It got so that whenever I went into my office I avoided looking at that thin pile on the shelf next to my typewriter.

But, as He had with everything else, God already had a solution for that, too. In May, I was speaking in Providence, Rhode Island, when Bob Veasey who had arranged the trip told me of an added talk that he had penciled into the schedule. It was at the Community of Jesus, an ecumenical residential community on Cape Cod.

"You may not want to do this one," Bob said as we drove away from the airport. "But there's a guy who lives there who is a writer, and he sent me a letter asking if you would be interested in some help with your book. He's done sixteen books, the majority of them collaborations."

My first reaction was to say no. It wasn't the first time such an offer had been made to me. But for some reason,

I was interested in this one. I told Bob that I didn't mind going there for the talk, and that I would meet with the gentleman, but that I really wasn't looking for anyone to do my book. "It's something I have to do myself, Bob," I added.

The directors of the Community of Jesus were two women, Cay Andersen and Judy Sorensen, who had been to Medjugorje themselves the previous November, as had several other members. So what I would be sharing would be more in terms of an update. It turned out to be one of the easiest talks I had ever given — and one of the most pleasurable.

After a wonderful lunch with the directors, I met privately with David Manuel, the man who had offered to help me with my book. He had done this for a number of authors, he said, and what he did basically was interview the author in depth, then edit the transcribed material into narrative form. "It would be your own story in your own words," he assured me, "told the way you want to tell it. All I would do is facilitate getting it done."

I firmly assured him that the final draft would have to be written my way, but that I needed aid in structure and editing. "What I really need," I added, "is someone to prod me along to get it done."

Somehow, after saying no to so many others who had offered help, David Manuel seemed to be the right person in the right place at the right time. We prayed that God would lead us to the right decision.

He did. Within the next two weeks, we were planning a quick trip to Medjugorje to orientate David to Medjugorje, and to squeeze in a few more interviews with the key personalities involved. However, there were a few obstacles to overcome.

First, there was a scheduled second trip to Ireland, that would leave only a few days between my return and our departure for the village. To further complicate matters, I would be leaving for a ten-day trip to Trinidad two days after arriving home from Medjugorje. Added to this was the fact that I had not as yet told Terri about our impromptu excursion back to the village. I waited until the morning I was leaving for Ireland to tell her.

She hit the ceiling. "Are you absolutely crazy?" she fumed. "You must think you're Superman or something! Let David go by himself and find out about Medjugorje as you and I did!"

"Okay, okay, I'll cancel my ticket," I said, trying to appease the situation. "I just wanted David to experience—"

"Listen, David's a big boy and will be able to go it alone. Maybe he doesn't realize you have a family and a full load of travel already; I really can't believe you'd even think about going at this time."

It was not the best of good-byes at the airport. Later, when I called her just prior to my Ireland flight and again tried to explain my reasons for having agreed to go with David, Terri resumed the offensive. Giving up, I assured her I would not go and that she was truly right. I wanted this Irish trip to be a good one and starting out with my wife angry with me wouldn't lead to the peace and joy Mary promised through the messages given at Medjugorje.

Vera McFadden, the driver assigned to bring me to my first speaking engagement in Northern Ireland, continued to motor along the beautiful roadway, lined with ancient stone fences and beautiful green shrubbery. Having finally quieted from the alarm of British armored personnel carriers swooping past us with rifles aimed at us, we resumed our conversation about the message of Medjugorje in Northern Ireland.

"You'll find the people receptive — they know about you, you know," she said in her heavy Northern brogue.

That surprised me some. Vera went on to say that they knew me as "that Protestant American" who gave a talk on Medjugorje in the church there. Evidently, the tape copied by Mary O'Sullivan was still making its rounds. "We also get a few of your columns," she added, "but they're scarce. I surely wish someone over here would see to their distribution — it's such a beautiful message!"

A little after two, we arrived at the first speaking site — a hotel with a turnout of only around fifty people. I began to wonder if it had been a good idea to come to Northern Ireland.

"This is just a quick stop and since it's in the middle of the day, we didn't expect too many people," Vera stated, as if reading my thoughts. I nonetheless gave the full story of Medjugorje and its effect on my life, just as though I was speaking in an auditorium filled with thousands.

That evening we went to another location in Derry, and, as in the afternoon, the turnout was low. But the spirit was high. It was a holy time of sharing and of listening to the witness of Catholics and Protestants. I was ecstatic to learn that there were many prayer groups — of which this was one — that were mixed. The next evening, the auditorium was packed. Trying to maintain an openness and a lightness to the event, I began by asking, "Are there any other Protestants here in attendance tonight?"

Not one hand went up. A bit dismayed, I continued by saying that since I was the lone Protestant there, I was at their mercy, and went on with my presentation. Afterwards, when a member of the group which had sponsored my trip was expressing his appreciation for my coming, I asked him, "Why were there no Protestants here tonight? I thought you told me that they were interested in hearing about the apparitions?"

He paused a moment before saying quietly, "Wayne, there *were* Protestants here tonight, but they were not about to identify themselves. You never know when the wrong people might be present."

That brought me back to the reality of the Northern Ireland problem. While the message of Medjugorje might be that small drop of the oil of peace, the daily lives of these people were still threatened by the radical groups on both sides. Fear was part of that daily living.

I was glad I had come to Northern Ireland as part of this second tour; it was actually the main reason I had agreed to return. The three days spent in this breath-takingly beautiful but strife-torn part of Ireland were priceless. It was a time of learning, filled with wonderful memories.

One I would never forget occurred when I had a chance to meet with a lady who was reported to be having visions of the Blessed Virgin Mary in a church at a place called Bessbrook. From her description, they appeared to be the same as were occurring in Medjugorje. After visiting with her and her priest, Father Gerald McGinity, in Armagh, I was convinced she was authentic. In fact, I felt assurance upon meeting her. She displayed the same spontaneous honesty and self-effacing humility that I had come to expect from Marija and the other Medjugorje visionaries. The essence of the messages she was receiving was identical, in spirit as well as content: fast, pray, do penance, convert, and make Christ the center of your life.

But she related something I had not heard before: the Blessed Mother had told her the previous year that the world had about ten more years in which to change its ways back to God. That meant we had until about 1997. This particular message was given not as a threat but rather as a time of grace for as many as possible to follow the road to conversion to God. I could find nothing phony about this new visionary's reports.

The rest of the trip was similar to the first; I traveled to many counties to proclaim the message, ending in County Cork. I returned home fully exhausted, but again filled with the joy of the mission.

Another "little miracle" occurred just a few days prior to my leaving Ireland. I called Terri to let her know that so far, everything had gone well, and that I would be returning as scheduled. I quickly added how much I was looking forward to coming home for ten days before the trip to Trinidad, hoping that all was forgiven and forgotten concerning my unscheduled trip to Medjugorje. Then, I asked somewhat tentatively, "By the way, did you call David for me, to tell him I was not going with him to Medjugorje?"

There was a pause and then a deep sigh. "No," Terri said softly, "but I have booked your ticket to Chicago."

"Terri, I'm not going to Medjugorje with David; I told you, it's okay —"

"I know you did, but I think Mary wants you there — so I booked you to Chicago."

I was dumbstruck. What had changed her mind? When she met me at the airport, that was the first thing I asked her. With a wry smile she said, "Let's just say that when Mary wants you to do something, she makes sure you do it!"

I laughed. Terri's conversion was certainly different from mine; but there was no doubt that she truly was learning to take everything to God in prayer. What was even better, she was responding to the answers.

A few days later I was headed to Chicago to begin trip number seven to Medjugorje. We would be under the wing of Lois Malik, the head of Peace Center Tours which probably arranged more pilgrimages to Medjugorje than any other organization. Lois was the original diamond in the rough. A seasoned professional in the travel business, when it came to looking after the well-being of her charges, she was as tough as a drill sergeant — which came in handy with the inevitable snafus of group travel.

And as with others for whom spreading the message of Medjugorje had become their life's work, she had quite a story. Born and raised in Chicago, at the age of nine she announced to her mother that she wanted to transfer from public school to parochial school. She didn't know why; she just wanted to. Until that point her family was unchurched, but her mother agreed, and she was baptized and received her first Communion on the same day.

The remainder of her education was in Catholic schools, culminating with Loyola University. Travel had always intrigued her, and she held jobs in all aspects of the business. But she wasn't really happy, and nothing seemed to satisfy her or fulfill her. Nor did church help; on the contrary, the thought of it made her feel guilty. For Lois, ever the perfectionist, had become an extreme anorexic. The thought of going to Confession was more than she could bear, and since you couldn't receive Communion unless you were in a state of grace. . . . But for some reason, she clung to the rosary. No matter how far from God she felt, she always felt close to "Our Lady." A mother could forgive anything.

Her problem eventually led her to a twelve-step program similar to Alcoholics Anonymous, and like AA, a key step was establishing a relationship with God and submitting to His will. This step took Lois to a prayer group and a "healing priest" — and back to church. As soon as she heard about Medjugorje, she went there, and then back and then back again. On her 45th birthday, she was invited into the apparition room, where she felt the Blessed Mother's presence — and realized that she could relax and trust God and that nothing else mattered but God.

But how to discern His will from hers? For she felt that she was supposed to start bringing pilgrims to Medjugorje. She brought her problem to Father Tomislav Pervan who made a special petition to Marija for her. All during that service Lois was anything but relaxed, but when it was over Father Tomislav met her, and with a smile gave her the answer: "Lois, Our Lady said, *Do not be afraid; I will be beside you in all that you do.*"

It was a word that she would frequently remind herself of, for on her first trip bringing others, there were eight pilgrims, and on the second trip, six. At that rate she would be bankrupt before too many more trips. But she trusted God and carried on, and today she was responsible for more than a hundred pilgrims a week. Under her efficient direction, this Yugoslavian Air Lines departure went as smoothly as any I'd been on, and soon David and I were 30,000 feet over the Atlantic, getting to know one another.

We were the same age, but there the similarity ended. Our backgrounds could not have been more different: he had gone to Yale and lived all his life in the Northeast. An editor at Doubleday when he first felt the waves of conversion through the Charismatic Renewal in 1970, he had gone on to head up the book division of Logos, the first Charismatic publishing house, turning to full-time writing in '73, at his community on the Cape. Yet the more we talked, the more I realized we were not so different, after all. We had both committed our lives to serving God, and believed that if we would trust and obey, He would lead us, providing the necessary grace.

The one place where we differed was on the question of Mary. It was the same story as with so many Protestants. By now David was familiar with my story and had heard the positive response of his friends who had been to Medjugorje. His own wife Barbara had returned home profoundly moved, with a renewed and lasting hunger for the things of God and a new appreciation of Mary. Moreover, he had collaborated on the last book of David du Plessis, the father of modern Pentecostalism, who had visited Medjugorje and was convinced of the authenticity of what God was doing there. But while David was prepared to accept that, it was almost as if he wished that Mary had had nothing to do with it.

It was hardly the first time I had encountered such resistance; my own pastor had been strenuous in his objections — not to what God was doing in Medjugorje, nor in the undeniably good fruit it was bearing world-wide. But he, too, would have preferred to have had it happen without the Blessed Mother being involved. Evangelicals of all stripes, I had discovered, had a deep-seated resentment of what they saw as Catholics elevating Mary to divine status. They viewed this as worshipping her, in place of her Son.

It was sad, because nothing was further from the truth; most Catholics venerated Mary as a human mother given a special status as the example, the image, the one who always leads us to her Son. That had also been my experience, as I continued to return to Medjugorje. While the mother of Jesus would forever have an extremely special place in my heart, with each trip I found myself being drawn closer to Jesus, wanting to live more for Him and surrender more to Him.

I was anxious to see what effect Medjugorje would have on David. If his wife Barbara had come home from the little village with a new perspective on Mary, why not David? I hoped that he also, would change.

We reached St. James at sunset — just in time for Mass. As usual, the church was crammed with people, and we stood in the midst of the crowd at the back. David was awed by the throngs and the strong singing. "I can't believe this!" he whispered. "They're singing 'The Battle Hymn of the Republic' — in Croatian!"

"It's one of the Blessed Mother's favorites," I whispered back.

When the service was over, we went to Marija's home where we would be staying. After having heard my story of conversion and mission, Marija had insisted that from then on, I stay nowhere else. She was in Italy now, on an extended retreat with several other young people from her prayer group. But Milka was there, and she made us feel at home — in the room which was normally hers and Marija's. We chatted for awhile but went to bed early; we'd been up for over 30 hours.

In the morning, Milka and her sister-in-law Macha fixed us breakfast — piping hot cafe espresso, sliced oranges, goat cheese, and slices of fresh-baked bread. As we were enjoying this simple but delicious food, a woman I had never seen before let herself in the front door and came into the dining room. She started speaking rapidly in Italian to Milka, who wiped her hands on her apron and answered with a smile. But the woman seemed angered at Milka's response and now spoke in a peremptory, demanding tone. While I didn't understand Italian, I *did* understand rudeness, and I found myself getting angry at this intruder. But Milka never stopped smiling. With a weary sigh she nodded to the window and pointed up the road, and the stranger, without so much as a word of thanks, abruptly turned and left.

"What was her problem?" I asked Milka.

"She is tour guide, looking for Marija. She is mad Marija is not here. Then she want to know where Ivan live."

"Does that happen often?" asked David. "Strangers coming into your kitchen?"

"Yes," she replied matter-of-factly, "all the time."

David just stared at her.

"I can't get over her reaction," he said to me later, as we walked over the footpath through the fields to the church. "If that had been my kitchen, I would have taken that woman and escorted her out the —"

"The Blessed Mother has told the villagers that they are to open their homes and their hearts to the pilgrims."

"Yes, but —"

"And Milka wasn't exaggerating; it is like that all day long."

Overhead a military helicopter swooped over the valley, and my friend squinted up at it.   "Government?" he asked.

"Yes, just letting us know who's in charge. Let's pray the rosary on the way to church; it'll take our minds off the intrusions."

"You go ahead," David answered. "I'm not really into the rosary — I prefer to go straight to Jesus."

I didn't answer at first. It was the same response I had heard from so many Protestants; I began to wonder if I could really work with him.

But, it was a beautiful morning, and the sights surrounding us reminded me of the peace she had come to give to the world through this little village. We saw a man forking hay onto a wagon with an ancient three-pronged wooden fork that was surprisingly efficient. There was a woman leading a big cow by a rope, and next to a barn we passed a rooster who was trying to steal some grain from a goat's bowl. David chuckled, "It's been a long time since I've seen such things."

"And smelled them, too, I'll bet."

"Yes, now that you mention it," he said, smiling, "but you don't notice it. In fact, it's kind of neat."

"Not everyone thinks so," I added with a shrug. "In Ireland I watched an interview by a very cosmopolitan talk show hostess. She had been here, and her dominant

memory was the awful barnyard odor of Medjugorje —
I mean, what's a barnyard supposed to smell like?"

David snorted. "She would have complained about the
manure on the floor of the stable at Bethlehem!"

I sighed. "You're right. So many people miss the point
here. They see the exterior and fail to take the time to
really listen and see God's work."

Then, thinking this might be a good time to emphasize
to David that Mary had asked us to pray the rosary as
part of the conversion experience, I added, "But David,
just as that woman failed to see the significant part of
Medjugorje's message, maybe you're missing the point as
well by not accepting her request to pray the rosary."

"Listen, I've always prayed directly to Jesus or to the
Father, and if my heart's right, They hear me. I'm not
about to change now."

"Well," I pushed on, "do you believe Mary is appearing
here?"

David looked a bit annoyed. "Of course I do, or I
wouldn't have offered to work with you on the book!"

"And you believe her messages are inspired by her Son?"

"They appear to be — what's your point?"

I stopped walking and turning to him, said, "Then why
is it you have such a hard time accepting the rosary which
she has asked us to pray?"

David turned red. "You know, you're more Catholic than
any Catholic I've ever met!"

I laughed. "Well, if I'm Catholic, it's with a little c. I'm
only telling you what I've been given through the
messages." We walked along in silence to the church.

Following the English-speaking Mass, Father Philip
Pavic, the American Franciscan priest assigned to
Medjugorje, had some strong words of advice. He
cautioned the pilgrims not to gaze up at the sun, that
a number of people had done permanent damage to their

retinas by tempting God in that way. He then asked them to respect the dignity of the church and the grounds around it by maintaining the spirit of reverence that it deserved. There was to be no conversation inside the church, and only appropriate attire, inside or out — no shorts or sleeveless dresses or sun-bathing.

Afterwards, we went up Mt. Krizevac, pausing at the Stations of the cross, where bas relief scenes, portraying Jesus' passion, had been cast in bronze. Graphically and viscerally the artist had captured the hatred of His accusers and the shock and stunned grief of the men and women who loved Him. It was impossible to look at them and not be profoundly moved. At almost every Station there would be a group of pilgrims, heads bowed in prayer or singing softly. At one point we heard both French and German being sung — and were struck by the fact that once-hated enemies could be reconciled on the Way of the Cross.

It was not an easy climb, though the rocks and stones had been worn smooth by the soles of literally millions of pairs of shoes. It took anywhere from one to two hours, depending on how long one paused at the different stations. Yet there were a number of old people on the path, and even one man on crutches.

Reaching the top, we sat down a bit away from the base of the cross and shared a bottle of mineral water. There were small clusters of pilgrims all over the summit, some were praying, some were singing, some were meditating. "You know," David said, "I feel such quiet joy. It began as soon as we started climbing, and it's been building ever since." He looked over at the cross. "So many pilgrims have said so many prayers here, it's as if the stones themselves are redolent with them."

Behind us, a group of Italians began the rosary. Earlier, when I had suggested that he pray the rosary, he had refused, calling it vain repetition. But now, as he listened to the gentle, deeply felt prayer of this group, his expression softened. "I'm seeing a lot of things," he mused, "and they're coming to me straight through the heart without having to be filtered through the intellect. For one thing, God does not care nearly as much as we do about what form our prayers take. As we pray, He is looking into our hearts, not listening to the words that pass our lips. The rosary can be mindless rote, or it can be opening of the heart to God. But that is equally true of the Lord's Prayer. . . who am I to judge the condition of the heart of the one who prays?"

I nodded. There was much I wanted to say, but I felt constrained to wait until he was finished. "So, I'm going to continue praying as I have been, straight through to the Lord," he said thoughtfully. "Because it works: He hears me, and if my heart's right, I can hear Him." He smiled. "But I am not going to say that others are wrong, because they don't pray as I do. Only God can see into the depths of their hearts—and to Him what resides *there* is all that matters."

I just nodded; there was nothing more to say.

That afternoon Father Svet came down from Konjic to give a talk at the church, after which he took us over to the rectory for a visit. From his shirt pocket David drew his ever-present cassette recorder, and we asked him to comment on the transformation that had occurred in the countryside as a result of the events at Medjugorje. Had it permeated all of Yugoslavia?

He thought for a moment before replying. "It's beyond Yugoslavia; the transformation is taking place all over the world. In this country you will not hear of Medjugorje on television, nor are they allowed to speak of it in churches. But," he smiled, "you might see the word on a bumper-sticker, and that car will be going many places."

What had Medjugorje meant to his own life?

"It has been my second ordination. It has challenged me and given new meaning and purpose to my priesthood. That was the easy part. It has also given me the calling to be holy. And that is a constant search and struggle every day to find one's own soul and the face of God in the midst of the temptations of the world. To praise Him and be holy and meet the demands of the priestly vocation, in spite of television programs and distractions and one's daily agenda, is sometimes wearing."

David smiled. "It would be easier to be a hermit."

"Oh, yes! How much easier to be holy, secluded in a monastery or in some protected environment!" He smiled. "But now I feel I must live in both. I must bear witness to my monastic life in a world that is not monastic." He smiled. "I am like a mailman, bearing this letter of the inner experience of the spirit, of life with God, to the world."

"Which encourages them in their own struggles: 'If I can do it, you can do it. . . .' "

"Absolutely! I always emphasize that we are pilgrims together. You did not come to me, nor I to you, but together we climb the hill of the Cross of Calvary."

He asked how the work on our book was coming, and I told him that this was a research trip. We were counting on the Holy Spirit to fill in the blanks. "But there's one thing I would like your help in doing. I've worked with you on your second manuscript, which contains such a long interview of Father Jozo, but I've never met him. Could you maybe take us to his parish sometime?"

Typically, Father Svet clapped his knees and said, "Why not right now?"

Five minutes later we were tucked into his little white Volkswagen, on our way to Tihaljina, some 35 kilometers distant. I reminded David that Father Jozo was the pastor at St. James when the apparitions had begun, and that he had doubted at first, but had protected the children and had later been imprisoned for refusing to curtail their activities. Even now he was forbidden by the bishop to celebrate mass in Medjugorje. So, the pilgrims came to him — every day, by the busloads. And for many, his talk was the highlight of their trip.

We arrived just at sundown and were shown into Father Jozo's office. He was a big man with dark, penetrating eyes and a flashing smile that could melt a heart of stone. Through Father Svet, I told him who we were and what we were hoping to accomplish, and he nodded and asked a sister to bring some coffee.

I asked about his time in prison — what was it like?

He smiled, then spoke rapidly in Croatian, pausing every so often to allow Father Svet time to translate. "I had always wanted to get into prison with the Gospel, but this was not exactly how I planned to do it. I prefer not to speak of details, except to say that it took the pride out of me and introduced simplicity. When you receive every kind of punishment, they think they have conquered you, and you are finished. But they were only preparing the ground for the seed of faith."

Did it grieve him not to go to Medjugorje now?

He shook his head and smiled. "Medjugorje is not tied to a particular location anymore. It is more a spirit, a spirit that can grow anywhere."

If he had to sum up all the messages of the Blessed Mother, how would he do it?

He looked out the window at the darkening sky. "When David confronted Goliath, God told him to take up five stones and go in His name. Those stones are in your hands today, and Our Lady has told us what is written on each: prayer, fasting, confession, the Bible, and the Eucharist. . . . Our Lady was crying when she told us of

the Eucharist, the symbol of her Son's sacrifice for us.
It reminds us that our lives are to become a sacrifice for
all. She understood that He had to go to the Cross. Despite
the pain she was suffering, she did not try to hold Him
back. She accepted God's plan: go and die, that all men
might be reborn and live."

David shook his head. "I knew what her obedience had
cost her at the time of His birth — but I never thought
about what it cost her at His death."

At the end of our time with Father Jozo, he prayed
for us: "Put your lives under the Cross, in the open
heart, in the open hands, in front of the open heaven
from where one can hear *This is my beloved son*. Hear
it. Thank you, Jesus, for the Cross. Thank you, Jesus,
for the open heart. Thank you, that from your hands
all blessings come. Thank you, that from your heart
comes peace and love. Put your hands upon us and bless
us."

I cannot remember ever being so affected by a
benediction.

That evening in our room, as David was laying out tapes
and film for the next day, he said, "You know, there are
three pairs of shoes outside the door across the hall. And
that other door down the hall, the one across from the
living room?"

I nodded. "Antonio and Macha's room."

"Well, ever since we came, it's been closed. Only this
morning, someone left it ajar. And as we were going out
— I know it was none of my business, but I glanced in.
There were four mattresses on the floor." He paused.
"Wayne, four people are sleeping on the floor in there,
so that you and I can sleep in beds, in a room to ourselves."

I nodded and sighed. "And when we leave, they won't let us give them any money. I know; I've tried."

"It just blows my mind."

"Mine, too," I replied. "But that's what the Blessed Mother has asked of them: welcome the pilgrims as if they are family. Let them see my Son in you."

"Well," David murmured, "I can."

The next morning we were alone at the table, savoring the bittersweet coffee and enjoying the luxury of having half an hour with nothing scheduled before we had to leave for Mass.

Suddenly David exclaimed, "You know, what we've got here is nothing less than full-scale, Holy Spirit revival!"

My friend was warming to his subject. "In all the great revivals of the Eighteenth and Nineteenth Centuries, in England and Wales as well as America, people were caught by surprise. Suddenly the reality of a personal Savior and the possibility of complete forgiveness overwhelmed them. Their lives changed, and relationships which had been broken for years were reconciled. The things of God were simply more important to them than anything else." He paused. "That's what I see happening here."

I smiled and poured some more coffee into the little cups. David was very different in his approach to God from what I was used to, but still, the result was the same. "There are still a few hold-outs," I replied, "but you're right; nearly everyone in this village is involved. And eight years ago, that ratio was reversed. This was a hard-bitten, cynical valley with neighbors feuding and farmers at the mercy of a government-controlled market, and the young people living for the day when they could leave and go to the cities. A few of the older folk regularly attended church, but they were definitely the minority. Even so, despite the hard times and the oppressive measures against religion, there was a deeper faith here than in most places in Yugoslavia." I looked out the window at Mt. Krizevac. "They did build that cross. . . . and in 1967, a church far larger than they could possibly need. The faith was still here — which, according to the visionaries, was one of the reasons why God picked this place."

David finished his cup and held it out for a refill. "I've been thinking about that, too," he said. "In fact, I prayed about it this morning. Why, of all countries, did God pick Yugoslavia?" He smiled. "You know what came to me? When God first called upon Mary to introduce His Son to mankind, it took place in a stable. Now that He has called upon her to re-introduce His Son, He has picked a stable-nation."

"Makes sense," I said, deciding that through all of these words and thoughts, David in his own way was getting the message of Medjugorje.

He got up and went to the window. In the valley the farmers were already out in the fields. "The path to conversion may be a little different from the one I'm used to," he said thoughtfully, "but the results are the same. If anything, the seeds seem to be going a little deeper here. . . ."

"The conversion that the Blessed Mother is calling for is the old-fashioned kind," I said, smiling. "And she's not kidding: by fasting, she means bread and water. And as for prayer — do you know how much the young people in the prayer groups here pray? *Three hours a day.* Until I came here, I don't think I prayed more than five minutes a day — if that."

David agreed. "I've seen it in my own wife," he said quietly. "When Barbara came here last November, she was already a committed Christian. She had loved God for sixteen years. But here — she fell in love with Him. That's the difference — and it's lasted."

I took my cup and saucer and dish in to the kitchen sink. We had about 25 minutes to get to the English Mass — just enough time if we left now. We headed down the path at a pace that would get us to the church on time — barely.

"Sparks borne on a divine wind, starting forest fires everywhere," David mused. "Well, it was certainly foretold: the Bible says that in the last days there will be a final great outpouring and multitudes will be converted." He snapped a photo of the twin-spired church in the distance. "You think we're in the last days?"

"You think we're not?"

"No, I'm sure we are," he said, putting his camera away.

I nodded. "It's the final harvest," I said, trying not to sound over-dramatic, "our last chance. If we miss it, I don't think we're going to get another."

We walked the rest of the way in silence.

31
Voices from Medjugorje

To my surprise, the guest celebrant at the English Mass that morning was an old friend. In honor of the 17th anniversary of his ordination, Father Jack Spaulding from Scottsdale, Arizona, had been invited to lead the service. Father Jack had been drawn to Medjugorje many times, and as our trips had overlapped, we had grown to be friends. So, to cap the occasion, after the service we invited him to lunch.

As usual, he and I started playing catch-up, and as usual he was being used in unusual ways. With another priest from the Phoenix area, Father Dale Fushek, Father Jack co-hosted a national TV talk show for teenagers that aired over the EWTN network. It was in this capacity that he and Father Fushek had recently flown to San Francisco, where Mother Teresa had come from Calcutta to witness the first vows of some new sisters entering her order. For nearly half an hour they had talked and prayed with her.

"Describe her," asked David, producing his recorder, as we settled on a semi-shaded grassy knoll in the grove behind the church.

"Well — I'm 5'6", and she barely comes to my shoulder. She's so small that when she comes into a room you don't

notice her, not at first. But then. . . before long, everyone is quiet. No one wants to miss what she has to say,
and she doesn't raise her voice to say it. Like when she
said that in abortion there are two killings: one is the
baby, and the other is the conscience of the mother.
And the only thing that can take care of that is the
sacrament of reconciliation, for the great gift of that
sacrament is that it enables us to begin to forgive
ourselves."

"I see what you mean," I said. "I've used her as an
example of what Jesus is asking us to be through Mary's
messages here in Medjugorje. She literally *lives* the Gospel
message." Mother Teresa had always been very special
to me, and I was glad to have an opportunity to learn
more about her. "What is the thing you will most remember
about her?"

"The thing that hit me the hardest," said Father Jack
laughing, "was that she refused to bless me. Everyone else
bent down, and she put her hands on their heads and
blessed them. But when she came to me, she wouldn't.
She said, 'You are a priest. It is for you to bless me.' "

"Did you?" David asked.

"Of course. Then she said: 'You priests do not
understand how precious you are. Because of you, Jesus
is here. You bring Him to us in the Eucharist.' "

I had to ask: did he ask her if she thought the Blessed
Mother was appearing in Medjugorje?

Father Jack nodded. "She said, 'Of course she's
appearing there!' Then she added, 'That's my home, you
know.' I had forgotten she was from Albania, which is
now part of Yugoslavia. And then she added, 'But I would
never go there, because I might be a distraction from what
God is doing there.' She was a little sad about that. She
said, 'I did send the visionaries a letter for them to give
Mary, asking her to come to Calcutta.' And I said, 'Well,

Mother, Mary won't come there, because she's using you there,' and we all laughed."

What was it like, leading the service today?

"Celebrating the Eucharist here is as close to home as I will ever be, until the Lord comes to take me back home with Him."

I nodded. "The first thing I thought when I came here was that I was on the edge of heaven."

Father Jack looked at the cross on Mt. Krizevac, which was directly behind us. "You begin to understand what it means to be in exile here," he mused. "It is just close enough to being home that it makes you really homesick. When you come here, you imagine that you're home — but that only makes it harder when you have to leave and go back to your worldly home."

David nodded. "You're describing my wife. She's so homesick for this place, she's reading everything on Medjugorje she can lay her hands on." I nodded in agreement, remembering how difficult it had been to leave the first time, and each time thereafter.

"She's really homesick for heaven," Father Jack smiled. "She touched heaven here." He paused. "Or rather, heaven touched her."

I asked him if he remembered the first time it struck him that this was a special place of reconciliation and conversion. "Oh, very definitely," he answered. Father Jack paused a moment and then, gazing at the mountain, continued: "My first time here, I came with a group of teen-agers. We were so busy taking care of them that I didn't have time for quiet prayer and meditation, as recommended by the local priests. Then, one afternoon as we were returning to the church from Vicka's house, my companion suggested we pray the rosary as we walked. We did, and in the praying of that rosary, I experienced for the first time, deep prayer from the heart." He suddenly teared up and through quiet sobs continued, "That was my moment of conversion, my real conversion."

I was touched that a priest would feel such emotion. Father Jack spoke of a moment of enlightenment for him that had occurred two years ago; yet it still affected him as though it had just happened.

"Well, why don't we move along to the restaurant, so that we can enjoy our luncheon celebration," I said trying to lighten the moment.

"You know," said Father Jack, as we settled into our seats at the little outdoor restaurant, there are priests who won't come here, because they're afraid of conversion. They're professionally spiritual but not personally. Their lives are comfortable now, and they're afraid of what might be required of them and how they might have to change."

David looked at the mountain. "Sometimes one can be rich in things other than money or comforts or a predictable routine. . . . We were talking about that yesterday, about how conversion means so much more than just being born again. How it means becoming holy. . . ."

Jack smiled. "Conversion is such a personal thing. And it's not something we do once; it's something we do every day." He paused. "You know, just before Marija left for Italy, she said to me, 'Father, please pray for my conversion.' "

"Marija?" I exclaimed, "I would have thought that if anyone —"

The priest nodded. "That was when I realized how important it was that we pray for each other's conversion. That was the gift of that trip. But I've stopped talking about that," he sighed, "because people started saying to me, 'Father, if you need conversion, then there's no hope for me!' "

We laughed, but I knew what he meant.

That afternoon, I was interviewed by a TV camera crew from WBRZ, the ABC-affiliate in Baton Rouge, Louisiana. Medjugorje had captured the imagination of that city, as much as it had New Orleans, and this crew was over here to make their station's *second* documentary. When we had finished, I asked the interviewer, John Pastorek, and cameraman Robert Chandler about their first documentary. "When we got home," John said, "everyone wanted to know if we'd seen the sun dancing and the cross turning, and stuff like that. Well, we had seen those things, but what had most impressed us and what we had concentrated on in the documentary was the human miracles — people whose lives were changed, whose faith was deepened or restored, that sort of thing."

He told of one woman in particular from Apaloosas, Louisiana who was on their pilgrimage with her mother. Partially blind, partially crippled, and with a hearing loss, she'd had over 60 operations and shouldn't be alive at all. Like so many others, she had come in hopes of a miraculous healing, and though she was admitted to the apparition room which was then in the rectory, she did not receive one. Instead, she received something else.

"When I looked around and saw people who couldn't walk at all," she'd told John, "people who were totally blind and had never seen in their lives, I thought, 'God, I've been praying for the wrong thing! I've been asking You for a miracle, when I should be asking You for forgiveness for an ungrateful heart.' Well," John smiled, "you could see the peace settle over her! And to cap it off, we went to see her a week after we got home, and she and her mother were beaming. They'd been to the doctor, and he had informed her of a new shoe that was now available, and that with some minor surgery she could be free of her wheelchair. In fact, she wouldn't even have to use a cane!" He paused. "But the real miracle was what happened in her heart, as she asked God to forgive her."

We went with John and Robert the next morning, as they interviewed Vicka in her home. They were professionals, setting up lights and camera quickly and putting Vicka and her interpreter at ease. John was a gifted interviewer, instinctively asking the questions that would be foremost in his viewers' minds. Even as they were about to begin, there was a group outside from the Philippines, standing in the road, waiting their turn to talk to her. And behind them, another group from Italy. . . . So his first question was: how did she feel about literally thousands of people invading her privacy every day?

Vicka shrugged and smiled. "For me it has become normal. I know that the people are coming here to hear Our Lady's words, and I feel lucky that these words are coming through me."

Next came a question that I had wanted to ask her many times: It had been six, seven years since the apparitions first started; did she ever get to sit by herself alone and think about who she was talking to?

"I feel like a lucky person that Our Lady chose me, and I am very, very glad that I can give the messages that I get from her to people. I think also sometimes about these people, and I know that most of them are coming here for religious reasons, but I also know that some of them are just curious."

When was the last time she had an apparition?

"Last night. I had the apparition, but there was nothing special, no special message. Usually when there is nothing special, I pray together with Our Lady and we pray for all the pilgrims. . . ."

What kind of a personality did the Madonna have?

"Sometimes she's sad, sometimes happy — just like any other person."

What was her reaction when she saw the apparition the first time?

"When I first heard that Our Lady had appeared, I couldn't believe it. I could not imagine that she would appear to anyone. Then when I saw her myself, I didn't know whether I was scared or happy."

How did she know it was the Blessed Virgin Mary and not something else?

"We knew it was Our Lady, because there is nothing similar on earth, and because we had already had one apparition the day before. We were quite sure it was her."

What was the strongest message she had given them?

"To pray for peace — that has been the strongest message."

Why?

"Because Our Lady says that prayers are so powerful, they can stop wars. But before we can pray for peace in the world, we must have peace in our hearts and in our families. If we have peace in our hearts, then we can understand all the other messages that Our Lady gives us here."

A lot of people out there were saying that this whole thing was a hoax — what did she have to say to those people?

"I don't have anything to say to them. Our Lady once said, 'You can pray for those people.' "

Had this whole thing changed her life? Had it made her a better person, or more religious?

"I'm trying to change, but I don't know how successful I am."

John ended the interview by asking what message would the Virgin Mary have for those people who couldn't come here?

"The main messages from Our Lady are for prayer, fasting, penance, conversion and peace. She has asked us to pray the rosary. She wants us to fast one day a week on bread and water, and to have strong faith. She asks us to pray, but she asks us from day to day to open our hearts so that we can feel joy in our hearts, so that we think about every word we are praying. Our Lady says when you start to pray, you start with one Our Father, because our Father is like one big father who is in heaven. We have to get rid of the things that disturb us, and we have to give them to Our Saviour and have Him lead us. Mary is like our mother, and she can see us with the eyes of God. Pray like this, and then it will not be hard for you to pray the rosary every day. You think when you are in trouble that God and Mary are far away from you, but that's not true; they are always close to you. She asks us to give up some things, give up sins. . . . She says that Satan is strong now and wants to disturb us in everything. That's why she asks us to put more into our prayers so that we can keep him away from us. . . ."

It was simple and direct — like most of the messages coming from the Madonna throughout the past seven years. I sat there, deeply touched by this last answer. Vicka had put so much energy into it, more than I had ever witnessed from her before. She looked at me with that smile that filled you with total trust in her words. "Look at you," she laughed, "I have made you cry!"

I smiled at her and shook my head. "I never get tired of hearing the message, and you expressed it better than I have ever heard you express it before. It really touched me."

Vicka gave me a hug, and as we said good-bye I said to her, "Tell Our Lady I love her very much, and I'm glad she chose you."

That evening, we were fortunate to be able to ascend Podbrdo for a late-night apparition. I was glad that David would have the opportunity to experience this, as I had

on my first trip. There was a lot of singing and David
was startled to hear,'The Saints Go Marching In', sung
in Croatian. The message from the Blessed Virgin Mary
that evening fit in perfectly with the ending of Vicka's
interview: beware the wiles of Satan, who would seek to
divert us from obedience to her Son.

As before, when we descended the hillside, there was
soft singing filling the air, mingled with the happy chirping
of thousands of birds. It was a beautiful ending to what
had been a full day.

A little after four in the morning, we were startled awake
by the mightiest thunderclap either of us had ever heard.
I reached over to switch on the light — which didn't work.
"You awake?" I called quietly to David.

"Are you kidding? That had to be as close to the Crack
of Doom as I ever hope to get!"

"Whatever it was, it seems to have knocked the power
out." When he didn't respond, I repeated the observation.
Still no reply. "You okay?"

"I'm listening for the first shouts," he chuckled.

"What are you talking about?"

"Of the people, calling their friends to the hillside to
see the sign."

Then I knew what he was talking about — and that
chances were, he was only half-kidding. The previous
afternoon I had told him about the permanent sign which
God would send, to let man know that He was the author
and finisher of the work at Medjugorje. What the sign
would be, only the visionaries knew. It was one of the
ten secrets, or future events that would happen in the
world, which she would tell them, and which would not
be revealed until she instructed them to do so.

Outside the rain started pouring. Listening to it pound
on the roof, I doubted that either of us would be getting
back to sleep that night. "About the secrets," David said,

"why are they secret? Nothing else she's allegedly told them has been."

"Historically she has done this. There were secrets given at Lourdes and at Fatima. At the latter, one was that Russia would be converted to Christianity."

David laughed. "Before *Glasnost,* I would have thought that was impossible. But the way things are going, it just might be the last chapter. So tell me more about the secrets given here in Medjugorje."

The first three, I told him, would be warnings to mankind and the permanent sign. The fourth, fifth and sixth had to do with the personal lives of the visionaries and the village, and the remainder were the final chastisements. But the seventh had been mitigated, because of all the prayer and fasting that had come as a result of the millions who had visited Medjugorje.

Of course, I added, these were simply my own thoughts; other than the visionaries themselves, no one knew for sure the order or the contents.

"What sort of timetable are we looking at?" my friend asked.

"As soon as all six of the visionaries have received all ten of the secrets, the apparitions will stop. Then, after a short while, it begins."

"Have any of them received them all?"

"Ivanka and Mirjana have. The Blessed Mother appears to them now only on the anniversary of the first day, and on their birthdays, or occasionally when they are in great personal need."

"What about the other four?"

"They've received all but the last secret."

There was silence in the darkness. Then he said, "So we're close to the end, right?"

I did not reply at first. "A year ago, I would have said yes. Now — I'm not so sure. For one thing, all of them have had the ninth secret for more than three years, yet the apparitions continue, as everyone plays guessing games as to when they will end. Frankly, I think they will go on for several more years."

"Why?"

"Well, there has been so much prayer and such a positive response to her coming, that the time of the apparitions is apparently being extended. Again, that's just my own personal opinion."

"And that didn't happen before?"

"Not like this. Lourdes and Fatima each did have profoundly beneficial effects — but nothing like what's happening now. Of course, by comparison she appeared only briefly at those places. Here, it's been constant for seven years. But also here the seed has fallen in fertile soil. Anyway, it's been responsible for millions of conversions. In fact, I personally think it is the most significant event in Christendom since Jesus ascended and the Church was formed."

David thought about that for a moment. "So God has finally gotten man's attention — now what?"

I told him that when the last secret was revealed to the last visionary, then Mirjana, the first to receive all the secrets, would, at the bidding of the Blessed Mother, reveal the first secret to a priest of her choosing. She had already chosen Father Petar Ljubicic, who had been posted near Zagreb but who by coincidence was re-assigned to Medjugorje not long after she had made up her mind that he was to be the one. After receiving the secret from Mirjana, he would fast for seven days and then reveal the first secret to the world. It was to take place three days later. This process would be repeated until all ten secrets were revealed.

"You have no idea, then, how much longer the apparitions will continue?"

"None," I answered. "Possibly until everyone who is supposed to come here or be otherwise touched by Medjugorje has had that opportunity."

"And do you have even a feel for how long that might be?"

"Well, as I said, possibly for several more years. But it wouldn't surprise me if they stopped tomorrow — or if they continued on for nine more years. In messages given to the visionary I met in Northern Ireland in May, the Madonna had told her the year before that the world had ten more years to return to God's ways, which would make it '97."

"And this is the last time she's coming?"

"That's what she has said. But at the same time, there are reports of her also appearing other places — in Japan, in Russia, and as I said, in Ireland. But after this period, no more. . . ."

"Which brings us back to the secrets; what has she said about the chastisements?"

"Very little, except that they will be global. And that we are not to speculate on them."

There was prolonged silence, and I wondered if David had drifted off to sleep. Then he said, "Well, I won't speculate on them, but the sensationalists will. As it becomes more widely known, they'll take it out of context and blow it up: Catholic Apocalypse!"

"They already have," I said softly.

"Most of my evangelical friends expect that we will experience a catastrophic Tribulation in our lifetimes. But of course, believers have been predicting the Apocalypse ever since the time of the Apostles."

"How do they think it will happen?"

David sighed. "Well, a lot of people think it will be annihilation by nuclear holocaust, but I don't. I think the disasters will be natural — acts of God, not man."

I didn't say it, but I disagreed with David. Man, as he has always done, would unleash a self-destructive fury as the abundance given us by God begins to dry up. Nation would fight against nation. . . .

The morning dawned bright and clear, and everything had that freshly-washed look from the recent rain. We were scheduled for an interview with Ivan and found him at home, in his living room. He was a very serious young man, quiet and reserved, who had recently celebrated his 23rd birthday. Through an interpreter I asked him if he ever had any free time, in which he could just do anything he wanted.

"One can always find some free time for oneself, if one wants to. I do sports for recreation, and I watch them sometimes. But they won't take you to heaven. So I often set sports aside. Our Lady didn't tell me to; I just did."

I told him that I was concerned about the changes I had observed in Medjugorje — not just the souvenir stands and the cafes, but in the people. It seemed that there were not as many villagers in church as there used to be. And the youngsters seemed to be hanging out in the cafes, most of which now contained small bars — places where they shouldn't be. Was the sudden influx of money affecting them? The young people's prayer groups, for instance; were they still continuing?

"Yes," he replied. "There are three of them now. Two were formed by the church and are led by Father Slavko and Father Petar. I lead the third one. In the groups we try to involve as many of the young people as possible. But there are many outside influences now, competing for their attention. Sometimes their parents are too occupied — too many guests in the house, and not enough time for their children. So some of the people in our prayer group go from family to family, talking to them. In some families we are not welcome, but we are coming as Mary's messengers, and sooner or later they realize this. We work especially with the young children, and have had some good effects. But we must persevere."

I was extremely impressed with the fact that this young visionary, so long regarded as too shy to greet crowds as Vicka and Marija did, was now himself going door-to-door in his community, trying to convert his peers.

I asked him about receiving the monthly message, the one meant for the entire world which was given by Mary on the 25th of each month; I had noticed that the October message seemed to be much longer than usual. . .

Ivan responded, "This message comes through Marija."

"But don't you hear it at the same time? Don't all four of you hear it together?"

"No, I cannot hear that message (the monthly one); only Marija hears it."

I was surprised by that, as I had always thought that they all received it simultaneously. I pressed on by asking if some of the daily messages had more impact than others.

"I don't think so; every message has a special reason for being given. It is all to help us."

I hoped Ivan would understand the next question, and why I was asking it. "Ivan, many people who will be reading my book are not Catholic. In America, seventy-five per cent of the people are Protestant, and they do not know Mary, and do not accept her as one to go to in prayer. Maybe with a Protestant writing about her, they will listen. Is there anything that can be said to a Protestant to open them up to Mary?"

"It is very important to emphasize that the Blessed Mother came for all of us. Mary's messages refer to the whole world. Her messages throughout have been that we must pray for all religions, because we know that we have divided ourselves by religion. God did not divide us; He does not give us wars . . . ."

"But still people have drawn those lines; they think she is taking the place of Jesus."

"How can they think that?" he answered with a touch of irritation. "She was sent by her Son, by Jesus."

I pointed out to him that they do not find such a role for Mary in the Bible.

"We have to go much more deeply into this, even from the theological side, we have to find meaning to the words. She is asking us to pray with the heart; to pray with the heart so that we can understand the meaning of the words."

I wanted to get back to the young people of Medjugorje. I had noticed in the last trips that many of them were staying out late, hanging around the cafes, and not attending the services as they had before; did he see this happening in Medjugorje?

"Yes, we can talk about those that are rich and those that are poor. Many people are poor today, but they have a very good and happy family life. With many others, I am looking and I see there is no family unity, no unity between husband and wife. They never have time for their children, they never pray with their children . . ."

As Ivan paused, David said, "Keep going."

Ivan smiled and said, "This is the topic I like to talk about. When you are talking with young people today, it is a burning question, it is almost like a fire that is going to hit the ceiling — like a fire in the house. The young people on the streets today — drugs, alcohol, and other things they are offered. And the parents seem deaf and blind. They are more occupied with the material things than with their children. When I was in Austria, Italy and Germany, I could see the differences in the youths. Italy is something special." He did not mean this as a compliment, adding that they had more problems than the others.

I laughed. "Wait until you see America!"

I was seeing and hearing a different Ivan than the one

I had met two years ago. He had matured considerably and was comfortable in interviews now. There was a time that he would not talk to the media, and would not meet with pilgrims. A year in the military had helped.

Last question: at one point he had considered entering the priesthood — was that still a possibility?

"That is a private thing. When Mary first came, she brought freedom, and told all of us that whatever we did with our lives was our decision."

It was a good answer and a good place to end the interview.

That evening, Father Slavko invited us up to the choir loft where the apparitions were now taking place. The television crew from Baton Rouge was there, as were a journalist from France, a priest from England, and a theologian from Germany. Ivan was the only visionary. As the apparition began, Father Slavko motioned to David that it was all right for him to come forward, so that he could take a picture of Ivan's face as he spoke to her, and I nudged him with my elbow, but he was immobilized. Finally, he was able to take a couple of pictures.

We went downstairs for the Croatian Mass, and afterwards, as we came out, David looked stunned.

"What's the matter?" I asked him.

He just shook his head. "It's just that our trip is about over. I'm having a hard time with that."

As the next day was our last, we went up on Podbrdo in the early morning to watch the light of the rising sun make its way across the sleeping valley. Already in the street far below there were people gathering outside of Vicka's house.

David shook his head. "How anyone could believe that those kids are perpetuating a hoax is beyond me. All you have to do is look at their lives: what possible gain is there from what they're doing? They're not getting any money." He paused. "They've got fame, I suppose — but honestly, who would want it? Ivan says they're free to choose, but they've got far less freedom than they had before. And they've got to put up with the same questions, the same rudeness and insensitivity, day after day, year after year." He paused. "Ivan and Vicka are the only ones I've met, but having spent an hour with each of them, I would have to say they are without guile."

I nodded. "Marija is the same. The last night I stayed at her house, the time before, we stayed up late having tea and cookies, while she showed me her photo album. There were typical teen-age snapshots of her and friends mugging for the camera or picnicking, or whatever. And the others are the same — just ordinary young people given a very special mission as visionary and messenger for the Blessed Virgin Mary." And then I added, more to myself than to David, "You know, that's really no different than the mission she has given me. . . ."

David took a picture of the valley below. "It just occurs to me: maybe that's another reason why the apparitions have been going on for this long. These kids are normal kids. There's no way they could keep a hoax going this long! Maybe one or two days, perhaps, or even a week. But not for seven straight years. Not with people constantly trying to catch them up or trap them in lies. Not with scientists hooking them up to electro-encephalographs right at the time of the apparition!" He took another picture. "No, the detractors are going to have to come up with another explanation, I'm afraid."

"Some say that the priests are controlling them, using them and perpetuating the hoax for their own ends," I mused.

"Well, I don't see that, either," he replied. "Here the bishop's doing everything in his power to shut them down. And the priests are still flat out from dawn till dusk."

"Their accusers say they're in it for the power."

David scoffed. "They don't even have to spend an hour with Svet or Jozo, or any of them. If they have a scrap of discernment, ten minutes will be enough time to see how patently ridiculous that is!"

"Hey," I laughed, "I'm on the same side, remember?"

He laughed, too. "Those guys are human; they're no race of supermonks. And I've heard the rumors about this one or that one — in fact, if there were no rumors, I'd be suspicious; maybe they weren't doing their job. But the very fact that they *are* human and not brown-robed heroes, makes the example of their surrender the more compelling."

I laughed again. "Then there must be an alternative explanation."

We went to the English Mass, and afterwards we went out to the cemetery in the cedar grove which had become his favorite place, as it was mine. During the week I had watched him become progressively more peaceful and pensive. "Talk about sensory deprivation," he murmured, "even the food is simple and rustic. God has your complete and undivided attention here, for an entire week! And I'll bet for many that come here that may be the first time in their lives that's been the case."

"I think you've got it," I said, smiling at him.

In the cemetery, a light breeze stirred the uppermost branches of the cedars, and in the distance the full sun shone on Mt. Krizevac. There were only a few scattered clouds in the sky. As we were preparing to wrap up the day's work, David held up his hand. "Do you hear that?"

I listened. From the vineyard out the gateway came the sound of someone saying the rosary. It seemed to be coming closer. We could see an old woman now, working her way up the row towards the cemetery, pruning off low-hanging leaves so that the vine's growing energy would be centered in its grapes. We stepped out of her line of sight and watched as she approached.

She turned in the gateway, and we noticed that in her arm she was carrying some fresh-cut lilies. These she laid tenderly under a new headstone, and then crying, returned to her work in the vineyard. She had never stopped saying the rosary.

We went over to see the stone. Someone named Ivan had been buried there a few months before, and from his birth-date we worked out that he had been 82 — undoubtedly her husband. We could still hear her praying, as I suggested to David we separate to pray and have a few moments to ourselves, this being our last day in the little village. I walked towards the field where the old woman had returned. She was still reciting her prayers. Gazing up at the sky, I realized that I had never been more peaceful than I had been on this trip. I felt like I had finally entered into "that peace which passeth understanding."

A half-hour later I returned to the cemetery, and came upon David praying, with tears in his eyes. Startled, he looked up, and for a moment my normally always-in-command friend flushed in embarrassment. Then, in a voice filled with emotion, he said softly, "I don't know how I'm going to leave this place."

Jesus' message of love, peace, and conversion — conveyed by the Blessed Virgin Mary, the most holy of messengers, had captured yet another heart in the little hamlet of Medjugorje.

Epilogue

Dear children, today I call you to live the messages which I have been giving you for the past eight years. This is a time of grace, and I desire that the grace of God be great for every single one of you. I am blessing you, and I love you with a special love. Thank you for responding to my call . . .*

Thus, it has continued. On June 25, 1996, the Blessed Virgin Mary gave a message to the four visionaries who still have daily contact with her. It was the fifteenth year of daily, consecutive appearances, an event unprecedented in Marian apparition history.

Many changes have occurred in Medjugorje, in Bosnia-Hercegovina, and in the federation of Yugoslavia. A horrible war, stoked by the fires of ethnic hatred, has divided the federation into independent republics. For more than three years, the war raged on, destroying everything in its path and killing hundreds of thousands of people. It was a desperate act by Satan to cap the fountain of grace pouring out of the little village of Medjugorje. But it failed to accomplish its goal.

Even in the throes of war, pilgrims continued to make the trek to Medjugorje, although in far fewer numbers. And even in the face of such horror, the light of God was present, as thousands of former pilgrims returned to bring food, clothing, medicine—and prayers—to the victims of the war.

---

* *This message and the excerpts at the beginning of each chapter are taken from the messages received by the visionaries of Medjugorje.*

Now, with an end to the fighting and an uneasy peace plan in place, Medjugorje continues to be a place where the Blessed Virgin Mary comes to speak to the world through these young visionaries. The crowds have returned in large numbers and the work of conversion goes on.

All of the visionaries, with the exception of Vicka, are married now, and they have families of their own. Marija, Ivan, Jacov and Vicka still have daily apparitions. And Mirjana now sees Our Lady on the second day of each month, an event that has been taking place now for more than two years. As of this recording, the apparitions continue. What wonderful grace!

So . . . where do we go from here? I think the answer can be found in the message received by Mirjana on her birthday in March, 1987. It is a succinct summation of the more than fifteen years of grace given us by the appearance of the mother of Jesus.

It is as follows:

"My dear children, I have come to lead you to purity of the soul, and thus, to God. How have you accepted me? In the beginning with disbelief, fear and distrust towards the children whom I had chosen. Then, most received me in their heart and began to carry out my motherly requests.

"But unfortunately, this did not last very long. Wherever I manifest myself, and with me, my Son, Satan turns up also. You have allowed him to control and guide you without your being aware of it. You are sometimes aware that your behavior is against the law of God, but you quickly suppress it. Do not give in, my children! Dry away the tears on my face, tears that I have shed when I see how you behave. Look at what is going on around you!

"Take time to get together as a family and pray for the grace of God; do not scorn the poor who beg for a crust of bread. Do not refuse them the overabundance of your meals. Help them and God

will also help you. Do not delude yourselves by thinking that you are good, but that your brother who lives near you is not. You would not be right in doing so.

"I am your mother and that is why I am warning you. There are some secrets, my children, and you do not know what they are; but when they will be known, it will be late. Go back to prayer! Nothing is more necessary than prayer! I would have liked the Lord to let me enlighten you at least a little on the secrets, but He is already offering you enough graces. Reflect on this! How much do you offer yourselves to Him? When was the last time you gave up something for the Lord?

"I want to call you once again to prayer, to fasting and to penance. If you wish to obtain the grace of God through fasting, then let no one know you are fasting; if you wish to obtain the grace of God by giving alms to the poor, let no one know you are doing so.

"Meditate in prayer, my dear children, on this message which I am giving you."

May this beautiful message from the Mother of God, along with the message of this book, bring you the peace, the love and the grace of our Lord, Jesus Christ.

Wayne Weible
June, 1996